Realms of Gold:

A Sketch of Western Literature

by L. James Hammond
author of *Conversations With Great Thinkers*

cover design: Elliott Banfield
                 elliottbanfield.com

Published by: Noontide Press
                 58 Jacob St.
                 Seekonk, MA 02771
                 508-336-5556

                 New Century Publishing, Taipei, Taiwan (in
                 translation)

Third English Edition
Copyright © 2017 L. James Hammond
All rights reserved.

ISBN: 978-0-615-31798-4

Contents

Preface

Much have I travelled in the realms of gold,
And many goodly states and kingdoms seen...

In this book, I propose to discuss the Western classics, beginning with philosophy and psychology, then going on to literature and history, and finally concluding with miscellaneous and scientific works. Although the focus is on Western works, I also look briefly at works from China, Japan, India, Iran, etc. Although the focus is on the humanities, I also suggest books about the sciences. I intend this essay to be a map of the literary world, like a map that shows a miner where he can find gold. I myself read many books that weren't worth reading; I was like a miner without a map, hence I can appreciate the value of a map. If people find just one book in this essay that they enjoy reading, my goal will have been reached. I'm not trying to dilute or popularize the classics; if the most gifted and ambitious reader in the world asked me what books I recommend, I would say just what I say here.

I. Philosophy

1. Schopenhauer

The nineteenth century produced three philosophers who combined depth of thought with elegance of style: Schopenhauer, Kierkegaard, and Nietzsche. These three philosophers have a certain family resemblance. All three were solitary and unmarried, all three had a certain disdain for the masses. The later two (Kierkegaard and Nietzsche) read the eldest of them (Schopenhauer) with keen interest, though none of them ever met. Though they questioned the importance of reason, all three belong to the classical-Western tradition, not the mystical-Hermetic tradition.

Just after the last of them died, two great intellectual revolutions occurred: depth psychology and Eastern philosophy. These two revolutions are having a profound effect on philosophy in our time, and are diminishing the importance of these three philosophers. This wouldn't come as a surprise to the three philosophers, since they knew that philosophy evolves, and a philosopher's influence gradually wanes. But though their influence is waning, their work will be read as long as literature is respected, as long as man seeks to understand the human condition. Let's discuss these three philosophers chronologically, beginning with the first, Schopenhauer.

I recommend Schopenhauer's essays and aphorisms. If you think that philosophy is dry or obscure, this book will change your mind. Schopenhauer's style is always lucid, and he often gives one a deeper understanding of daily life. Schopenhauer's essays and aphorisms contain the sort of wisdom that never grows old, and never becomes obsolete. For example, Schopenhauer speaks of, "that optical illusion of the mind from which everyone suffers, making life, at its beginning, seem of long duration; and at its end, when one looks back over the course of it, how short a time it seems!"[1] Schopenhauer's essays and aphorisms total about 800 pages; since some of them are of little interest, they should be read in an abridged version, such as the Penguin Classics version.

Schopenhauer displayed a certain disdain for his essays; he gave them the title *Parerga and Paralipomena*, which is Greek for *Scraps and Leftovers*. He treated his essays and aphorisms as minor works, less important than his two-volume work, *The World As Will and Idea*. The *World As Will and Idea* is as clear and readable as his essays are, but it deals with metaphysical abstractions rather than everyday reality. Though one need not read both volumes, it's still a harder book to read than Schopenhauer's essays.

In *The World As Will and Idea*, Schopenhauer expresses his view that the world is hell, and that one should renounce life, not seek happiness. His pessimism is apparent in this aphorism: "No rose without a thorn. But many a thorn without a rose."[2] His pessimism is also apparent in his famous porcupine parable: Some porcupines come together on a cold winter day, in order to share each other's warmth. But when they're pricked by each other's quills, they move apart. And so, like mankind, they move back and forth, satisfied neither with the cold of solitude, nor with society's quills.

Schopenhauer is best known for his pessimism and his misogyny. These qualities have blinded many modern readers to the merits of his work. Those who are serious about philosophy will find *The World As Will and Idea* to be a work of the highest quality.

Schopenhauer wrote *The World as Will and Idea* when he was in his twenties; it was published in 1818, when Schopenhauer was thirty. It aroused no response from the public. For the next 35 years, Schopenhauer lived in obscurity in Frankfurt-am-Main, a bachelor, supporting himself with inherited money, confident of future fame. Schopenhauer's favorite philosopher was Kant, who lived according to a fixed routine; Kant's neighbors could set their clocks by his afternoon walk. Following Kant's example, Schopenhauer lived according to a fixed routine: he rose every morning at seven, skipped breakfast, and wrote until noon. Then he quit work for the day, and practiced the flute for half-an-hour. He lunched at The English House, and always laid a gold coin on his table, promising to give it away if the English officers at nearby tables talked about anything except horses and women. After lunch, he read until four,

---

[1] *Counsels and Maxims*, 1
[2] *Essays and Aphorisms*, "Aphorisms: On Various Subjects."

then took a two-hour walk, regardless of the weather. At six, he went to the library and read newspapers. Then he went to a play or a concert, had dinner, and went to bed.

In 1851, he published his essays, and said,

> I am right glad to witness the birth of my last child, which completes my mission in this world. I really feel as if a load that I have borne since my twenty-fourth year had been lifted from my shoulders. No one can imagine what that means.[1]

This book of essays brought him the fame that he had long sought; an English literary critic was impressed with Schopenhauer's essays, and wrote a laudatory review of them, thereby starting a chain reaction that soon made Schopenhauer famous the world over.

Schopenhauer died in 1860, secure in the knowledge that his works would never die. In the 1890s, Schopenhauer's fame was eclipsed by Nietzsche. Though he is still in Nietzsche's shadow today, Schopenhauer will long be viewed by discerning readers as one of the deepest thinkers, and one of the best stylists, ever to put pen to paper.

Where does Schopenhauer fit in the history of philosophy? Schopenhauer was the enemy of Hegel, the student of Kant, and the teacher of Nietzsche. He despised Hegel; having seen Hegel in person, he said that he could tell by the shape of his head and the look in his eye that he wasn't a genius. Meanwhile, Schopenhauer regarded Kant as a great thinker; Schopenhauer's metaphysics picks up where Kant left off. Schopenhauer's influence on Nietzsche was considerable. But Nietzsche disagreed with many of Schopenhauer's views. Much of Nietzsche's work was an attempt to justify life, and affirm life; Nietzsche was steadfastly opposed to Schopenhauer's pessimism.

Biographies of Schopenhauer have been written by (among others) Helen Zimmern, Bryan Magee, and Rüdiger Safranski. Zimmern's biography is one of the earliest (Zimmern was an acquaintance of Nietzsche), and is still one of the best. Bryan Magee became well known in Britain for his TV shows on philosophy. His book *Confessions of a Philosopher* is an introduction to philosophy in autobiographical form; it contains an attack on analytic philosophy that runs for several chapters. More recently, Magee wrote an award-winning autobiography called *Clouds of Glory: A Hoxton Childhood*. Magee's *Philosophy of Schopenhauer* is one of his best-known works. Rüdiger Safranski has

---

[1] *Schopenhauer: His Life and Philosophy,* by Helen Zimmern, ch. 10

written biographies of Schopenhauer, Nietzsche, Heidegger, etc. Safranski hosts a philosophy show on German TV.

2. Kierkegaard

Like Schopenhauer, Soren Kierkegaard developed under the shadow of Hegel. But while Schopenhauer despised Hegel and ignored him, Kierkegaard took Hegel seriously, adopted much of Hegel's terminology, and devoted much time to answering Hegel's arguments. Hegel concentrated on metaphysics, logic and history; he paid little attention to the individual, little attention to ethics. Kierkegaard insisted that the individual was of primary importance—the individual's ethical choices and religious decisions. Kierkegaard's work is addressed to the solitary individual. While Schopenhauer was an atheist, Kierkegaard was a passionate Christian. Kierkegaard combines religiosity with a sense of humor. Kierkegaard is the most humorous of all philosophers; his sense of humor is on a par with Kafka's. If you want a taste of the humorous and poetic side of Kierkegaard, read the first few pages of *Either/Or*.

Walter Lowrie wrote two biographies of Kierkegaard, one short and one long. The long one is one of the best biographies ever written; indeed, it's one of the best books ever written. It contains so many quotes from Kierkegaard's works that one could say Kierkegaard wrote most of it. Anyone interested in Kierkegaard should start with this book. Some of Kierkegaard's own books are slightly dry, abstract and Hegelian. Another starting-point for the study of Kierkegaard is *The Essential Kierkegaard*, an anthology edited by Howard and Edna Hong.

Among Kierkegaard's books, my favorites are his *Journals* (in an abridged version), *The Point of View*, *The Present Age*, and *Attack on Christendom*. Kierkegaard was capable of the deepest seriousness; this is evident from his *Attack on Christendom*, which is a work of extraordinary rhetorical power. Here's a sample of the *Attack*: "It is a crime, a great crime, to take part in the public worship of God as it now is; for this is at the greatest possible remove from being divine worship."[1] The *Attack* is clear and readable; its only weakness is that it's too long, it needs to be abridged.

---

[1] *Attack on Christendom*, "What Christ's Judgment Is About Official Christianity"

3. Nietzsche

Nietzsche was born in 1844. He was born into an upper-class family, and as a youngster, he attended Schulpforta, Germany's most prestigious school. The first decisive event in his life occurred when he was four: the death of his father. This event must have had a profound impact on the young Nietzsche, and must have been an important factor in creating the instability that later developed into madness. Nietzsche exemplifies the idea that genius is akin to madness; as Plato said, genius is "divine madness."

Nietzsche was an outstanding student, and when he was only 25, he became a professor of philology (ancient language and literature). At about the same time, he discovered the works of Schopenhauer, which made a deep impression on him. Nietzsche regarded himself not only as one of Schopenhauer's readers, but as one of his "pupils and sons"[1]; Schopenhauer was a father figure for Nietzsche. To follow in Schopenhauer's footsteps, to become a philosopher, became the goal of Nietzsche's life.

When he was 24, Nietzsche met Richard Wagner, the creator of operas. At their first meeting, they discussed Schopenhauer, whom they both admired. Wagner was 31 years older than Nietzsche, and Wagner was an established figure, so it was natural for Wagner to become a father figure for Nietzsche. Nietzsche was so fond of Wagner's operas that he wanted to devote himself to explaining them to the world. Nietzsche's first book, *The Birth of Tragedy*, glorified Wagner's operas by comparing them to Greek tragedy. Though Nietzsche eventually broke with Wagner, it was a peaceful break; Nietzsche looked back on his friendship with Wagner as the best experience of his life.

When Nietzsche was in his early thirties, he became seriously ill— so ill that he resigned his professorship, and seemed close to death. He withdrew into himself, and took stock of himself. It was time for Nietzsche to become Nietzsche. Now he must cease to be Wagner's son or Schopenhauer's son, now he must become his own man, now he must become a father figure in his own right. He parted ways with Wagner and Schopenhauer, and lit out on his own. His next two books—*Human, All-Too-Human* and *Dawn*—are declarations of independence from Wagner and Schopenhauer.

Like Kierkegaard, Nietzsche became happier, and more at peace with himself, as he grew older. In his next book, *The Gay Science*,

---

[1] Nietzsche, *Untimely Essays*, "Schopenhauer as Educator"

Nietzsche wrote, "What is the seal of liberation? No longer being ashamed in front of oneself."[1] Nietzsche had finally liberated himself from inner obstacles. He accepted himself, he accepted his life, including sickness and death, and he accepted the world. Indeed, he went beyond acceptance to ecstatic affirmation. In his next book, *Thus Spoke Zarathustra*, Nietzsche reached heights of inspiration rarely, if ever, reached in the history of literature.

One of the main themes of Nietzsche's work is the critique of morality. Nietzsche argued that morality, as practiced by saints and preached by philosophers, is not as pure and holy as we think, and it's not as healthy, not as beneficial to mankind as we think. According to Nietzsche, the saint, the "good man," is driven by a variety of motives, including perhaps a lust for power, a hostility to other people, and a hostility to life itself; in short, the saint is driven by motives that are "human, all-too-human."

Nietzsche's view of morality is at odds with Schopenhauer's. Schopenhauer rejected traditional religion and espoused atheism, but he was sympathetic to traditional morality. Nietzsche went further than Schopenhauer insofar as Nietzsche rejected traditional morality as well as traditional religion. While most moralists, including Schopenhauer, preached renunciation of life, Nietzsche affirmed life and espoused earthly values. Nietzsche deplored the old emphasis on the "other world": "The concept of the 'beyond', the 'true world' invented in order to devaluate the only world there is—in order to retain no goal, no reason, no task for our earthly reality!"[2]

Nietzsche's work is free from the Kantian verbiage that one finds in Schopenhauer, and free from the Hegelian verbiage that one finds in Kierkegaard. Nietzsche rejected the German philosophical tradition, the tradition of Kant and Hegel. Nietzsche emulated French philosophers like Montaigne, La Rochefoucauld, La Bruyére, etc. But while Nietzsche's words are plain, his sentences are slightly precious and his thoughts are often strained. Thus, Nietzsche's work, especially his early work, is difficult to read. His later work is strident, but more readable than his early work.

The most readable, concise and powerful book that Nietzsche wrote is his autobiographical work, *Ecce Homo*. I also recommend two of his late works, *Twilight of the Idols* and *The Antichrist*, and Part I of *Thus*

---

[1] Nietzsche, *The Gay Science*, #275
[2] *Ecce Homo*, "Why I Am A Destiny"

Spoke Zarathustra. Those interested in Nietzsche's personality should read *Conversations With Nietzsche* (edited by Sander Gilman). Nietzsche wrote a lot; though he preached brevity, he didn't practice it. If his books were skillfully abridged, they would be incomparable. Nietzsche is unsurpassed in profundity and also in pathos. If anyone doubts Nietzsche's genius, they should consider three things:

1. his gift for psychology; Freud said that Nietzsche's "guesses and intuitions often agree in the most astonishing way with the laborious findings of psychoanalysis"[1]
2. his style, his ability to express himself in German; Thomas Mann said that Nietzsche and Heine were the supreme masters of German prose
3. his gift for prophecy; though he died in 1900, he foresaw many of the major events of the 20th century, such as the world wars, the rise of psychology (Freud), etc.

4. Emerson

One of Nietzsche's favorite writers was Emerson. Nietzsche admired the cheerful, positive, affirmative tone of Emerson's work. Emerson's cheerfulness is the opposite of Schopenhauer's pessimism. Emerson's favorite writer was Montaigne, the most cheerful of philosophers. Emerson tried to write essays similar to Montaigne's essays. Emerson's goal was not to extend the boundaries of knowledge, but rather to help people to live, to inspire people. "The characteristic of heroism," Emerson wrote, "is its persistency. All men have wandering impulses, fits, and starts of generosity. But when you have chosen your part, abide by it, and do not weakly try to reconcile yourself with the world."[2] Influenced by Romantics like Coleridge, Emerson championed intuition rather than logic, spontaneity rather than reason.

Emerson's best book is his *Journals*; I recommend Bliss Perry's abridgment, which is about 300 pages long. This is the best American book—better than Emerson's *Essays*, better than Thoreau's *Walden*. In its variety and profundity, it reminds one of Eckermann's *Conversations*

---

[1] Freud, *An Autobiographical Study*, 5
[2] "Heroism"

With Goethe. Like Kierkegaard's *Journals*, Emerson's *Journals* are actually a book of aphorisms. As for Emerson's essays, my favorites are "The American Scholar," "Self-Reliance," and "Thoreau." Emerson's prose is excellent, but his essays are occasionally windy. If you want to read a biography of Emerson, consider *Emerson: The Mind on Fire*, by Robert Richardson.

5. Thoreau

Emerson's friend and neighbor, Thoreau, is best known as the author of *Walden*. The first three chapters of *Walden* are among the finest of all philosophical writings. Thoreau's style is earthy, lively and eloquent. His cheerfulness reminds one of Emerson. Thoreau argues in favor of a simple, frugal life, and criticizes the complex, hurried life that most men lead. "Men's minds run so much on work and money," writes Thoreau, "an Irishman who saw me in the fields making a [note] in my notebook took it for granted that I was casting up my wages and actually inquired what they came to, as if he had never dreamed of any other use for writing."[1]

Thoreau's love of nature has made him very popular with readers in our time—more popular than Emerson. "In Wildness is the preservation of the world," said Thoreau; "I believe in the forest, and in the meadow, and in the night in which the corn grows.... Hope and the future for me are not in lawns and cultivated fields, not in towns and cities, but in the impervious and quaking swamps."[2] Thoreau could make friends with all sorts of wild animals, including birds, frogs and woodchucks; he would call his animal friends by whistling, and they would eat out of his hand.

He spent his days wandering in the woods and fields around Concord, Massachusetts, collecting arrowheads, plants, birds' nests, etc. and bringing them back to his private museum in his parents' attic. Occasionally he ventured farther afield, taking trips to Cape Cod, Mt. Katahdin, the White Mountains, etc. He wrote several travel books, the best of which may be his book on Cape Cod. Like Emerson, Thoreau often gave lectures and readings at the Concord Lyceum. Thoreau's

---

[1] *The Selected Journals of Henry David Thoreau*, edited by Carl Bode, 4/3/59

[2] "Walking," an essay by Thoreau

works are filled with puns and witticisms. When Thoreau lectured on Cape Cod, Emerson said that the audience "laughed until they cried."[1]

Emerson allowed Thoreau to build a cabin on his land at Walden Pond; thus began Thoreau's famous experiment in simple living. In a lecture at the Concord Lyceum, Thoreau described his lifestyle at the Pond; Emerson said that the audience was "charmed with the witty wisdom which ran through it all,"[2] and Thoreau was asked to repeat it the following week for the benefit of those who had missed it. This enthusiastic response prompted Thoreau to expand the lecture into a book—his most famous book, *Walden*. I recommend the Norton Critical Edition of *Walden*—or better yet, Jeffrey Cramer's *Walden: A Fully Annotated Edition*.

While he was living at Walden Pond, Thoreau was arrested and jailed for non-payment of taxes. Thoreau was fervently anti-slavery, and he didn't want his tax money to support government policies that he viewed as pro-slavery. When a relative paid Thoreau's tax, and Thoreau's jailer told him that he had to leave, Thoreau was "mad as the devil,"[3] and refused to leave, since he wanted to call attention to his political views. Out of this incident grew Thoreau's famous essay, "Civil Disobedience," in which he argued that the individual should obey conscience rather than law, and that passive resistance by numerous people could change government policy. "Civil Disobedience" influenced Gandhi's struggle against British rule in India, and also influenced Martin Luther King's struggle on behalf of American blacks.

Thoreau devoted most of his afternoons to walking in the woods and fields around Concord.

> He set out each afternoon well prepared for his hikes. Under his arm he carried an old music book in which to press flowers. In his hand was a cane... its edge marked off in feet and inches for quick measuring. On his head was his size seven hat with a special shelf built inside on which to place interesting botanical specimens.... His clothes were chosen to provide a natural camouflage in the woods and fields.... He rejoiced that he could easily walk ten, fifteen, or twenty miles from his own door without going by any house.[4]

---

[1] *The Days of Henry Thoreau*, ch. 14
[2] ibid, ch. 10
[3] ibid, ch. 11
[4] *The Days of Henry Thoreau*, XIV, 8

Thoreau foresaw that, in a few decades, it would no longer be possible to take such walks; he realized that open space was diminishing. "Let us improve our opportunities, then," he wrote, "before the evil days come."[1]

Sometimes, instead of walking on dry land, he walked through streams for long stretches, and sometimes, instead of walking by the light of the sun, he walked in the middle of the night, by the light of a full moon. "Will not my townsmen consider me a benefactor," Thoreau wrote in his journal, "if I conquer some realms from the night, if I can show them that there is some beauty awake while they are asleep?"

Many abridgements of Thoreau's *Journals* have been published; I recommend *The Heart of Thoreau's Journals*. I also recommend two essays by Thoreau, "Walking" and "Life Without Principle." Walter Harding has written an extraordinary biography of Thoreau, *The Days of Henry Thoreau*; fans of Thoreau will find this book difficult to put down. Richardson's biography—*Henry Thoreau: A Life of the Mind*—is also top-notch.

In January, 1862, Thoreau was 45, and he was dying of tuberculosis. Two of his friends, who skated down the river to visit him, reported later that

> he seemed glad to see us; said we had not come much too soon.... There was a beautiful snowstorm going on the while which I fancy inspired him, and his talk was up to the best I ever heard from him—the same depth of earnestness and the same infinite depth of fun going on at the same time.

When he was asked if he put his faith in Christ, he said that a snowstorm meant more to him than Christ. One of his friends said to him, "you seem near the brink of the dark river. What do you think of the next world?" Thoreau responded, "One world at a time." In March, 1862, a neighbor visited Thoreau and later told Emerson that he "never spent an hour with more satisfaction. Never saw a man dying with so much pleasure and peace." In his final days, Thoreau worked on his book about Maine, and his last sentence contained only two distinct words: "Moose" and "Indian."[2]

6. Carlyle

---

1 "Walking"

2 On Thoreau's final months, see *The Days of Henry Thoreau*, ch. 20

Carlyle was born in 1795, 8 years before Emerson and 22 years before Thoreau. Though he was one of the leading intellectuals of his time, Carlyle is largely forgotten today. He wrote essays and several long historical works. Carlyle is known for his hero-worship; he emphasized the importance of great individuals in history. The best government, in Carlyle's view, is one in which a great individual has unlimited power.

Carlyle is also known for introducing German writers and German thought to the English-speaking world. He learned German at a time when few English intellectuals knew German. He wrote a biography of Schiller, the German poet and dramatist, and a multi-volume work on Frederick the Great, the German military hero.

Carlyle's conversational talent was legendary; Darwin said that Carlyle was "the best worth listening to of any man I know."[1] Emerson traveled to England partly in order to converse with Carlyle; Emerson called Carlyle, "an immense talker... as extraordinary in that as in his writing; I think even more so. You will never discover his real vigor and range, or how much more he might do than he has ever done, without seeing him."[2] Carlyle was a keen observer of people, and he left memorable sketches of many of his contemporaries, including Coleridge, Wordsworth, and Queen Victoria. Emerson said that Carlyle's forte was not abstract thinking, but rather grasping the essence of a man or an epoch.[3] Carlyle used this ability to create a highly poetic type of historical writing. Mill said that Carlyle's *French Revolution* "is not so much a history as an epic poem [and yet] the truest of histories."[4]

Carlyle was a right-wing thinker who rejected the liberalism and Utilitarianism that was popular in his time, and criticized the democratic, business-oriented society that was developing around him. He was especially critical of the U.S., the nation in which democracy and capitalism were most fully developed:

> My friend, brag not yet of our American cousins! Their quantity of cotton, dollars, industry and resources, I believe to be almost unspeakable; but I can by no means worship the like of these. What great human soul, what

---

[1] *The Norton Anthology of English Literature*, 4th edition, volume 2, introduction to the section on Carlyle

[2] *The Heart Of Emerson's Journals*, edited by Bliss Perry, October, 1847

[3] See Frank T. Thompson, "Emerson and Carlyle," *Studies in Philology*, XXIV, 1927

[4] *The Norton Anthology of English Literature*, 4th edition, volume 2, footnote in the excerpt from Carlyle's *French Revolution*.

great thought, what great noble thing that one could worship, or loyally admire, has yet been produced there?[1]

Among Carlyle's works, my favorite is *Sartor Resartus*, an auto-biographical novel. Though Carlyle lacks wit and grace, he's one of the most profound thinkers that the English-speaking nations have produced. If you'd like to read a biography of Carlyle, consider Fred Kaplan's biography.

7. Wilde

Oscar Wilde possessed the wit and grace that Carlyle lacked. Though Wilde is known as a dramatist, he wrote superb philosophical dialogues. Wilde reached the peak of his fame in the late 1800's, shortly after Carlyle had died. Like Carlyle, Wilde was critical of modern society. Wilde was especially critical of modern journalism: "In America," Wilde said, "the President reigns for four years, and Journalism governs for ever and ever.... In America journalism has carried its authority to the grossest and most brutal extreme."[2] In fact, all of the philosophers we've discussed so far loathed modern journalism.

Wilde was a witty talker, and his writings are filled with clever epigrams. "To be Greek," said Wilde, "one should have no clothes: to be medieval one should have no body: to be modern one should have no soul."[3] When Wilde visited the U.S., he passed through customs with the remark, "I have nothing to declare except my genius."[4] Wilde's best works are his dialogues—*The Critic As Artist* and *The Decay of Lying*—his essay, "The Soul of Man Under Socialism," and his fairy tales. Wilde's dialogues are as good as the best of Plato's dialogues. Wilde's dialogues deal mainly with aesthetics, but they also discuss modern life and modern society. Wilde's fairy tales are suitable for readers of all ages; "The Happy Prince" is especially good. His novel, *The Picture of Dorian Gray*, is morbid, but it's also well-written and interesting. His plays are graceful and readable, but they lack imaginative power. Wilde was too good an essayist and critic to be a great artist.

---

[1] *Latter-Day Pamphlets*, "The Present Time"
[2] *The Soul of Man Under Socialism*
[3] *Oscar Wilde*, by R. Ellman, ch. 3
[4] ibid, ch. 6

Like Kierkegaard, Wilde had a short, eventful, tragic life. Like Kierkegaard, Wilde was cruelly satirized by the press. After achieving fame at a young age, Wilde seemed to feel a self-destructive urge. His homosexual affairs led to a highly-publicized trial and to imprisonment. He died at age forty-six. Ellman's biography of Wilde would be good if it weren't so long; like most modern biographies, it needs to lose a lot of weight.

8. Mill

In the late 1700s, at the time of the French Revolution, the remnants of feudalism were being swept away, Utopian ideas were in the air, and it seemed that reason, democracy, and education could create a new, better world. Among the English proponents of these radical ideas, two of the leading figures were Jeremy Bentham and James Mill. Bentham and Mill advocated the philosophy of Utilitarianism, that is, they believed that the goal of government was the greatest happiness of the greatest number of people. They believed that their writings could improve the world, and they wanted someone to carry on their work after their deaths. Since Bentham had no sons, they chose as their successor John Stuart Mill, eldest son of James Mill.

John Stuart Mill was born in 1806, and by the time he was 2, Bentham and James Mill were drawing up plans for his education. When John was 3, he began learning Greek, and a few years later, he took up Latin. The education of John Stuart Mill was one of the most rigorous and systematic in history. It exemplifies the view of the English Radicals that reason and education can reshape human nature, and reshape society.

When John Stuart Mill was 20, he began to question his goals. Hitherto he had striven to educate himself and to reform society, but now he realized that if all the reforms he was aiming at were achieved, he would not be happy. He fell into a deep depression, which lasted for many months. When he finally climbed out of this depression, he was a different person: he was receptive to poetry, art, music, and nature, he respected feeling as much as reason, and he insisted that any Utopian scheme should leave room for individual inclinations and eccentricities.

Though Mill had emerged from his depression, he had also lost the companionship of his fellow reformers, and he felt isolated. Then he met Harriet Taylor, with whom he had a long, Platonic relationship. His high opinion of Harriet Taylor's mental powers was doubtless a factor in making Mill an advocate of women's rights.

Mill wrote ambitious works on logic and economics, but his most popular book today is a short book called *On Liberty*. In this book, Mill criticizes his contemporaries in the tone of a prophet:

> The greatness of England is now all collective: individually small, we only appear capable of anything great by our habit of combining; and with this our moral and religious philanthropists are perfectly contented. But it was men of another stamp than this that made England what it has been; and men of another stamp will be needed to prevent its decline. [1]

Mill's criticism of collective action and of associations reminds one of Kierkegaard. In his book *The Present Age*, Kierkegaard lamented that the individual was now lost in the Public; Mill makes the same argument in *On Liberty*. The embodiment of the Public is the newspaper, and both Kierkegaard and Mill discuss the enormous power of newspapers in the modern world.

Mill regarded Harriet Taylor as his muse, even his co-author. When Harriet's health began to fail, Mill was eager to preserve the thoughts that they had shared, before Harriet died. He urged Harriet to assist him in writing works that would serve as "mental pemmican" for future thinkers, works that would preserve their thoughts in concentrated form, works that could later be diluted for a popular audience. *On Liberty* was one of the results of this project, and it did indeed serve as pemmican for future thinkers. *On Liberty* contains the seeds of two of the most famous theories of the 20th century: Ortega's theory of the "revolt of the masses," and Riesman's theory of "inner-directed" and "other-directed" character types.

Mill warned against the dangers of communism, against the dangers of utopian schemes that would result in the death of liberty. His interest in economics did not prevent him from appreciating the importance of non-economic factors. "Among the works of man," wrote Mill, "which human life is rightly employed in perfecting and beautifying, the first in importance surely is man himself." [2] Mill's humanism made him an opponent of communism.

Mill believed that a good man can give reasons for his conduct. He opposed those who argued that a good man follows his instincts, or his innate moral sense. Likewise, in the field of epistemology, Mill argued

---

[1] *On Liberty*, ch. 3
[2] ibid

that one should be able to defend one's beliefs with reasons, not by appealing to intuition or feeling. Thus, Mill's views on ethics and epistemology were consistent; in both fields, Mill was a champion of reason.[1]

Emerson said that great minds are distinguished by "range and extent."[2] Like most philosophers, Mill wrote on a wide range of subjects: politics, aesthetics, economics, epistemology, ethics, even botany. While many philosophers lived solitary lives, Mill was involved in reform movements, reading groups and debating societies, worked for the East India Company for twenty years, and was even elected to Parliament, despite his refusal to campaign.

As a stylist, Mill has few equals in English literature. Mill's most popular book today (besides *On Liberty*) is his *Autobiography*, in which he describes his education, his depression, his relationship with Harriet Taylor, his political activity, etc.

Mill had no children, but he was regarded as a father figure by his disciples. One of his disciples, John Morley, described Mill as "the best and wisest man that I can ever know... one whose memory will always be as precious to me as to a son."[3]

9. Leopardi

Leopardi is the most interesting Italian philosopher. Like Schopenhauer, Leopardi was born in the late 1700's; like Schopenhauer, Leopardi was a pessimist and an atheist. Leopardi is best known for his poetry; his philosophical output is small, consisting chiefly of his *Pensieri* (*Thoughts*) and a few dialogues. Leopardi's aphorisms are first rate. He notes that it's difficult to appreciate a great literary work; in order to appreciate such a work, one must almost be capable of producing such a work: "There is little or no difference between appreciation and accomplishment."[4]

---

[1] see "John Stuart Mill As Moralist," by H. S. Jones (*Journal of the History of Ideas*, April–June, 1992, vol. 53, #2)

[2] see Emerson's essay, "Shakespeare; Or, The Poet"

[3] "John Stuart Mill As Moralist," by H. S. Jones (*Journal of the History of Ideas*, April–June, 1992, vol. 53, #2)

[4] *Parini's Discourse on Glory*, §2

While we're on the subject of Italian philosophy, we should mention the famous Italian political theorist, Machiavelli. Machiavelli is best known for his short work, *The Prince*, which takes a cold, amoral view of politics. Machiavelli also wrote *Discourses on Livy*, in which he reflects on the history of Rome, as narrated by the Roman historian, Livy. The *Discourses* are neither as concise nor as readable as *The Prince*. Machiavelli's *History of Florence* is his longest and least interesting work; "I have tried to read Machiavelli's histories," wrote Emerson, "but find it not easy. The Florentine factions are as tiresome as the history of the Philadelphia fire-companies."[1]

10. Ortega

The best twentieth-century philosopher is the Spaniard, José Ortega y Gasset. Ortega's *Revolt of the Masses* is an extraordinary work—one can't praise it too highly. In this work, Ortega discusses modern society and the dangers that threaten it. No one understands modern society better than Ortega. "There is one fact," Ortega writes, "which [is] of utmost importance in the public life of Europe at the present moment. This fact is the accession of the masses to complete social power. As the masses, by definition, neither should nor can direct their own personal existence, and still less rule society in general, this fact means that actually Europe is suffering from the greatest crisis that can afflict peoples, nations, and civilization."[2]

Ortega's father ran a newspaper, and Ortega was active in journalism and politics; he was also a philosophy professor. During the Spanish Civil War, he went into exile, returning to Spain at the end of his life; he died in 1955.

Ortega attended German universities, and his work was influenced by the German metaphysical tradition. Some of his books are dry. Aside from *The Revolt of the Masses*, his best works are *Notes on the Novel*, *The Dehumanization of Art*, *Man and Crisis*, *The Modern Theme* and *On Love*.

---

[1] *The Heart of Emerson's Journals, edited by Bliss Perry, journal entry of 1/10/47*
[2] *Revolt of the Masses*, 1

11. Hoffer

Another interesting twentieth-century philosopher is the American,
Eric Hoffer. Hoffer never attended any schools. During the Depression,
Hoffer was jobless, became depressed, and decided to commit suicide.
He bought some poison, walked out on the highway, and started to drink
the poison. Then he had a vision of life on the road, spat out the poison,
and spent the next twenty years living his vision, living as a tramp,
walking up and down California, following the harvests, picking crops,
doing odd jobs, and consorting with prostitutes. During World War II,
Hoffer got a steady job as a longshoreman in San Francisco, and lived
there until his death in 1983.

Like Emerson, Hoffer loved Montaigne. Like Emerson, Hoffer
wasn't a systematic philosopher, but rather a wise and gifted observer of
mankind. Hoffer's books are short, and they consist of either essays or
aphorisms. Of the philosophers we've discussed so far, Hoffer is the
most readable. Hoffer's chief interest is society and politics, but he
addresses a wide range of subjects, including psychic phenomena:

> The capacity for transcending the senses—for telepathic transmission and
> for sensing the unseen—is an animal characteristic.... A misunderstanding
> takes place not when people fail to understand each other, but when they
> sense what is going on in each other's mind and do not like it.[1]

Hoffer's best works are *Before the Sabbath* and his autobiography, *Truth
Imagined*.

12. Ancient Philosophers

If you want to read about ancient philosophy, consider

- Alfred Edward Taylor, who wrote studies of Socrates and Plato
- Pierre Hadot, author of *What is Ancient Philosophy?*, *Philosophy as
  a Way of Life*, etc.
- Gregory Vlastos, author of (among other works) *Socrates: Ironist
  and Moral Philosopher*
- I. F. Stone, an American journalist who studied Greek in his
  retirement years, and wrote an unscholarly but interesting book
  called *The Trial of Socrates*

---

[1] *Reflections on the Human Condition*, §21

- Diogenes Laertius, who wrote short biographies of ancient philosophers; it's thought that he lived around 230 A.D.
- Xenophon, who knew Socrates, and wrote about him in works such as *Memorabilia* and *Symposium*
- Gilbert Murray, prominent writer on ancient literature, who wrote a book called *Five Stages of Greek Religion*, which is a good introduction to ancient philosophy; Murray's style is graceful, his knowledge deep, his ideas profound
- Walter Pater, the renowned English writer, who wrote *Plato and Platonism*
- Kierkegaard wrote *The Concept of Irony, with constant reference to Socrates*

My favorite ancient philosopher is Plato. No one combines the poetic and the profound better than Plato. But in several of his dialogues, Plato becomes entangled in metaphysics, hence many readers (including Montaigne and Nietzsche) have found Plato boring. Plato's best dialogues are *Apology, Symposium* and *Republic*; also of interest are *Gorgias, Laws, Crito* and *Phaedo*. *Apology* is short, interesting and readable—a good introduction to philosophy. *Symposium* is delightful on the whole, though slow at times. *Republic* is Plato's greatest achievement, a profound discussion not only of politics, but also of religion, morality and art. I recommend reading Plato in an annotated edition, such as the two volumes published by John Burnet; these volumes contain a total of four dialogues.

Gorgias may be the source of one of Nietzsche's best-known theories: *Gorgias* contrasts the morality of the strong with the morality of the weak. Plato reminds one of Dostoyevsky insofar as Plato is friendly to religion and morality, but has a deep understanding of the arguments against religion and morality. Plato's comments on democracy are still fresh and relevant; in a democracy, Plato says, there are "subjects who are like rulers, and rulers who are like subjects."[1] Plato was convinced that every form of government was flawed.

In addition to being a profound philosopher, Plato is a shrewd psychologist; "In all of us," Plato writes, "even in good men, there is a lawless wild-beast nature, which peers out in sleep."[2]

---

[1] *Republic*, 8. This remark contains the seed of Ortega's theory of "the revolt of the masses."

[2] *Republic*, 9

Aristotle lacks the poetry of Plato; if Plato is sometimes dry, Aristotle is frequently dry. *Poetics* is Aristotle's most interesting and readable work; it's very short, about forty pages. Though *Poetics* concentrates on drama, it also discusses epic poetry. Like all of Aristotle's works, *Poetics* is weighed down with distinctions and definitions; here's an example: "A whole is that which has a beginning, a middle, and an end. A beginning is that which does not necessarily come after something else, although something else exists or comes about after it...." Aristotle's *Ethics* and *Politics* are occasionally interesting.

The dominant philosophies of later antiquity were Epicureanism and Stoicism. Epicureanism has come down to us chiefly in Lucretius's long poem, *On the Nature of Things*. Though this work contains flashes of brilliance, I don't recommend it highly. Stoicism has come down to us chiefly in the works of Marcus Aurelius, Epictetus and Seneca. The *Meditations* of the emperor Marcus Aurelius is a clear and concise expression of the Stoic philosophy; it has sincerity, but it lacks vitality and profundity. The *Manual* of the slave Epictetus is generally considered to be better than Marcus's *Meditations*. Seneca is more interesting than Marcus or Epictetus; Seneca was a favorite of Montaigne.

Before we leave antiquity, we should say a few words about Cicero and Plutarch. Cicero's treatises have little originality or profundity; the best that can be said of them is that they lucidly summarize ancient philosophy. Cicero is best known for his orations and for his *Letters to Atticus*.

Plutarch is best known for his short biographies of famous Greeks and Romans. Plutarch's biographies contain many clever epigrams and interesting anecdotes; those interested in ancient history shouldn't ignore Plutarch's biographies. Plutarch's philosophical essays had a great influence over Montaigne, just as Montaigne's essays had a great influence over Emerson. Though Montaigne is sometimes credited with being the father of the essay form, he actually borrowed that form from Plutarch. Originality often consists in reviving what is old and forgotten.

13. Montaigne

Montaigne is one of the finest fruits of the Renaissance, and one of the best-loved of all philosophers. Montaigne was a student of the history, poetry and philosophy of antiquity; he was cool toward Christianity. Montaigne sprinkles his essays with quotations from ancient writers. But Montaigne isn't pedantic; his books carry us beyond books and they bring us into contact with life itself. Montaigne often expresses disdain for books; he says that he only resorts to books when he lacks friendship, conversation and love. Montaigne argues that the purpose of philosophy is to live better, to overcome anxieties. According to Montaigne, philosophy

> preaches nothing but jollity and merry-making. A sad and dejected air shows that here philosophy is not at home.... The most manifest sign of wisdom is a constant happiness; its state is like that of things above the moon: always serene.[1]

Many of Montaigne's essays are dull, hence they need to be edited and abridged. Among Montaigne's essays, my favorites are "On Friendship," "On Vehicles," "On Physiognomy," "On Democritus and Heraclitus," "To Study Philosophy is to Learn to Die," and "We Taste Nothing Pure." A book called *The Autobiography of Michel De Montaigne* arranges excerpts from Montaigne's essays to form an autobiography.

14. Descartes and Pascal

Descartes, who was born about fifty years after Montaigne, is generally considered to be an important French philosopher. Descartes was a pioneer in science and math. Though Descartes's works are historically significant, they're of little interest to modern readers. Descartes lacks the humanity and pathos of Montaigne. Descartes's *Discourse on Method* is concise and readable, but dry.

Pascal has the humanity and pathos that Descartes lacks. Born in 1623, about twenty-five years after Descartes, Pascal was a child prodigy with a gift for math. Like Kierkegaard, Pascal was a fervent and impassioned Christian. Pascal opposed Descartes's belief that reason alone could lead one to truth; "the heart," wrote Pascal, "has its reasons, of which reason knows nothing." Pascal's *Pensées*, written in aphoristic form, is a powerful and interesting work. Though its chief aim is to defend Christianity, it also discusses the human condition generally.

Pascal argues that one of man's basic desires is a desire for diversion, for something to fill up the time. Pascal argues that man would rather have something to do, even if it's unpleasant, than have nothing to do; Pascal says, "When a soldier complains of his hard life (or a labourer,

---

[1] "That to Study Philosophy is to Learn to Die"

etc.) try giving him nothing to do."[1] Man is incapable (says Pascal) of sitting quietly in his room.

In the field of math, one of Pascal's achievements was the theory of probability. As a young man, his doctor told him that he was working too hard, he should relax. So he went to the clubs and casinos of Paris, and applied his knowledge of probability to games of chance. Pascal's *Pensées* contains his famous wager theory. This theory states that God may or may not exist, just as a coin may be heads or tails. Everyone must wager, that is, everyone must choose whether to live as if God exists, or live as if God doesn't exist. If we choose to live as if God exists, we may win eternal happiness. If we choose to live as if God doesn't exist, we may win some trivial worldly goods. Since eternal happiness is so valuable, so much more valuable than worldly goods, we should bet on God, we should live as if God exists.

Pascal is considered one of the supreme masters of French prose. Tocqueville said that the age of Pascal was the golden age of French literature, since style was then only the vehicle of thought; the writers of that time aimed only to communicate their thoughts clearly and concisely, and didn't aim at an elegant style.[2]

15. Other French Philosophers

During the seventeenth and eighteenth centuries, a number of Frenchmen— including La Rochefoucauld, La Bruyère, Vauvenargues and Chamfort—wrote philosophical works in aphoristic form. La Rochefoucauld's *Maxims* are famous for their penetrating analysis of mankind. "We are equally unhappy," wrote La Rochefoucauld, "when we are deeply in love, and when we have no lover at all." La Bruyère's *Characters* is also interesting; the first chapter, "On Books," is the best. An excellent book could be compiled from the best of La Rochefoucauld, La Bruyère, Vauvenargues and Chamfort.

During the eighteenth century, the dominant figures in French thought were Voltaire and Rousseau. Both were extremely influential in their day, though neither looms large in the history of philosophy. Voltaire and Rousseau were famous for their imaginative works as well

---

[1] *Pensées*, §415

[2] *Correspondence and Conversations of Alexis de Tocqueville With N. W. Senior*, 8/26/50

as their theoretical works. They were neither true artists nor true philosophers, but they had genius and they had a mastery of the French language.

Voltaire was a popular dramatist, and even wrote an epic poem, the *Henriade*, which deals with Henry IV. Voltaire also wrote tales and stories, of which the most famous is *Candide*. Like Swift's *Gulliver's Travels*, *Candide* is a vehicle for the author's ideas rather than a purely imaginative work. But *Candide* is more concise and readable than *Gulliver's Travels*; Voltaire is unsurpassed in wit and taste. Voltaire's wit is at its best in his *Philosophical Dictionary*, in which he pokes fun at the religious and political establishment. Voltaire's *General History* is an entertaining survey of Western history; his *History of Louis XIV* is also a readable work. I highly recommend André Maurois's biography of Voltaire.

Almost everything Rousseau wrote created a sensation. Rousseau broke onto the literary scene with his *Two Discourses*, in which he glorified the simple, uncivilized life of primitive man. While Voltaire had generally worked within the classical tradition, Rousseau introduced a new, sentimental, romantic style; Rousseau is often called the father of Romanticism. His long novel, *The New Héloïse*, concerned itself with the emotions of young lovers. In his novel *Émile*, Rousseau expounded his innovative theories on education. Rousseau's political theories were also innovative; he anticipated the French Revolution, and helped to incite it with his book, *The Social Contract*, which begins with the famous words, "Man was born free, and he is everywhere in chains." Rousseau's *Confessions* is of greater interest to modern readers than his other works; it is one of the best autobiographies ever written—intimate and poetic, long but rarely dull.

16. Bacon

Francis Bacon was one of the leading intellectuals of the Renaissance era. Bacon is best known for his ideas on scientific method and for his interest in the natural world. Like Pliny the Elder, Bacon died from a scientific experiment; Pliny died while gathering data on a volcanic eruption, Bacon died from a cold that he contracted while trying to freeze meat in snow. Bacon's most popular book is his *Essays*, which was inspired by Montaigne's *Essays*. Bacon's *Essays* aren't as intimate and sincere as Montaigne's *Essays*; Montaigne put his whole soul into his *Essays*, while Bacon wrote with his mind. Nonetheless, Bacon's *Essays* are interesting and his style is lively. Bacon's archaic language has a certain charm: "Those that want friends [i.e., lack friends] to open themselves unto," writes Bacon, "are cannibals of their own hearts.... This communicating of a man's self to his friend works two contrary effects; for it redoubleth joys, and cutteth griefs in halves."[1] Besides his intellectual work, Bacon was actively involved in English politics, and held high government positions. I recommend Macaulay's essay on Bacon, which is profound and well-written. I also recommend Catherine Bowen's biography of Bacon; it's one of those rare books that one wishes were longer. "In the House of Commons," Bowen tells us, "Bacon was at his best. When he rose to speak, the crowded benches were quiet. We have Ben Jonson's testimony: 'The fear of every man that heard him was, lest he should make an end.'"[2] Lisa Jardine has written several books about Bacon, and edited some of Bacon's own books; Jardine has also written about Erasmus, Robert Hooke, and Christopher Wren.

17. Other British Philosophers

Hobbes is best known for his book, *Leviathan*, which argues in favor of absolute monarchy; *Leviathan* is occasionally interesting. Locke was important in his time for his political writings, which advocated limited monarchy, popular representation and religious toleration. Locke was also important for his epistemological writings, which criticized the concept of innate ideas, and argued that the mind was a blank paper, a *tabula rasa*, that acquired ideas through experience. I don't recommend any of Locke's books. Berkeley is famous for his radical idealism, for saying that matter doesn't exist, only ideas exist. Berkeley, like Hume, expressed his views in the form of dialogues as well as treatises.

Hume is more interesting than Locke or Berkeley. Hume's best work is his *Dialogues Concerning Natural Religion*, which discusses God and the origin of evil:

> Epicurus's old questions are yet unanswered. Is [God] willing to prevent evil, but not able? then is he impotent. Is he able, but not willing? then is he malevolent. Is he both able and willing? whence then is evil?[3]

---

[1] "Of Friendship"

[2] *Francis Bacon: The Temper of a Man*, by C. D. Bowen, ch. 5

[3] *Dialogues Concerning Natural Religion*, §10

Of all the philosophers before Schopenhauer, Hume is the most irreligious. Hume's *History of England* is eloquent but somewhat dull; it was overshadowed by Macaulay's *History of England*. Hume's essays are of little interest.

18. Lichtenberg, Kant and Hegel

While Kant is the most famous eighteenth-century German philosopher, Lichtenberg is the most interesting. Schopenhauer called Lichtenberg one of the few genuine philosophers. Lichtenberg's best work is written in aphoristic form. His aphorisms are lively and witty, as well as profound. "When a book and a head collide," Lichtenberg asks, "and there is a hollow sound, is it always in the book?"[1] Lichtenberg's thought covers a broad range of subjects. He jots down whatever thoughts and experiences he finds interesting; anticipating Freud, he says, "a philosophical dream book could be written.... I know from undeniable experience that dreams lead to self-knowledge."[2] Various collections of Lichtenberg's writings have been made; I recommend *The Lichtenberg Reader*.

Kant's works are dry and obscure; perhaps Kant's most readable book is his *Prolegomena to Any Future Metaphysic*. I recommend a book called *The Last Days of Kant*, written by Wasianski, and translated into English by Thomas De Quincey; it's an intimate sketch of Kant in his old age.

If Kant is obscure, Hegel is even more so; those of Hegel's books that deal with metaphysics and logic are especially obscure. But two of Hegel's books are somewhat readable: *The Philosophy of History* and *The Philosophy of Right*. *The Philosophy of History* summarizes world history. Though Hegel's observations on history are sometimes profound, he often insists on interpreting history in terms of his religious and philosophical preconceptions. *The Philosophy of Right* takes a right-wing view of politics; Hegel argues that the state doesn't exist for the individual, but rather the individual exists for the state. Hegel rejects the common view that war is purely destructive: "Just as the blowing of the winds preserves the sea from the foulness which would be the result of a prolonged calm, so also corruption in nations would be the product of

---

[1] *The Lichtenberg Reader,* Boston, Beacon Press, 1959, Introduction
[2] ibid, Aphorisms, 1775-1779

prolonged, let alone 'perpetual' peace."[1] Both Kant and Hegel were first rate thinkers in terms of depth of thought, but second rate in terms of elegance of style.

19. Weininger, Spengler, etc.

Weininger and Spengler both wrote in the early 1900's. Weininger is the author of a book called *Sex and Character*. Weininger is known for his misogyny and for his anti-Semitism; he was anti-Semitic despite being Jewish himself. Weininger was one of the most precocious philosophers in history; Weininger wrote *Sex and Character* when he was in his early twenties, showed it to Freud and others, and then committed suicide. *Sex and Character* contains some interesting comments on genius, but it's too long-winded, especially on the subject of women.

Spengler's *Decline of the West* created a sensation when it was first published in 1918. But few have ever accepted its thesis, and today *The Decline of the West* is largely ignored. Spengler suffocates his thesis under a mountain of evidence. But like Weininger's work, Spengler's work contains some profound remarks; Toynbee said that Spengler's work was "teeming with firefly flashes of historical insight."[2] Like Weininger's *Sex and Character*, Spengler's *Decline of the West* might be worth reading if it were abridged.

One final word about histories of philosophy: beware! Most histories of philosophy are preoccupied with metaphysics and episte-mology. They over-emphasize philosophers who deal with those subjects, such as Aristotle and Kant, and they under-emphasize philo-sophers who deal with life itself, such as Montaigne and Thoreau. They over-emphasize systematic philosophers, and under-emphasize apho-ristic philosophers. Those who approach philosophy by reading a history of philosophy may well decide that philosophy is abstract, cold and impersonal. If, however, one is already acquainted with philosophy, one can learn much from a history of philosophy. I recommend a history of philosophy by Julián Marías, a Spanish writer, though I don't share Marías' approach to philosophy.

---

1 *The Philosophy of Right*, §324
2 *Civilization On Trial*, "*My View of History*"

I also recommend *Sophie's World: A Novel About the History of Philosophy*. *Sophie's World* is a very popular book, an international bestseller. It's ideally suited for young people, and for people who are new to philosophy. It introduces the reader to Western philosophy, and to Western civilization as a whole. Though *Sophie's World* is ideally suited for young people, it's deep enough to stimulate experienced readers. Like Marías, the author of *Sophie's World* (Jostein Gaarder) ignores philosophers like Montaigne and Thoreau. An admirer of reason, Gaarder scorns psychic phenomena, passes over Zen in silence, and has no interest in Jung. In short, *Sophie's World* has the shortcomings and biases of most histories of philosophy, but it's more readable than most histories of philosophy.

Another popular history of philosophy is Will Durant's *Story of Philosophy* (Durant also wrote *The Mansions of Philosophy*, which is sometimes called *The Pleasures of Philosophy*). Durant is best known for his 11-volume *Story of Civilization*. Durant wrote good prose, and his work is useful as a summary/introduction.

If you're looking for a history of religion, try Huston Smith's *The World's Religions*. Aldous Huxley compiled a book called *The Perennial Philosophy*, which blends the spiritual traditions of East and West.

Huxley was one of the outstanding intellectuals of his day. Born into a family of distinguished intellectuals, Huxley became a leading novelist, a biographer, and an explorer of the mystical, the Eastern, and the occult. Huxley's biography of Richelieu, *Grey Eminence*, was praised by no less a critic than E. M. Forster. Huxley's brother Julian was as renowned in biology as Aldous was in the humanities.

II. Psychology

1. Freud

As a Jewish boy growing up in Vienna, Freud was a top-notch student. In the 1870s, he studied medicine at the University of Vienna. He had vast intellectual ambitions, and as he walked beneath the statues of the great scholars of old, he fancied that someday his statue would be there, inscribed with the words that were spoken of Oedipus: "He solved the famous riddle and was a most mighty man."

Freud was a profound thinker and a superb stylist. He can teach one as much about human nature as any writer can. It may be said that others discovered the unconscious before Freud. It may be said that the psychology of the unconscious was "in the air" during Freud's time, and that if Freud had never been born, someone else would have made the discoveries that Freud made. It may be said that Freud made mistakes during the course of his long career—overlooking some things, exaggerating others. But none of this should prevent us from appreciating the importance of Freud's work. What most impresses me about Freud is

1. his discovery of techniques for grasping the unconscious
2. his ability to cast a bright light on the study of literature, biography, etc.
3. his ability to set forth philosophical ideas that are remarkable for their originality and profundity

One of Freud's best books is *Civilization and Its Discontents.* Written when he was 75, this little book is full of profound ideas. It isn't an easy book to read; the reader must strain to grasp all the ideas that it contains. It's a penetrating analysis of human nature, it throws light on the dark side of human nature. Based on his analysis of human nature, Freud makes predictions about the future, predictions that proved to be accurate. All things considered, one must regard this book as a philosophical work of the highest order.

Pascal once said, "All men naturally hate each other."[1] This is what Freud discusses in *Civilization and Its Discontents*: the dark side of human nature, the hostile, violent impulses in human nature. This book alone can refute the myth that Freud is obsessed with sexuality, that Freud finds sexual motives behind all human actions.

Freud mentions the religious commandment, "Love thy neighbor as thyself," and calls it, "a commandment which is really justified by the fact that nothing else runs so strongly counter to the original nature of man."[2] Freud says that each of us, drawing on our own life experience, can prove his assertions about the original nature of man:

> The time comes when each one of us has to give up as illusions the expectations which, in his youth, he pinned upon his fellow-men, and when he may learn how much difficulty and pain has been added to his life by their ill-will.[3]

Nor is it only our neighbor who harbors hostile impulses, we ourselves harbor them; Freud speaks of "this inclination to aggression, which we can detect in ourselves and justly assume to be present in others."[4]

Freud scoffs at communism, which blames private property for the evil in human society; "Aggressiveness was not created by property."[5] If you abolish private property, says Freud, people will fight over sexual relationships. If you declare complete sexual freedom, and abolish the family, it is impossible to foresee how civilization will develop, but we can be sure of one thing: aggression will continue to be part of it.

How is it possible for people to cooperate with each other? Freud says that two people can be bound together if they have a third person on whom they can vent their aggressive impulses. "The dream of a Germanic world-dominion called for anti-Semitism as its complement."[6] Russian communists were bound together by their hostility to the bourgeois; "one only wonders, with concern, what the Soviets will do

---

1 *Pensées*, Penguin Classics, #210
2 *Civilization and Its Discontents*, ch. 5
3 ibid
4 ibid
5 ibid
6 ibid

after they have wiped out their bourgeois."[1] These sentences were written before Stalin and Hitler committed their worst atrocities. The accuracy of Freud's predictions validates his analysis of human nature.

Freud's broad education is evident throughout *Civilization and Its Discontents*. He frequently quotes Goethe, and occasionally Shakespeare. He also quotes Heine:

> Mine is a most peaceable disposition. My wishes are: a humble cottage with a thatched roof, but a good bed, good food, the freshest milk and butter, flowers before my window, and a few fine trees before my door; and if God wants to make my happiness complete, he will grant me the joy of seeing some six or seven of my enemies hanging from those trees.[2]

One reason I enjoy reading Freud is that he treats the reader with courtesy, he treats the reader like a friend, like a companion who is joining him on a search for truth. As an example of Freud's courtesy, permit me to quote the start of the book's final chapter: "Having reached the end of his journey, the author must ask his readers' forgiveness for not having been a more skillful guide and for not having spared them empty stretches of road and troublesome detours. There is no doubt that it could have been done better."

When you read Freud, you feel that you are in the company of a great intellectual—bold and original, yet also cautious and skeptical; searching for ultimate truths, yet also admitting when truth is uncertain or elusive. Like all great intellectuals, Freud has a deep love for civilization, for cultural tradition. This is apparent in the first chapter of *Civilization and Its Discontents*, when Freud discusses the history of Rome. This discussion of the history of Rome is occasioned by a discussion of the nature of the mind; Freud mentions that nothing is ever completely forgotten, that everything is preserved in the mind, and can be recalled in certain circumstances. He compares this to the history of Rome, in which earlier buildings are preserved alongside later ones. Freud's lengthy, detailed description of Rome shows his respect for tradition, for civilization.

Freud scorns American civilization, perhaps because it lacks the respect for tradition, the courteous tone, that one finds in Freud's own work. Though Freud anticipated the atrocities of Hitler and Stalin, he felt that one of the greatest threats to civilization was the American spirit—the un-civilized, un-traditional, un-respectful tone of American culture.

---

[1] ibid
[2] ibid

I strongly recommend Freud's book, *Leonardo and a Memory of his Childhood*; it's a fascinating sketch of Leonardo, as well as a good introduction to Freud's ideas. Freud's *Totem and Taboo* teaches one much about primitive man and about human nature; I recommend it highly. "What primitive man regarded as the natural thing," writes Freud, "was the indefinite prolongation of life—immortality. The idea of death was only accepted late, and with hesitancy. Even for us it is lacking in content and has no clear connotation." *The Future of an Illusion* is a clear and concise attack on religion; like Schopenhauer and Nietzsche, Freud is an uncompromising atheist.

If you want to read a book about Freud, consider Ruitenbeek's *Freud As We Knew Him*; also consider Ernest Jones' 3-volume biography.

In 1906, when Freud turned 50, his friends presented him with a medallion; on one side was Freud himself, on the other was Oedipus solving the riddle of the Sphinx. The inscription read, "He solved the famous riddle and was a most mighty man."

What one longs for in youth, one attains in old age.

2. Jung

I recommend *Memories, Dreams, Reflections*, which is Jung's summary of his life and work, as dictated to Aniela Jaffé. Much of it deals with the occult. Jung believed that, in the unconscious, time and space have no effect, so the unconscious can perceive future events, and events taking place elsewhere. Before World War I broke out in 1914, Jung anticipated the outbreak of a pan-European war from which only Switzerland would emerge unscathed:

> In October 1913.... I lost consciousness of time and place and [had] an hallucination, a waking dream. I was looking at the map of Europe and saw how, country by country, beginning with France and Germany, all Europe became submerged under the sea. Shortly afterwards, the entire continent was under water with the exception of Switzerland: Switzerland was like a high mountain that the waves could not submerge.... I realized that the sea was of blood. Floating on the waves were corpses, roof tops, charred beams.

In the 1950s, when Jung was about 80, he appeared on British television. He impressed many viewers, and he was urged to write a book that would make his ideas accessible to a wide audience. He enlisted the help of several of his disciples, each of whom wrote a chapter of the book, following Jung's outline; Jung himself wrote the introduction. The book was called *Man and His Symbols*, and it's an excellent introduction to Jung's theories. Though it isn't as concise and well-organized as Freud's works, *Man and His Symbols* contains an abundance of provocative ideas and fascinating stories. It's a readable book, liberally sprinkled with illustrations (avoid the paperback version, which contains fewer illustrations). *Man and His Symbols* was Jung's last project; Jung died in 1961, just before the book was finished. If you want to read a biography of Jung, consider Barbara Hannah's *Jung: His Life and Work*. Remarks by people who met Jung can be found in *C. G. Jung: Interviews and Encounters*.

I recommend Jung's *Symbols of Transformation*, which discusses the hero archetype and mythology. Jung's interest in mythology is related to his concept of the collective unconscious. Myths are expressions of the unconscious, and because the unconscious is collective, the same myths are found in different peoples. Jung felt that myths, like religious creeds, helped to integrate consciousness with the unconscious:

> Myths and fairytales give expression to unconscious processes, and their retelling causes these processes to come alive again and be recollected, thereby re-establishing the connection between conscious and unconscious.... Since the symbol derives as much from the conscious as from the unconscious, it is able to unite them both.[1]

Jung's *Psychological Types* is an excellent book; no one ever knew more about human nature than Jung did. *Answer to Job* is an interesting work about Christianity. *Aion* deals with astrology and alchemy, and their relation to Christianity. Jung had a strong interest in alchemy—its psychological meaning and its symbolism. Jung's psychology is a search for the self, for wholeness, for the integration of consciousness with the unconscious, and Jung thought that alchemy was also a search for the self and for wholeness. Like some of Jung's other books, *Aion* is interesting and profound, but dry and long-winded.

Unlike Freud, Jung was friendly toward religion. Jung was not an atheist; he believed in God as an unconscious entity, an archetypal being. Jung didn't scoff at the notion that Jesus was the son of God; he believed in Jesus as the incarnation of the son-of-God archetype. Jung believed that modern man needed to re-connect with myths, with dreams, with the unconscious. He believed that modern man had bought technological progress at the price of spiritual sickness:

---

[1] Jung, Collected Works, vol. 9, part II, ¶280

Reforms by advances, that is, by new methods or gadgets, are of course impressive at first, but in the long run they are dubious and in any case dearly paid for. They by no means increase the contentment or happiness of people on the whole. Mostly, they are deceptive sweetenings of existence, like speedier communications which unpleasantly accelerate the tempo of life and leave us with less time than ever before. [1]

For Jung, expressing his ideas on paper wasn't enough: "I had to achieve a kind of representation in stone of my innermost thoughts." Jung constructed a stone tower on the shore of a Swiss lake, and he lived there as Thoreau lived on the shore of Walden Pond:

I have done without electricity, and tend the fireplace and stove myself. Evenings, I light the old lamps. There is no running water, and I pump the water from the well. I chop the wood and cook the food. These simple acts make man simple; and how difficult it is to be simple! [2]

During Jung's last years, his secretary was Aniela Jaffé, a disciple who wrote one of the chapters of *Man and His Symbols*. Jaffé's memories of Jung can be found in a wonderful little book called *From the Life and Work of C. G. Jung*; this book is a good introduction to Jung's ideas, as well as a lively portrait of Jung himself.

As I sat for the first time in the office [Jaffé writes], I waited tensely for what was about to come.... At ten o'clock he appeared, and that was the hour when our daily work began. Generally it lasted until midday. I could hear his slow, rather dragging step as he passed through the hallway. I must confess that the approach of the old magician never lost its excitement in all those years. With my inner ear I still hear it to this day. [3]

3. Adler

Like Jung, Adler was initially one of Freud's disciples, then broke with Freud and set up his own school. Adler originated the concept of the inferiority complex. According to Adler, the feeling of inferiority is often caused by a physical defect, a physical handicap of some kind. The feeling of inferiority can inspire great achievement, or prompt a retreat from life.

---

[1] *Memories, Dreams, Reflections*, ch. 8
[2] *Memories, Dreams, Reflections*, ch. 8
[3] Aniela Jaffé, *From the Life and Work of C. G. Jung*, ch. 4

Like Nietzsche, Adler argued that the desire for power was a fundamental part of human nature. But while Nietzsche had said that the desire for power generally has positive effects, Adler insisted that the desire for power was harmful to others and to oneself. While Nietzsche had glorified the loner, the solitary beast of prey, and criticized the herd animal, Adler criticized the beast of prey and glorified the amiable herd animal. "Education in the home," wrote Adler "...commits the gravest of psychological errors in inoculating children with the false idea that they must be superior to everyone else and consider themselves better than all other human beings."[1]

While Freud had said that a psychologically healthy person should be able to love and to work, Adler added a third ingredient, social interaction: "The three great problems of life," said Adler, "[are] the question whether [the individual] has fostered his contact between himself and his fellows in an approximately correct manner, or has hindered this contact.... the problem of profession and occupation, and the problem of love and marriage." Many of history's outstanding figures have failed to solve what Adler calls "the three great problems of life." Kierkegaard, for example, wrestled unsuccessfully with the problem of love and marriage. One of the paradoxes of our species is that great men aren't healthy, and healthy men aren't great. The great man is generally unhealthy, unbalanced, half-mad. Adler's healthy man, on the other hand, though he may be an excellent neighbor, an excellent friend and an excellent parent, isn't likely to be a great man. Should we not strive for both greatness and health? Would it not be a mistake to pursue only one of these goals, and forget the other? Should we not try to reconcile these goals, however difficult that may be?

Adler was sympathetic toward feminism, and his political views were left-wing. Those interested in Adler should read his book, *Understanding Human Nature*. Though this book is neither well-written nor well-organized, it contains some shrewd observations about human nature; for example, Adler points out that "a pampered child, as much as a hated one, labors under great difficulties."[2]

4. Other Psychologists

---

[1] *Understanding Human Nature*, Appendix

[2] *Understanding Human Nature*, I, 3

The fertility of the line of inquiry that Freud initiated is shown by the number and quality of Freud's disciples. One of Freud's most talented disciples was Ernest Jones, an Englishman. I recommend Jones's work, *Hamlet and Oedipus*. I also recommend several essays by Jones: "The Significance of Christmas," "Psycho-Analysis and the Christian Religion," "Psycho-Analysis and Folklore," "A Psycho-Analytic Study of the Holy Ghost Concept," "Anal-Erotic Character Traits," and "The Influence of Andrea del Sarto's Wife on His Art."

Karl Abraham was another of Freud's disciples. Abraham wrote a fascinating essay on Giovanni Segantini, an Italian painter. He also wrote an excellent essay on Amenhotep IV, an Egyptian pharaoh, and an interesting essay on "Character-Formation on the Genital Level of Libido-Development."

Freud's daughter, Anna Freud, followed in her father's footsteps and pursued a career as a psychoanalyst. While her father had concentrated on the psychology of the unconscious, Anna Freud concentrated on ego psychology. She specialized in the study of children and adolescents. I recommend her lucid and interesting book, *The Ego and the Mechanisms of Defense*.

Erik Erikson continued along the same path that Anna Freud had trodden. Erikson specialized in ego psychology, and is best known for his work on adolescence and for his theory of "identity crisis." I recommend his book *Youth: Identity and Crisis*. Erikson illustrates his theories about youth by discussing the identity crises of George Bernard Shaw and William James. Erikson insists that adolescence must be viewed in its social context: "We cannot separate personal growth and communal change, nor can we separate [the] identity crisis in individual life and contemporary crises in historical development."[1]

Though one can learn much from Freud's disciples, one can learn even more from Jung's disciples, such as Marie-Louise von Franz. Von Franz lived a long life, and was a prolific writer. The depth of her thought is astonishing, and she often speaks to one's most personal experience. Unfortunately, her books are somewhat unpolished, consisting of lecture notes, seminar transcripts, etc. Von Franz's specialty was fairy tales; she wrote several books about fairy tales, discussing tales from many different countries, and enriching her discussion with comments on her patients. She also wrote books about other Jungian topics—dreams, divination, alchemy, etc. She collaborated with Jung's wife, Emma, on a

---

[1] *Youth: Identity and Crisis*, Prologue, 3

major study of the Grail Legend. Emma Jung also wrote a small book called *Animus and Anima* which is highly regarded.

Another prominent Jungian is Edward Edinger, an American, who wrote psychological works (such as *Ego and Archetype*), and also studies of literature (Shakespeare, The Bible, *Faust*, *Moby Dick*, etc.). Mary Esther Harding was born in England, studied with Jung at his home in Switzerland, and spent most of her career in the U.S. Perhaps her best-known book is *The Way of All Women*. Among her other books is *Psychic Energy: Its Source and Transformation*.

Jung is more popular today than Freud, and Jungian books like Thomas Moore's *Care of the Soul* often become bestsellers.

Elisabeth Kübler-Ross, an American psychiatrist who worked with terminally-ill patients, is the author of numerous books, including the well-known book, *On Death and Dying*. She argues that in modern society, the subject of death is taboo; "the more we are making advancements in science, the more we seem to fear and deny the reality of death."[1] She argues that the process of dying usually occurs in five stages: denial, anger, depression, bargaining and acceptance; her theory has become known as "The Five Stages of Grief." I can't wholeheartedly recommend *On Death and Dying* because it isn't well-written; the classic work on this important subject remains to be written. Kübler-Ross also wrote a short book called *Life After Death*.

M. Scott Peck, an American psychiatrist, is the author of a book called *The Road Less Traveled*. Peck's book is popular rather than scholarly, inspirational rather than scientific, sincere rather than original. Though the style is second rate, it's clear and readable. Peck's book isn't a classic, but it does contain considerable psychological wisdom; the first half is especially interesting.

Peck uses case histories to illustrate the importance of early childhood and of parental love. He says that parental love indicates to the child that he's valuable. A child who feels itself to be valuable will take care of itself and discipline itself. Thus, parental love, according to Peck, is the source of self-discipline.

Peck's book shows how important psychotherapy is in the modern world. Many other interesting books will doubtless be written by psychotherapists in the future.

I recommend Malcolm Gladwell's bestseller, *Blink: The Power of Thinking Without Thinking*; it's highly readable and highly interesting. Since I'm a champion of the classics, I hate to admit how enjoyable a

---

[1] *On Death and Dying*, ch. 1

contemporary bestseller can be. *Blink* was difficult for me to put down, it made me late for appointments. Gladwell tries to present psychology research in a manner that laymen can understand. Gladwell discusses non-rational thinking—intuitive, unconscious thinking. Gladwell's thesis is interesting, and the stories with which he supports his thesis are also interesting. Popular as *Blink* is, Gladwell's other book, *The Tipping Point*, is even more popular. *Tipping Point* is described as "social psychology"; it discusses fads, "social epidemics."

Those interested in the occult should consider Dean Radin's book, *The Conscious Universe: The Scientific Truth of Psychic Phenomena.* Radin describes the careful, controlled, verifiable experiments that have been made over the last hundred years, and how these experiments have built a strong case in favor of psychic phenomena. Radin takes a scholarly, statistical approach to the occult; his book isn't anecdotal or literary. Though he knows how stubborn skeptics are, Radin looks to the future with confidence: "The eventual scientific acceptance of psychic phenomena is inevitable. The origins of acceptance are already brewing through the persuasive weight of the laboratory evidence."[1]

Colin Wilson is a popular and prolific English writer who often writes about the occult, crime, and sex. Compared to Dean Radin, Wilson discusses the occult in a manner that's more literary, less laboratory. *The Occult: A History* is Wilson's chief work in this field. Now in his seventies, Wilson burst into prominence at age 24 with a book called *The Outsider*, which discussed outsiders and outcasts in the works of Kafka, Nietzsche, Dostoyevsky, and others. Wilson has written studies of Rasputin, Gurdjieff, Jung, Aleister Crowley, Henry Miller, Rudolf Steiner, and others. Wilson says that his best book is a mystical work called *Beyond the Occult*.

5. Psychological Interpretations
of Literature and Art

Hitschmann has written a superb collection of biographical sketches, *Great Men: Psychoanalytic Studies*. This book is a goldmine of psychological wisdom. I recommend it highly.

Phyllis Greenacre wrote a highly-regarded book called *Swift and Carroll: A Psychoanalytic Study* (Jonathan Swift is, of course, the author

---

[1] Introduction

of *Gulliver's Travels*, and Lewis Carroll is the author of *Alice in Wonderland*).

Dalton's *Unconscious Structure in "The Idiot"* is an excellent study of the famous novel by Dostoyevsky. One should read the novel before reading Dalton's book. (Dalton was a disciple of Lionel Trilling, who had a deep appreciation of literature, and also a keen interest in Freud and Freudian interpretations of literature.)

Ruitenbeek has compiled an extraordinary anthology of essays and articles, *Psychoanalysis and Literature*. The essays on Poe, Hawthorne, Kafka, Lewis Carroll, and Hamlet are excellent. Kazin's essay on modern literature is full of interesting ideas. Kazin argues that modern English and American writers are isolated within their own selves, and can't make contact with the external world: "The world—the surrounding and not always friendly reality of nature, history, society—has disappeared for these writers." The world no longer offers people anything to respect, anything to be enthusiastic about. Modern man has fallen into an abyss of nihilism.

The Creative Unconscious, by Hanns Sachs, is a collection of essays, most of which deal with literature. It's an interesting book, though the style is second rate. Theodor Reik's *Secret Self* is also badly-written but interesting. Reik's book includes sketches of Goethe, Heine and Anatole France. Reik wrote a number of other books, the best of which may be *A Psychologist Looks At Love*. Otto Rank is the author of two books that are interesting but badly written: *Psychology and the Soul* and *The Don Juan Legend*.

Eissler is a major figure among psychologists who study literature and art. Eissler is an expert on genius, and his work is often interesting. But Eissler wrote carelessly; though he studied literature, he didn't try to create literature. Eissler is the author of two huge tomes: one on Leonardo, the other on Goethe. I recommend Eissler's essay, "Psychopathology and Creativity," which discusses the nature of genius with reference to Goethe. I also recommend Eissler's essay, "Talent and Genius."[1] Eissler notes that the genius suffers more than other people: "Many a reader of the works of a genius may feel an ardent wish to

---

[1] "Talent and Genius" is a chapter in a book by Eissler called *Talent and Genius: The Fictitious Case of Tausk contra Freud*. Another interesting chapter in that book is "Remarks on Freud's Psychopathology." "Psychopathology and Creativity" is an article in the magazine *American Imago* (spring-summer, 1967). See also "Eissler's 'Goethe'," by H. Slochower (*American Imago*, winter, 1965).

achieve an equivalent greatness on his own, but it is more than likely that he would not have been able to endure the pain to which most geniuses are subjected."[1]

[1] *Talent and Genius: The Fictitious Case of Tausk contra Freud*, ch. 7

III. Literature

1. Kafka

Kafka's works certainly rank among the classics of modern fiction, yet one can't call them "classics" without qualification. Most of Kafka's novels are unfinished, perhaps because Kafka could find no way out of a hopeless dead-end, perhaps because Kafka thought they were unworthy of being finished. "My scribbling," Kafka told an acquaintance, "[is] only my personal specter of horror... It is without meaning."[1] In his will, Kafka left instructions that most of his works be destroyed.

Kafka was born into Prague's Jewish community. Prague was then inhabited by Czechs, Germans, and Jews. In his famous "Letter to His Father," Kafka said, "You were capable... of running down the Czechs, and then the Germans, and then the Jews... and finally nobody was left except yourself." Kafka could sense that there was intense hostility toward the Jewish community: "Anti-semitism [will] seize hold of the masses."[2] Kafka died before Hitler came to power, but his prophecies came true; his three sisters died in the Holocaust.

While Kafka's historical circumstances influenced his work, his temperament probably influenced his work more. Kafka was afraid of life, and had a deep sense of guilt. Kafka's father was a big, boisterous businessman who didn't appreciate the delicate, conscientious intellectual who was his son. Kafka could never please his father, or be like his father, and he became filled with guilt:

> From the many occasions on which I had, according to your clearly expressed opinion, deserved a whipping but was let off at the last moment

---

[1] *Conversations With Kafka*, by Gustav Janouch, p. 150
[2] ibid, p. 174

by your grace, [I] accumulated a huge sense of guilt. On every side I was
to blame, I was in your debt.

Kafka had several affairs with women, and was even engaged to be
married, but his diffidence, and his dedication to literature, prevented
him from "taking the plunge." He had trouble making a decision, and if
he finally made one, he soon had doubts and second thoughts. "When it
comes to indecision," Kafka wrote, "now there is something I know all
about; in fact, I know nothing else."[1] Kafka's fear of life, his inability to
let himself go, made it difficult for him to sleep, and he suffered from
severe insomnia. He died of tuberculosis at age 41.

For Kafka, as for other writers, the literary world was more real than
the "real world," and he never felt at home in the "real world." He told
his mother, "Certainly, you are all strangers to me."[2] Kafka's passion for
literature drew all his energy and talent away from the "real world", and
enabled him to create works that combine wild fantasy with vivid
realism, works that have a beautiful simplicity of style, and an
unsurpassed sense of humor. Kafka didn't try to create memorable
characters, or set forth philosophical arguments; he isn't part of the
classical tradition of Balzac and Tolstoy. He's part of the anti-hero
tradition, the tradition of humor and the surreal, the tradition of Gogol's
"Overcoat" and Dostoyevsky's "Crocodile".

Kafka loathed the decadent and the nihilistic, and liked literature
that was positive and affirming. Among Kafka's favorite writers were
Strindberg and Chekhov; "Chekhov I love very much," he once wrote,
"sometimes quite madly."[3] Kafka's favorite books were biographies and
autobiographies; he was especially fond of Ben Franklin's autobiography.[4]

Kafka earned a law degree, and found a job in a government
insurance company, part of the huge Austro-Hungarian bureaucracy.
Once a year, he wrote a long report for his boss. He treated this report as
a literary work, and gave copies of it to his friends. Once, when his boss
was addressing Kafka and a colleague, Kafka suddenly saw the literary
potential of this scene, and started laughing.

---

[1] *The Nightmare of Reason: A Life of Franz Kafka*, by Ernst Pawel, ch.
12
[2] *Franz Kafka*, by Max Brod, ch. 5
[3] *Letters to Milena*
[4] *Franz Kafka*, by Max Brod, ch. 4

Kafka had several friends in the Prague literary world, and he was able to publish some early stories. The first story that he was really proud of was "The Judgment", which he wrote in one night, one sleepless night. Kafka wasn't a craftsman who planned his writing in advance, and polished it afterwards; he wrote in moments of inspiration, he wrote automatically. He spoke of, "the time of inspiration, which I dread rather than long for."[1] On January 20, 1915, Kafka made the following entry in his diary: "The end of writing. When will it take me up again?"[2]

After completing "The Judgment," Kafka attempted to write a novel. "Kafka is in ecstasy," reported his friend Max Brod, "writes whole nights through. A novel set in America."[3] Of Kafka's three novels, *Amerika* is the most realistic, the most like other novels, the least "Kafka-esque." *Amerika* was influenced by *David Copperfield*; *Amerika* was Kafka's attempt to refine and modernize *David Copperfield*.

Kafka's second novel, *The Trial*, is the most finished, and the most popular, of his novels. It was written when Kafka was struggling to marry, and leave his parents' house—a struggle he ultimately lost. Who can forget the famous Cathedral scene?

> What stillness there was now in the Cathedral! Yet K. had to violate it, for he was not minded to stay; if it were this priest's duty to preach a sermon at a certain hour regardless of circumstances, let him do it, he could manage it without K.'s support, just as K.'s presence would certainly not contribute to its effectiveness. So he began slowly to move off, feeling his way along the pew on tiptoe until he was in the broad center aisle, where he advanced undisturbed except for the ringing noise that his lightest footstep made on the stone flags and the echoes that sounded from the vaulted roof faintly but continuously, in manifold and regular progression. K. felt a little forlorn as he advanced, a solitary figure between the rows of empty seats, perhaps with the priest's eyes following him; and the size of the Cathedral struck him as bordering on the limit of what human beings could bear.... He had almost passed the last of the pews and was emerging into the open space between himself and the doorway when he heard the priest lifting up his voice. A resonant, well-trained voice. How it rolled through the expectant Cathedral! But it was no congregation the priest was addressing, the words were unambiguous and inescapable, he was calling out: "Joseph K.!"

---

[1] *Franz Kafka*, by Max Brod, ch. 3

[2] ibid, perhaps ch. 8, perhaps an appendix

[3] I quote from memory, being unable to find the source of this quotation.

Kafka's last and longest novel, *The Castle*, was written in the shadow of death, and its snow-covered landscape contains no hint of green. Kafka didn't finish this novel, and he didn't want it to be published. Why did he write it? One suspects that he wrote it out of sheer love of literature, and out of a need to release what was on his mind. Although *The Castle* isn't a cheerful work, the reader will enjoy Kafka's prose, and he'll be amused by Kafka's wild fantasies.

Kafka's best short stories are as good as his novels, but his short stories aren't consistently high in quality, and therefore should be read selectively. I recommend "The Metamorphosis," "Josephine the Singer," "The Hunger Artist," "A Report To An Academy," and "The Burrow." Like his stories, Kafka's *Eight Octavo Notebooks* need to be edited; if edited, these notebooks could be an excellent book. Some of Kafka's letters are also interesting; I recommend his letters to Felice and also a collection of his personal writings called *"I Am A Memory Come Alive."* Those who want to read a psychological study of Kafka's writings have numerous works to choose from.[1] Finally, I recommend Brod's biography of Kafka, Janouch's *Conversations With Kafka*, and a little cartoon-book called *Introducing Kafka*.

2. Proust

Unlike Kafka, Proust was born into a family that respected literature. When Proust was still a boy, his mother and grandmother introduced him to French literature, and soon he realized that literature was his calling. But his literary ability developed slowly; he worried that he didn't have enough imagination to write a novel. He regarded himself as, "a man born sensitive to impressions but without imagination."[2] Finally he

---

[1] *Kafka's Prayer*, by Paul Goodman, is a comprehensive study of the man and the work; *Kafka's Prayer* is penetrating but obscure. Among the shorter works on the subject are Lesser's "The Source of Guilt and the Sense of Guilt—Kafka's *The Trial*" (an essay in Ruitenbeek's *Psychoanalysis and Literature*), Sebald's "The Undiscover'd Country: The Death Motif in Kafka's *Castle*" (*Journal of European Studies*, 1972, 2), Globus and Pillard's "Tausk's *Influencing Machine* and Kafka's *In the Penal Colony*" (*American Imago*, fall, 1966), and Webster's "Critical Examination of Franz Kafka's *The Castle*" (*American Imago*, March, 1951).

[2] *The Past Recaptured*, ch. 3

decided that he wouldn't try to write a work based on imagination, but rather a work based on his own experiences: his loves, his sorrows, his friendships, his social life, etc.

Proust doesn't write about exotic experiences, but rather universal experiences. For example, he writes about the death of an acquaintance:

> As I ran my eye over the newspaper, my attention was suddenly arrested by the announcement of [Swann's death], as though traced in mysterious lines interpolated there out of place. They had sufficed to make of a living man some one who can never again respond to what you say to him, to reduce him to a mere name, a written name, that has passed in a moment from the real world to the realm of silence.[1]

Proust makes universal experiences seem fresh, interesting and exotic, because he himself lived through those experiences fully and consciously.

One could summarize Proust's life thus: he was introduced to literature at an early age, and soon became preoccupied with literature. Later he became preoccupied with life itself, and despaired of becoming a novelist. Then he retreated from life, devoted himself entirely to writing, and transmuted his experiences into art. Finally, he said to his maid, Celeste, "Last night I wrote 'The End.' Now I can die."[2]

Like Kafka, Proust was a very unusual person, and he presents a new and different view of the world. But since Kafka presents his view of the world in a manner much like other novelists, he doesn't demand as much from the reader as Proust, who presents his view of the world in a manner that is both unusual and challenging. Proust's prose is ornate, his sentences long, his paragraphs long, his chapters long, and his book long. Furthermore, his work contains little action, little plot. Those who commit themselves to studying Proust will find these difficulties gradually melt away, and will realize that Proust is clear, though long-winded.

Some readers, unwilling to read all seven of the novels that comprise *Remembrance of Things Past*, choose to read only the first and last of the seven. Such readers may benefit from a book that summarizes the other five novels, such as Miller's book (*Nostalgia: A Psychoanalytic Study of Marcel Proust*) or Maurois' superb biography of Proust. Maurois' biography is half as long, and twice as good, as most modern biographies. George Painter's two-volume biography of Proust is well-

---

[1] *The Captive*, I, ii
[2] Celeste Albaret, *Monsieur Proust: A Memoir*, ch. 28

regarded, but the more recent biography by Jean-Yves Tadié seems to have become the standard biography of Proust.

I recommend *Monsieur Proust: A Memoir*, by Proust's housekeeper, Celeste Albaret. This memoir is an intimate and fascinating look at Proust. Proust told Celeste that if she ever recorded her memories of him, the book would sell like hot rolls in the morning, and indeed her memoir did become a bestseller in France. I recommend *A Reader's Guide to Marcel Proust* (a useful summary-and-analysis of Proust's work), *The Cambridge Companion to Proust* (a collection of essays), and a Proust essay in the Scribner Writers Series (an excellent introduction to Proust's life and work, written by F. Hemmings).

Like Kafka, Proust was deeply committed to literature. But Proust wasn't bookish or pedantic. Like Kafka, Proust was more fascinated by life itself than by literature. Kafka and Proust viewed life from a literary standpoint, and found life to be the most profound and the most humorous of authors. Proust would have agreed with Kafka's remark: "From life one can extract comparatively so many books, but from books so little, so very little, life."[1] The greatness of Kafka and Proust lies less in their learning than in their living. Proust learned a great deal from life, and his work is based on his own experience.

Proust's work is full of profound thoughts. He notes, for example, that people often overlook the ability of those who are close to them: "We can never believe in the genius of a person with whom we went to the Opera last night."[2] Proust's work is also full of humorous remarks; he says, for example, that

> When [M. de Charlus] had perfected... an entirely successful epigram, he was anxious to let it be heard by the largest possible audience, but took care not to admit to the second performance the audience of the first who could have borne witness that the novelty was not novel. He would then rearrange his drawing-room, simply because he did not alter his program, and, when he had scored a success in conversation, would, if need be, have organised a tour, and given exhibitions in the provinces.[3]

---

[1] *Conversations With Kafka*, by G. Janouch

[2] *The Captive*, II, ii

[3] *The Captive*, II, ii. Some interesting psychological studies of Proust have been written; for example, "The Discovery of the Oedipus Complex: Episodes from Marcel Proust," by G. Zilboorg, *Psychoanalytic Quarterly*, 1939, and "Marcel Proust and His Mother," by G. Bychowski, *American Imago*, spring, 1973.

No imaginative writer is more profound, or more humorous, than Proust.

3. Joyce

James Joyce was born in Ireland in 1882, eleven years after Proust was born. During his early years, Joyce went in and out of Catholic schools, while his father went in and out of jobs. As a teenager, Joyce went through moral cycles: sin, followed by repentance and asceticism, eventually giving way to renewed sin. Joyce later described these cycles in *A Portrait of the Artist as a Young Man.* Some may regard these cycles as typical of a Catholic adolescence, but I regard them as typical of adolescence in general.

While still a teenager, Joyce felt that he was called to a literary life. Like other adolescents, the young Joyce had moments of inspiration in which his calling, his destiny, appeared to him like a vision or dream; as Joyce described it in *A Portrait,*

> His thinking was a dusk of doubt and selfmistrust, lit up at moments by the lightnings of intuition, but lightnings of so clear a splendor that in those moments the world perished about his feet as if it had been fire consumed. [1]

Joyce was completely confident of his genius; George Russell, an Irish man-of-letters, said that the young Joyce was "proud as Lucifer." [2]

Though Joyce was influenced by the Irish writer Yeats, his ambitions transcended his native land; he was international. He admired Ibsen, and even learned Norwegian in order to read Ibsen in the original, and write Ibsen a letter. At 22, Joyce eloped with Nora Barnacle, left Ireland, and began a life of voluntary exile; as he later wrote (in the peculiar and playful style of *Finnegans Wake*), "He even ran away with hunself and became a farsoonerite, saying he would far sooner muddle through the hash of lentils in Europe than meddle with Irrland's split little pea." [3] Joyce lived most of his adult life in Trieste, Zurich and Paris. A student of foreign languages, Joyce earned some money as a teacher at a Berlitz language school. Later, he received assistance from wealthy patrons, and earned money from royalties.

---

[1] Ch. 5

[2] *James Joyce*, by R. Ellman, ch. 7

[3] *Finnegans Wake*, ch. 5

While still in Ireland, Joyce had begun writing short stories for George Russell's magazine. Eventually, he had enough stories for a book, which he called *Dubliners*. For years, he tried unsuccessfully to publish *Dubliners*; "publishers and printers alike," he wrote, "seemed to agree among themselves, no matter how divergent their points of view were in other matters, not to publish anything of mine as I wrote it." Joyce's career took a turn for the better when Ezra Pound and Yeats began to admire his work, and help him find publishers and patrons. By the time Joyce reached 40, he was internationally famous; the controversy surrounding *Ulysses* (it was initially banned as indecent) only enhanced Joyce's fame.

In addition to being controversial, *Ulysses* was also experimental; Joyce tried to capture the miscellaneous thoughts that flit through one's head, using a technique called stream-of-consciousness. In the following passage, Leopold Bloom is attending a funeral; after Bloom "moved behind the portly kindly caretaker," Joyce tries to follow Bloom's thoughts:

> Well cut frockcoat. Weighing them up perhaps to see which will go next. Well it is a long rest. Feel no more. It's the moment you feel. Must be damned unpleasant. Can't believe it at first. Mistake must be: someone else. Try the house opposite. Wait, I wanted to I haven't yet. [1]

Humor plays an important role in *Ulysses*, as it does in *Finnegans Wake*. It was said that "no one could laugh more wholeheartedly or more infectiously"[2] than Joyce. He worked on *Ulysses* at night, after his wife and two children had gone to bed, and his wife often heard his laughter ringing through their rented rooms.

Joyce's early works—*Dubliners* and *A Portrait of the Artist*—are extremely popular, while his later works—*Ulysses* and *Finnegans Wake*—are enjoyed by few readers. His play, *Exiles*, is largely forgotten. *Dubliners* is one of those rare books that one wishes were longer. Like Chekhov's stories, Joyce's stories contain little action—just enough to hold the reader's attention. But while Chekhov often wrote hastily—to meet a deadline or to generate some cash—Joyce wrote carefully and seriously. Joyce's stories may not be better than Chekhov's best stories, but they're more polished and more consistent than Chekhov's stories.

A Portrait of the Artist is neither as readable as *Dubliners* nor as obscure as *Ulysses*. Many readers of Joyce regard *A Portrait* as one of

---

[1] *Ulysses*, ch. 6
[2] *James Joyce*, by R. Ellman, ch. 24

their favorite books. Those who dedicate themselves to reading *Ulysses* will enjoy parts of it as much as *A Portrait*, if not more so. Few, however, will enjoy every chapter of *Ulysses*, and many won't want to make the commitment that reading *Ulysses* requires. *Ulysses* can't be read without help from an editor or commentator. Until *Ulysses* is published with notes on every page, as Shakespeare's works are, readers will have to turn to commentators like Tindall, Burgess and Thornton.[1]

Finnegans Wake also requires commentary. Perhaps the best-known commentary on *Finnegans Wake* is *A Skeleton Key to Finnegans Wake*, by Joseph Campbell (the mythology expert) and Henry Robinson. Campbell views *Finnegans Wake* as a mythological work, a work that deals with the circle of life—birth, death, rebirth. Indeed, the title of *Finnegans Wake* alludes to the circle of life: Finnegan alludes to the end of life (fin = end), followed by going around again (egan = again), and likewise Wake alludes to death (wake = funeral), and also to arising (wake = awake). Campbell insists that *Finnegans Wake* is a masterpiece, an immortal work.

Like many modern biographies, Ellman's biography of Joyce is overly detailed. It's sometimes interesting, however, and it helps one to understand Joyce's work. *Conversations With Joyce*, by Arthur Power, is an excellent book, a book that fans of Joyce will thoroughly enjoy.

4. Gide

André Gide was born in 1869, two years before Proust. Like Proust, Gide was born into a wealthy family, never had to earn money, and devoted himself to literature. Many geniuses mature slowly, and seem to remain stuck in childhood, instead of rapidly becoming an adult. Such was the case with Gide, who later wrote of, "the thick darkness that still

---

[1] *A Reader's Guide To James Joyce*, by W. Y. Tindall
Re Joyce (also called *Here Comes Everybody*) by A. Burgess
Allusions in Ulysses: An Annotated List, by Weldon Thornton
Ulysses Annotated, by Don Gifford with Robert Seidman.
Gifford also wrote *Joyce Annotated: Notes for Dubliners and A Portrait of the Artist as a Young Man*. Consider also *James Joyce's Dubliners: An Illustrated Edition With Annotations*, by John Wyse Jackson and Bernard McGinley

wrapped my tardy childhood."[1] Like Jung, Gide had a childhood neurosis that kept him out of school for long periods. Gide was born into a strict Protestant family. Like Joyce, he went through phases of piety and asceticism, and he also went through phases of hedonism; he made life experiments, moral experiments, philosophical experiments. He later wrote, "I do not think there is any single way of envisaging the question of religion or morals that at some moment of my life has not been mine."[2] (Tolstoy also tried different philosophies; Tolstoy experimented with Stoicism, Epicureanism, Skepticism, etc.) When Gide was 24, he visited North Africa, a visit that confirmed his choice of a bisexual lifestyle, and his rejection of Protestant asceticism and Victorian convention. The next year, he returned to North Africa, and became friends with Oscar Wilde, who encouraged Gide's hedonistic tendencies; "it is a duty to make oneself happy," Gide declared.[3]

Gide felt that destiny had marked him for literary greatness, and that whatever problems he encountered, whatever mistakes he made, would add to his life experience, and enrich his writings. "The kind of faith I had in my predestination as a poet," Gide wrote, "made me welcome whatever happened to me."[4] (Joyce had the same attitude, the same confidence in his destiny: "A man of genius makes no mistakes," wrote Joyce; "his errors are volitional and are the portals of discovery."[5])

Though Gide abandoned the Protestant faith of his ancestors, he always retained a vague piety. He said, "I am an unbeliever. I shall never be an ungodly man."[6] He had a vague love of Christianity, but rejected established Christianity; "Catholicism is inadmissible," he said, "Protestantism is intolerable; and I feel profoundly Christian."[7] One might say that Gide was casting about for new approaches to religion; doubtless he would have embraced Zen, if he had been introduced to it.

---

[1] *If It Die*, I, 1

[2] ibid, II, 2

[3] see the essay "André Gide," by Vinio Rossi, *European Writers*, Vol. 8 Pages 495–518, Copyright 1989, Charles Scribner's Sons, The Scribner Writers Series

[4] *If It Die*, I, 10

[5] *Ulysses*, ch. 9

[6] *The Journals of André Gide: 1889-1949* (edited and abridged by Justin O'Brien), 11/6/27

[7] see the article on Gide in Encyclopedia Britannica

Like Joyce, Gide wrote short works early in his career, works that are at least as good, if not better, than his later, larger, more ambitious works. Gide's best short works are based on his own experience, and combine sincerity with elegance. An example is *Strait Is The Gate*, which deals with Gide's platonic love for his cousin, whom he later married; Joyce called it, "a little masterpiece.... as fine as a spire on Notre Dame."[1] *The Immoralist*, another of Gide's short works, is based on Gide's experience in North Africa; *The Immoralist* is the story of a melancholy intellectual who learns to find joy in life. Gide wrote two autobiographical works, *If It Die* and *So Be It*. *If It Die* covers the early part of his life, and is one of his best books, better than *So Be It*, which covers the latter part of his life. Gide's journals contain many fine passages, but require drastic abridgment.

Gide was a prolific writer. In addition to writing fiction and autobiography, he wrote dramas, and he translated Shakespeare and Blake. He also translated Whitman, whose homoerotic poetry must have struck a responsive chord in Gide.

If one compares Gide with Kafka, Proust, and Joyce, one finds that Gide had the same serious commitment to literature as they did. One also finds that Gide was more widely read, more learned, than they were; Gide knew several foreign languages. Gide's commitment to reading reminds one not of an imaginative writer, but of a philosopher like Schopenhauer or Nietzsche. And indeed, much of what Gide wrote wasn't imaginative literature; Gide was a prominent critic and essayist, and he kept a journal throughout his life. Gide wasn't a pure artist, and he wasn't as creative as Kafka, Proust, and Joyce. Gide didn't create a distinctive type of literature, and he didn't have a distinctive worldview; one can speak of a "Kafka-esque" world, or a "Proust-ian" world, but not of a "Gide-ian" world. Instead of expressing his own worldview, Gide sometimes imitated Dostoyevsky, whom he greatly admired; Gide's chief novels—*The Counterfeiters* and *Lafcadio's Adventures*—have the atmosphere and characters of a Dostoyevsky novel.

When World War II broke out, it seemed that Western civilization, which had been dealt a heavy blow by World War I, was disintegrating completely. This disintegration was especially conspicuous to someone like Gide, who reached maturity before World War I. Gide spoke of, "the atrocities of war... that vast upsetting of all the values that constituted our

---

[1] *Conversations With Joyce, by Arthur Power, 10*

reasons for living."[1] Western civilization was in retreat, it doubted itself, it lost touch with the past. The modern world was an inhospitable environment for culture; "we are headed faster and faster," Gide said, "into a world in which [culture] will be denied, neglected and made fun of."[2]

Gide became a champion of civilization, of tradition, of humanistic values. One might compare Gide with Bernard Berenson, who was also a humanist, who also came to maturity before World War I, who also lived through both World Wars. Gide's bookish journals are similar to Berenson's journals. Gide and Berenson both aspired to self-culture, self-development, *Bildung*. Gide said that self-culture means exposing yourself to new things, stretching your boundaries: "real culture begins at the point where we approach what we don't already like."[3]

Like Goethe, the chief representative of *Bildung*, Gide was involved with political affairs. At 27, he became a mayor (the youngest mayor in France). Later he visited French colonies in Africa, and wrote about conditions there. For a time, he was attracted to Communism, and he visited the Soviet Union, but he returned disillusioned (he contributed to a famous anti-Communist book, *The God That Failed*). Gide was also actively involved in the French literary world; he helped to found *La Nouvelle Revue Française* (NRF), one of the chief literary periodicals of its time.

Though Gide's works aren't as popular today as the works of Kafka, Proust, and Joyce, they'll be read for many years to come; they combine elegance of style with depth of learning, and they represent a sincere attempt to answer ethical and aesthetic questions.

5. Mann, Hesse, and Goethe

Like Gide, Thomas Mann seemed to write with his mind rather than his soul. Like Gide, Mann wrote essays as well as imaginative works. Mann was a deep thinker, and his stories and novels contain many profound ideas. In *The Magic Mountain*, for example, Mann notes that work is of paramount importance in modern life, work has become "the

---

[1] *So Be It or The Chips are Down* (New York, Alfred A. Knopf, 1959), p. 5
[2] *Conversations With Gide*, by Claude Mauriac, 7/14/39
[3] ibid

most estimable attribute of life... the Absolute of the time... its own justification."[1] One of Mann's major works, *Doktor Faustus*, has parallels in Nietzsche's life; another of Mann's novels, *Lotte in Weimar*, is based on Goethe's life. Mann has neither the humor of Kafka nor the pathos of Proust nor the intensity of Tolstoy. Nonetheless, he was one of the outstanding novelists and thinkers of his time, and his work won't soon be forgotten.

Hesse lacks the profundity of Mann, and also lacks the imaginative power of Kafka. Hesse's novels depict states of being, approaches to life, the evolution of personality. When Hesse was young, one of his chief spiritual guides was Nietzsche, but during his later years, Hesse turned away from Nietzsche, turned toward Eastern philosophy, and decided that Nietzsche's approach to life was too dry and intellectual. Hesse's last major work, *The Glass Bead Game* (also called *Magister Ludi*) criticizes Nietzsche (without mentioning him by name). Hesse's best and most popular work is *Siddhartha*, a short novel set in India in the time of Buddha. *Siddhartha* is a delightful blend of fiction and philosophy, East and West, Buddhist ideas and Western preoccupation-with-self. I also recommend *Steppenwolf*; like Gide's *Immoralist*, Hesse's *Steppenwolf* is about a melancholy intellectual who learns to find joy in life.

Perhaps the best way to approach Goethe is through his *Conversations With Eckermann* and his autobiography, *Dichtung und Wahrheit* (*Poetry and Truth*). His novels are somewhat dated for a modern reader, and his poetry loses something in translation.

One of the leading Goethe scholars of our time is Cambridge professor Nicholas Boyle, who has completed two volumes of a Goethe biography, and is working on a third; Boyle's biography may be too detailed for the non-specialist. Rüdiger Safranski, whom I mentioned earlier in connection with Schopenhauer, has written biographies of Goethe and Schiller, as well as a book about their friendship, but none of these books has yet been translated into English. George Lewes wrote a well-known biography of Goethe shortly after Goethe's death, while T. J. Reed published a biography of Goethe in 1984.

6. Tolstoy

Like Kafka and Proust, Tolstoy was more fascinated by life itself than by literature. For Tolstoy, literature wasn't a game, hobby or craft,

---

[1] II, 2

literature was a quest for the meaning of life, a quest for something to live by. For Tolstoy, this quest began during adolescence, when he experimented with various philosophies—Stoicism, Epicureanism, Skepticism, etc. After writing *War and Peace* and *Anna Karenina*, and becoming an internationally famous author, Tolstoy felt that he still hadn't found the meaning of life. He had a religious conversion, turned his back on the work that had made him famous, and devoted himself to carrying out his religious ideals.

Tolstoy's literary work is a reflection of his personality, and is characterized by the same spiritual hunger, the same intensity, that one finds in Tolstoy himself. Tolstoy's biography sounds much like one of his novels. Tolstoy had exceptional vitality, a feeling of oneness with the universe; when he was nine, Tolstoy was so fascinated by the night sky that he jumped from a third floor window in an attempt to fly. One finds the same ecstatic feeling of oneness with the universe in Tolstoy's fictional creations; in *War and Peace*, for example, Tolstoy writes, "Pierre glanced at the sky, at the far-away, twinkling stars. 'And all that is mine, and all that is in me, and all that is I!'"[1]

Just as Tolstoy was more interested in life than in literature, so too he was more interested in people than in books. Gorky said that Tolstoy "was not very fond of talking about literature, but he was vitally interested in the personality of an author." In this respect, Tolstoy resembled Kafka, whose favorite books were biographies and autobiographies.[2] Some literary critics say that the personality of an author is irrelevant, and that literature should be objective and impersonal. Critics separate literature from life because they aren't fascinated by life, as great writers are, and they don't experience life as intensely as great writers do. This is why critics are critics, and not great writers.

Tolstoy's best work deals with the subject that interested him most, namely, life itself. While Kafka and Proust viewed life from one perspective, from an eccentric perspective, Tolstoy views life as a whole. In this respect, Tolstoy reminds one of ancient writers like Homer, rather than modern writers. Tolstoy is clear and readable, and he's popular both with the general public and with discriminating readers. Everyone likes Tolstoy. Joyce called Tolstoy, "a magnificent writer.... Head and shoulders over the others."[3]

---

[1] XIII, 14

[2] See Max Brod, *Franz Kafka*, ch. 4. The Gorky quotation is from Gorky's *Reminiscences of Tolstoy* (Dover, 1946), ch. 2.

[3] Richard Ellman, *James Joyce*, ch. 12

Though Tolstoy's best works are *War and Peace* and *Anna Karenina*, he also wrote some excellent short works, such as "Master and Man," "The Kreutzer Sonata," and "The Death of Ivan Ilych." During his long life, Tolstoy also wrote a good deal of non-fiction, such as *A Confession, What is Art?* and *My Religion.* Tolstoy's literary criticism was collected in a book called *Tolstoy on Art*, which Wilson Knight describes as "a massive collection of some of the most masculine, incisive, and important criticism that exists."[1] Troyat's biography of Tolstoy is interesting, though too long; as with many biographies, the second half is less interesting than the first. Gorky's *Reminiscences of Tolstoy* is first-rate.

7. Dostoyevsky

Dostoyevsky resembled Tolstoy in many ways: both were passionate about religion, both were capable of keen psychological insights, insights that anticipated Freud's theories, both made full use of plot and action in their writing, both filled their works with religious, philosophical and psychological ideas. But while Tolstoy's religiosity gave him a certain disdain for literature, Dostoyevsky's attachment to literature never flagged. In fact, Dostoyevsky's creative powers increased as he grew older; most readers consider Dostoyevsky's last work, *The Brothers Karamazov*, to be his best work.

Dostoyevsky criticized the view that man is rational, and argued that man is complex and irrational. Many admire Dostoyevsky's emphasis on the irrational, and believe that he anticipated modern psychology. Others, however, say that Dostoyevsky exaggerated the irrational side of human nature, that he was obsessed with the irrational and the morbid. Tolstoy, for example, said that Dostoyevsky's characters "are not real. It is all much simpler, more understandable"; Tolstoy said that Dostoyevsky's works were "painful and useless." Joyce's view of Dostoyevsky was similar to Tolstoy's.[2]

Dostoyevsky loved paradox. For example, he wasn't content to say (as Freud later said) that homosexual impulses exist in all men; he

---

[1] *The Wheel of Fire*, "Tolstoy's Attack on Shakespeare," #2

[2] See Frank Budgen, *James Joyce and the Making of Ulysses*, ch. 9. Tolstoy's remarks on Dostoyevsky can be found in Gorky's *Reminiscences of Tolstoy* (Dover, 1946).

insisted on going further, and saying that these impulses were actually stronger, in most men, than heterosexual impulses: "Can there be beauty in Sodom? Yes and, believe me, it is precisely there that beauty lies for most men."[1] Dostoyevsky annoys readers by his penchant for paradox and his exaggeration of the irrational side of human nature. Dostoyevsky himself wasn't far from mad. In fact, speaking of a two-year period in his twenties, Dostoyevsky said, "there was even a time when I lost my reason." He wrote a story called "The Double," about a young man with a split personality, and described it as "a confession." Dostoyevsky was an epileptic; according to Freud, "it is highly probable that this so-called epilepsy was only a symptom of his neurosis."[2] Dostoyevsky was also a compulsive gambler, and lost all he had in German casinos. Dostoyevsky utilized his epilepsy, his gambling and many other experiences for literary purposes. Dostoyevsky's novels often echo his biography, and many of his fictional characters represent facets of his own personality.

Dostoyevsky said that he had been tormented all his life by the question of whether God exists. Some of his characters are tormented by the same question. Dostoyevsky discusses the connection between atheism and socialism, and the connection between atheism and the collapse of traditional morality. Only Nietzsche had as deep an understanding of atheism as Dostoyevsky had. But while Nietzsche embraced atheism, Dostoyevsky rejected it, and sided with God, with Christianity, and with traditional morality. Dostoyevsky opposed those who wanted to Westernize Russia; his political views were conservative and nationalistic.

Several of Dostoyevsky's novels—*The Idiot, The Possessed,* and *The Brothers Karamazov*—are generally considered to be among the best novels ever written. Dostoyevsky also wrote some excellent short works, such as "Notes From Underground," "White Nights" and "A Gentle Creature." One of Dostoyevsky's best books is *The House of the Dead,* in which he describes his imprisonment in Siberia. Though it would be a mistake to overlook Dostoyevsky's weaknesses, it would be

---

[1] *The Brothers Karamazov,* I, iii, 3

[2] Freud, "Dostoyevsky and Parricide." On Dostoyevsky's bout of insanity, see Yarmolinsky, *Dostoyevsky,* ch. 5. For Dostoyevsky's description of "The Double," see ibid, ch. 8. In addition to Freud's essay, several other interesting studies of Dostoyevsky have been written. See the essays on Dostoyevsky in J. Coltrera, *Lives, Events, and Other Players,* and the essay by J. Maze in *American Imago,* summer, 1981.

a greater mistake to overlook his strengths; few writers in the history of literature have possessed the combination of pathos and profundity, imagination and humor, that Dostoyevsky possessed.

8. Chekhov

Chekhov aims to depict life, to depict the experience of living. He isn't as ambitious as Tolstoy and Dostoyevsky; he doesn't aim to change the world or to create a new religion. While Tolstoy and Dostoyevsky were masters of the long novel, Chekhov was a master of the short story. Chekhov describes routine, everyday matters; his work isn't as rich in plot and action as the work of Tolstoy and Dostoyevsky.

Chekhov came from a poor family; his father was a former serf. When Chekhov was a child, his father told him not to run around lest he wear out his shoes. While still young, Chekhov helped support his family by writing humorous sketches for newspapers. After attending medical school, Chekhov divided his time between practicing medicine and writing stories. As his literary reputation grew and his talent matured, he began writing longer, more serious stories. During his last years, he gave up medicine and story-writing, and wrote plays. He died of consumption at age forty-four.

Though Russia hasn't produced any major philosophers, Russian writers have a strong interest in philosophy. (As Chekhov said, "While there is no philosophy in Russia, everyone philosophizes, even the little nobodies."[1]) Chekhov's work contains many philosophical ideas. In "The Bet," for example, one of Chekhov's characters argues that since the sun will eventually burn out, and mankind will perish, all human activity is futile: "Your posterity, your history, your deathless geniuses— all will freeze or burn along with the terrestrial globe."

Like Dostoyevsky, Chekhov often depicts characters who express atheistic, anti-Christian, Nietzschean ideas. In "The Duel," for example, Chekhov depicts a character, Von Koren, who argues that the weak should perish for the sake of the species; Von Koren "works... not out of love for his neighbor, but for the sake of such abstractions as humanity, future generations, an ideal race of men." Like Dostoyevsky, Chekhov doesn't side with Von Koren and Nietzsche, he opposes them. While Dostoyevsky embraced a Christian worldview, Chekhov doesn't embrace any religion or philosophy; Chekhov always remains an artist.

---

[1] "Ward Six"

The prevalence of Nietzschean ideas in the work of Dostoyevsky, Chekhov and other writers indicates that these ideas aren't rare, and aren't found only in isolated thinkers; as Gorky said, Nietzschean ideas "are more persistent and more widespread than they are commonly thought to be."[1]

Though one finds ideas in Chekhov's work, Chekhov's specialty isn't ideas but rather daily life, the details of life, the details that often upset man's grand ambitions. Many of Chekhov's characters have ambitions and dreams that are never fulfilled; they never manage to bring daily life into harmony with their aspirations. They struggle with life, and life wins. In his memoirs of his trip to Siberia, Chekhov wrote:

A peasant moving to Siberia: "it can't be worse."
Another peasant, coming back from Siberia: "it will be worse."

All of Chekhov's plays are first rate, but the quality of his short stories varies considerably. Some of my favorite Chekhov stories are "Rothschild's Fiddle," "The Darling," "Three Years," "A Dull Story" and "The Kiss."

9. Other Russian Writers

Pushkin is revered in Russia, but less popular outside Russia, perhaps because much of his work is poetry, which doesn't translate well. Among his major works is a play, *Boris Gudonov*, and a verse novel, *Eugene Onegin*. (Nabokov made a multi-volume translation-with-commentary of *Eugene Onegin*.) If you want to read Pushkin's short stories, I suggest a volume called *The Captain's Daughter and Other Stories*.

While Dostoyevsky, Tolstoy, and Chekhov were part of the realistic tradition, Pushkin was part of the Romantic tradition. One of his inspirations was the English Romantic, Byron, who wrote fiction in verse. Some of Pushkin's works, like "The Queen of Spades," have an occult atmosphere, and remind one of Poe and other writers from the Romantic period. On the other hand, Pushkin's short novel, "The Captain's Daughter," can be compared to the historical fiction of Walter Scott, which was popular during the Romantic period. I found "The Captain's Daughter" rather dull, but I was entranced by "The Queen of Spades."

---

[1] See Gorky, *My Universities*.

Gogol was born in 1809, about ten years after Pushkin, about ten years before Dostoyevsky, about twenty years before Tolstoy, about fifty years before Chekhov, and about sixty years before Gorky. Some of Gogol's short stories—such as "The Overcoat" and "The Nose"—are still popular today. In these stories, Gogol depicts an anti-hero, a social outcast; Gogol influenced Dostoyevsky, who depicted anti-heroes in such stories as "Notes From Underground" and "The Double." I don't recommend *Dead Souls*, Gogol's only full-length novel. As for Gorky, the only one of his works that I recommend is *My Universities*, an autobiographical work.

10. Ibsen

Ibsen was highly influential during his lifetime, and he has remained popular ever since. Like Joyce, Ibsen lived most of his life in voluntary exile, critical of his homeland (Norway). Besides Ibsen and Joyce, many other intellectuals have been critical of their homelands; Nietzsche, for example, was critical of Germany. A true intellectual stands above nationality.

Like Nietzsche, Ibsen opposed the democratic trend of his time. In a letter, Ibsen spoke of his "contempt for political freedom.... The liberals are the worst enemies of Freedom. Spiritual and intellectual freedom flourish best under absolutism."[1] Ibsen expressed the same views in his play, *An Enemy of the People*. In that play, Ibsen argues that political power should be in the hands of the gifted few, not the mediocre many. Dr. Stockmann, the character who expresses these views, comes into conflict with his community; Stockmann is declared "an enemy of the people," and his house is stoned.

While *An Enemy of the People* deals with politics, *Brand* deals with religion. *Brand* isn't as dramatic and exciting as *An Enemy of the People*, but the theme of the two plays is similar: the conflict between society and a courageous, strong-willed, idealistic individual. Ibsen doesn't advocate a particular religious creed. Ibsen was neither as religious as Tolstoy and Dostoyevsky, nor as irreligious as Nietzsche. His attitude toward religion was similar to Chekhov's: detached and neutral.

Like many other imaginative writers, Ibsen was fascinated by parapsychology—by hunches, intuitions and communication via the

---

1 See M. Meyer, *Henrik Ibsen*, ch. 15.

unconscious. One of his characters says, "she believed I had said to her what I had only wished and willed—silently—inwardly—to myself."[1]

Ibsen has broad appeal: he appeals to those who enjoy an elaborate, exciting plot, to those who enjoy psychological analysis, and to those who enjoy philosophical ideas. I recommend the Norton Critical Edition of *Wild Duck*, which contains many superb essays.

11. Shakespeare

Few writers, if any, have ever dominated a nation's literature as Shakespeare dominates English literature. Vergil doesn't dominate Roman literature, nor Dante Italian literature, nor Goethe German literature, nor Tolstoy Russian literature, to the same degree that Shakespeare dominates English literature. Homer is the only writer who has ever played such a dominant role in a nation's literature as Shakespeare plays in English literature. Just as it would have been difficult for an ancient Greek to imagine another writer equaling the achievement of Homer, so too it's difficult for us to imagine another writer equaling the achievement of Shakespeare. What would Greek civilization be without Homer? What would English civilization be without Shakespeare? Writers like Homer and Shakespeare are nation-builders; they give nations a sense of identity—in fact, one might say that they give entire civilizations a sense of identity.

Shakespeare should be read intensively, not extensively; one shouldn't try to read all of Shakespeare's works. While Homer's works are consistent in quality, Shakespeare's works vary widely in quality. In choosing which of Shakespeare's works to read, let reputation be your guide.

As for biographies of Shakespeare, I recommend J. Thomas Looney's *"Shakespeare" Identified*. Around 1905, Looney discovered that "William Shakespeare" was the pen name of the Earl of Oxford. Looney's book contains not only a revolutionary theory but also good prose and a deep understanding of Shakespeare. Since the publication of Looney's book in 1920, many Oxfordian biographies have been published, such as Mark Anderson's *Shakespeare by Another Name* and Richard Whalen's *Shakespeare: Who Was He?* Charlton Ogburn wrote a big book about the Oxford Theory called *The Mysterious William*

---

[1] *The Master Builder*, Act I

Shakespeare. Ogburn also wrote an excellent 90-page summary of the case for Oxford, *The Man Who Was Shakespeare*.

Around 1930, Looney's followers discovered the Prince Tudor Theory, an outgrowth of the Oxford Theory. Like the Oxford Theory, the Prince Tudor Theory is most interesting, most exciting, and draws you into both Shakespeare's works and Elizabethan history. *Shakespeare and the Tudor Rose*, by Elisabeth Sears, is a good introduction to the Prince Tudor Theory. Hank Whittemore carried the Prince Tudor Theory further; I strongly recommend the 75-page introduction to Whittemore's massive *Monument*. You'll enjoy Shakespeare's Sonnets much more after reading Whittemore.

As for critical studies of Shakespeare, I recommend the works of G. Wilson Knight, such as *The Wheel of Fire*, which deals with the tragedies, and *The Crown of Life*, which deals with the last plays. If you want to try a short Knight essay, read "Myth and Miracle", which is the first essay in *The Crown of Life* (Knight's brother, W. F. Jackson Knight, was also an eminent critic, specializing in Roman literature). Another Shakespeare critic who has much to offer is A. C. Bradley. Bradley is better-known than Knight; Bradley was long considered the dean of Shakespeare critics.

Shakespeare is easier to read in translation than in the original. Translations can be revised as a language evolves, but Shakespeare's original language can't be revised; it would be considered blasphemy to revise Shakespeare's language. Hence those who read Shakespeare in the original have to struggle with archaic language. Shakespeare makes little effort to be clear; A. C. Bradley said that Shakespeare's language was often "obscure, inflated, tasteless, or 'pestered with metaphors.'"[1]

12. Other English Writers

Milton's language is more modern, more readable than Shakespeare's, and it has the beauty and richness of Shakespeare's language. Like Shakespeare, Milton was well-educated and widely read. But while Shakespeare's work is full of action, life and reality, Milton's work is somewhat dull, dry and bookish. Like a preacher, Milton often tries to convey religious and moral lessons to his audience. Milton is best known as the author of *Paradise Lost*, an epic poem, but his shorter works—

---

[1] *Shakespearean Tragedy*, Lecture II, "Construction in Shakespeare's Tragedies"

Comus, Samson Agonistes, Paradise Regained, etc.—are as enjoyable to read as *Paradise Lost,* if not more so.

Beowulf, the Old English epic poem, is an enjoyable book to read. I recommend the Seamus Heaney translation, which is in the series called Norton Critical Editions. There's energy in every line, the story is entertaining, and it has the atmosphere of an authentic ancient work. Beowulf is a warrior from one of the Norse societies of what is now Denmark. When the Norse people came to England in the Early Middle Ages, they brought the Beowulf legend with them; doubtless it was recited before many audiences, and it was finally written down in Old English. The king is often referred to as the "ring-giver", the lord of the rings; *Beowulf* inspired Tolkien's *Lord of the Rings.* Tolkien was an Old English scholar, and one of the commentaries in the Norton Critical Edition of *Beowulf* is by Tolkien.

Among early English novels, Fielding's *Tom Jones* and Sterne's *Tristram Shandy* stand out above the rest. Though Fielding and Sterne wrote in the mid-1700's, their work is still fresh and lively. Fielding's work has a mellow humor that reminds one of Cervantes. Sterne's work has an eccentric wit that reminds one of no other writer; Goethe called Sterne the freest spirit of the eighteenth century, while Nietzsche called him the freest spirit of all time.[1]

Swift, who wrote in the early 1700's, is known for his bitter satire, which dealt with politics, religion and mankind in general. *Gulliver's Travels* is Swift's most famous work. *A Tale of a Tub,* which satirizes established Christianity, is an extremely witty work. Leo Damrosch wrote an acclaimed biography of Swift; Damrosch has also written about Blake, Tocqueville, etc.

Like Swift, Byron is both a deep thinker and a superb stylist. Byron was more irreligious than Swift; while Swift poked fun at churches for distorting the original meaning of Christianity, Byron challenged the fundamental tenets of Christianity. In *Cain,* Byron argued that the existence of evil indicates that God is either not omnipotent or not benevolent. Like many of Byron's works, *Cain* is a drama that is designed to be read rather than acted. Byron's strongly-marked individuality makes him a modern figure, a nineteenth-century figure. This individuality is evident in Byron's drama, *Manfred;* Manfred says, "From my youth / My spirit walk'd not with the souls of men.... The lion is alone, and so am I."[2]

---

[1] See Nietzsche, *Assorted Opinions and Maxims,* §113.
[2] *Manfred,* II, ii and III, i.

As for the Romantic Poets in general, there are useful Norton Critical Editions on each of the "Big Six": Keats, Coleridge, Blake, Byron, Shelley, and Wordsworth. Northrop Frye wrote a classic study of Blake called *Fearful Symmetry*. Walter Jackson Bate wrote a well-regarded biography of Keats. André Maurois, whose biography of Proust I praised earlier, wrote biographies of Byron and Shelley. John Livingston Lowes explored the Hermetic sources of Coleridge's poetry in a book called *Road to Xanadu*. My favorite critic, G. Wilson Knight, discussed the Romantics in several different books.

13. Monsters

I recommend *Frankenstein* (by Mary Shelley) and *Dracula* (by Bram Stoker). Though they aren't my favorite novels, they're rich in imagination and symbol, and they call forth all the powers of the critic. Some of the critical essays written about them are so good that it would be worth reading the novels in order to appreciate the essays.[1]

Mary Shelley's father was the philosopher William Godwin, and her novel *Frankenstein* contains several philosophical ideas, as well as discussions of the classics. The main theme of *Frankenstein* is that those who follow a solitary path in the hope of reaching a lofty goal will come to grief; *Frankenstein* contrasts the happiness of family life and friendship with the misery of solitude. *Frankenstein* also touches on alchemical and Rosicrucian ideas; Victor Frankenstein seeks the elixir of life that alchemists had long sought, and he finally manages to manufacture a monster.

Dracula is more enjoyable to read than *Frankenstein*. If *Dracula* is occasionally tedious, it isn't because it's filled with bloody violence; rather, it's because it's filled with sugary sentimentality. *Dracula* has some memorable scenes, and some interesting remarks on occult matters.

---

[1] See
- "Philosophical and Literary Sources of *Frankenstein*" by Burton R. Pollin, *Comparative Literature*, vol. xvii, #2, spring 1965
- "Moral and Myth in Mrs. Shelley's *Frankenstein*" by Milton Allan Goldberg, *Keats-Shelley Journal*, VIII (Winter, 1959), pp. 27-38
- "Vindictiveness and the Search for Glory in Mary Shelley's *Frankenstein*," by Harry Keyishian, *The American Journal of Psychoanalysis*, vol. 49, #3, 1989

I recommend Mark Hennelly's essay "*Dracula*: The Gnostic Quest and Victorian Wasteland."[1] This essay throws a flood of light on *Dracula*, and raises one's opinion of the novel.

According to Hennelly, *Dracula* depicts both Victorian England and Transylvania as wastelands. Both areas need the other in order to be rejuvenated. Victorian England needs the passion, energy, and spontaneity of Transylvania, and Dracula needs the "man-brain", the self-consciousness, of England. On the surface, *Dracula* is a quest to kill a vampire, but under the surface, according to Hennelly, it's a quest for spiritual growth, for knowledge, for "gnosis." *Dracula* advocates open-mindedness: "The action of the novel," Hennelly writes, "dramatizes the Gnostic value of this 'open mind.'" We must keep an open mind toward the strange, the inexplicable, the occult.

14. Jane Austen

Jane Austen depicts everyday life, not the strange or the monstrous. Her work is respected by critics, and enjoyed by the general public. Unlike most writers, she seems to become more popular with the passage of time.

Austen's most popular novel is *Pride and Prejudice*. The style is clear, the plot easy to follow; it's never dull, and not very long. It's easy to see why it's popular. Austen focuses on people—their feelings, conversations, actions—and spends little time on descriptions of furniture, curtains, flowers, etc. Perhaps we can explain her popularity by saying "people are interested in people." Austen seems to enjoy writing, and this adds to our enjoyment of her works.

Her language is clear but not colloquial; one might describe it as literary language, formal and stilted by today's standards. For example, here's how Mr. Collins speaks to Mrs. Bennet when he wants to marry Mrs. Bennet's daughter: "May I hope, madam, for your interest with your fair daughter Elizabeth, when I solicit for the honor of a private audience with her in the course of this morning?"

The first novel Austen published was *Sense and Sensibility*, which she published at her own expense in 1811. She published three more novels before she died in 1817, at the age of 41. After her death, one of her brothers published her last two novels. She was quite a popular

---

[1] *English Literature in Transition (1880-1920)*, vol. 20, 1977, pp. 13-26, by Mark M. Hennelly, Jr.

novelist in her day; one of her fans was Walter Scott. Her name wasn't known, though, since she published anonymously. It seems that the first novel she started was *Pride and Prejudice*, which was initially called *First Impressions*. A writer's first book is often their best, the clearest expression of their deepest feelings.

Austen depicts upper-middle-class English society. She takes no daring flights of imagination, creates no dream worlds; she stays close to everyday life. As Walter Scott said, writers like Austen are "copying from nature as she really exists in the common walks of life, and presenting to the reader, instead of the splendid scenes of an imaginary world, a correct and striking representation of that which is daily taking place around him." Perhaps Austen would be surprised if she knew that she's far more popular today than Scott, whose novels were set in past ages. One might say that Austen is the opposite of Tolstoy and Dostoyevsky because they try to transcend everyday life through mystic ecstasy or sudden enlightenment. Austen is like a basketball player who makes no spectacular shots, but has good "shot selection," never forces a shot, never tries to do more than he's capable of.

She has no truck with the dark passions of the Romantic school. She has more in common with pre-Romantic writers like the rational moralist Samuel Johnson (she was a fan of Johnson). She often uses the word "rational" as a positive term; for example, when Mr. Bennett is annoyed with Kitty, he says, "you are never to stir out of doors till you can prove that you have spent ten minutes of every day in a rational manner."

Austen's philosophical remarks are often impressive. As A. C. Bradley wrote, "Like Johnson, [Austen is] a moralist. Her morality [is] not merely embodied in her plots, it is often openly expressed.... Her explicit statements and comments are often well worth pondering."[1]

Austen reminds me of Freud insofar as she believes that the feeling of guilt plays a key role in human nature, and human suffering. Austen speaks of, "the keenest of all anguish, self-reproach." Surely this is one of Austen's best aphorisms. When Mr. Bennett blames himself for letting Lydia go to Brighton, Elizabeth tries to raise his spirits: "You must not be too severe upon yourself," Elizabeth says. Mr. Bennett responds, "You may well warn me against such an evil. Human nature is so prone to fall into it!" One wonders where Austen acquired her understanding of guilt. Did this understanding come from her own experience, or from a philosophical writer like Johnson, or both?

---

[1] "Jane Austen as Moralist and Humorist," in the Norton Critical Edition of *Pride and Prejudice*.

After Austen's death, her brother wrote a short memoir of her. He says, "She read aloud with very great taste and effect. Her own works, probably, were never heard to so much advantage as from her own mouth; for she partook largely in all the best gifts of the comic muse." When she was growing up, literature was part of her life, and a primary means of entertainment. She began writing at a young age. She and her family also enjoyed drama, and staged their own plays.

15. Dickens

Dickens is a giant in English literature, and some of his works have attained mythic status. Characters like Scrooge are embedded in our culture, and are known even to people who haven't read Dickens. But Dickens' star seems to have dimmed somewhat in recent years, and his critical reputation has never been as high as that of Shakespeare, Tolstoy, etc. He has almost as many detractors as admirers.

Dickens enjoyed wide popularity because his work is bursting with vitality and humor, and his plots are elaborate and exciting. His work also has a theme or idea: he's a champion of feeling over reason, fairy-tales over economics. He argues that life is desiccated by reason, calculation, and economics, and saved by feeling, fairy-tale, and play. He opposes the attempt to arrange society and educate children in a rational-scientific way. He opposes Malthus and other economists, who try to regulate society by statistics, who overlook feelings and imagination.

Early in *Christmas Carol*, two men ask Scrooge to donate to a fund to help the poor. When Scrooge says the poor can go to prisons and work-houses, one of the men says, "Many can't go there; and many would rather die." To which Scrooge responds, "If they would rather die... they had better do it, and decrease the surplus population." This is the approach of Malthus, Nietzsche, and others.

Later in the story, the ghost throws this comment back at Scrooge, and Scrooge is "overcome with penitence and grief." The ghost asks Scrooge, "Will you decide what men shall live, what men shall die?" This is the tremendous question that hangs over the philosophy of the 19th century, and the politics of the 20th century. This question is only asked when people try to arrange society according to rational principles. It was first asked by the French revolutionaries, who enthroned the Goddess of Reason. It is this Goddess that Dickens tries to dethrone.

Dickens lived at a time when the middle class was expanding, and becoming more important in English society. Dickens was a product of the middle class, he wrote for the middle class, and he often wrote about the middle class. While Scott had written about the old aristocracy, Dickens wrote about contemporary society. One might say that Dickens modernized Scott, as Kafka later modernized Dickens.

Dickens is amusing and interesting, but he falls short of the sublime. He's a master of bathos, but falls short of pathos. He depicts many characters that you can ridicule or despise, some that you can pity, but few that you can admire. His characters are caricatures—exaggerated rather than life-like. His characters are too black-and-white, too one-dimensional, to be realistic; they aren't a mix of light and shadow, they're either all light or all shadow. Dickens covers romantic relationships with a thick layer of sugary, teary-eyed sentimentality.

Dickens' best short work is *Christmas Carol*, which is still enjoyable today. As for his best long work, everyone seems to have a different opinion. His later works (beginning with *Bleak House*) have a more elaborate plot than his early works, and are more strident in their criticism of contemporary society. Perhaps his most strident criticism of contemporary society is *Hard Times*, the shortest of his novels. I recommend reading Dickens in an annotated edition, such as the Norton Critical Edition. If you want to read Dickens criticism, I recommend *Dickens: The Novelist*, by F. R. Leavis and Q. D. Leavis. As for Dickens biographies, I recommend Christopher Hibbert's *The Making of Charles Dickens* (sometimes called *Charles Dickens: The Making of a Literary Giant*).

Dickens is a great affirmer of life, a great glorifier of existence. Isn't this the ultimate achievement for any artist?

16. Hardy

While Dickens often wrote of urban life, Thomas Hardy wrote of rural life. Hardy wrote a series of novels about Wessex, an area in the southwest of England. Like Dickens, Hardy weaves an exciting plot.

Hardy was born in 1840, about 30 years after Dickens. In the 1890s, Hardy's novels began to arouse criticism for violating the Victorian moral code. After *Jude the Obscure* was castigated as *Jude the Obscene*, Hardy quit writing fiction. Hardy lived until 1928, and during his latter years, he concentrated on writing poetry; he's regarded as one of the leading poets of his day. Hardy regarded himself primarily as a poet; he said that he wrote fiction merely to make money. Among Hardy's chief works are *Tess of the d'Urbervilles*, *Far From the Madding Crowd*, *Jude the Obscure*, *The Return of the Native*, and *The Mayor of Casterbridge*.

Hardy was married twice. He gradually became estranged from his first wife, but when she died in 1912, he was deeply affected, and his feelings overflowed in poetry. His second wife was his secretary, a woman much younger than he was. After Hardy died, his second wife published a two-volume biography of him; much of this biography was apparently written by Hardy himself, so perhaps it should be called an autobiography.

Hardy was not from the upper class (his father was a mason and builder), and his sympathies seem to lie with his working-class characters, rather than with his aristocratic characters. The hero of *Far from the Madding Crowd* is the shepherd Gabriel Oak, and the villain is the high-born soldier, Frank Troy. According to Wikipedia, "Hardy never felt at home in London. He was acutely conscious of class divisions and his social inferiority." George Meredith advised Hardy not to publish his first novel, *The Poor Man and the Lady*, because it was "too bitter a satire on the rich."[1]

Hardy is known for taking a rather dark, tragic view of the human condition; many of the characters in *Madding Crowd* meet misfortune. Hardy once said that we should take "a full look at the Worst." But his worldview is only dark if he's compared to other Victorian writers; if he's compared to modern writers, one is struck by his hopefulness, his lack of the morbid and cynical.

Hardy describes Gabriel Oak as "generous and true,"[2] and he describes one of his female characters (Fanny Robin) as a "gentle creature."[3] Can you imagine a more modern writer, like Forster or Lawrence, using such phrases? One might say that Hardy is the last of the morally simple writers, the last of the "generous and true" writers.

Hardy's morality is traditional, Western morality. Hardy praises Gabriel for his unselfishness: "Among the multitude of interests by which he was surrounded, those which affected his personal well-being were not the most absorbing and important in his eyes."[4] Hardy blames Bathsheba for following her feelings: "Her culpability lay in her making no attempt to control feeling by subtle and careful inquiry into

---

[1] Wikipedia article on Meredith
[2] Ch. 38
[3] Ch. 45
[4] Ch. 43

consequences."[1] Hardy's morality has more in common with the morality of Socrates and Jesus than with the morality of Forster and Lawrence. Hardy has none of the admiration for Eastern mysticism that we find in Forster; Hardy doesn't discuss spiritual growth, as Forster does, and he doesn't urge us to follow the wisdom of the body, as Lawrence does.

I recommend *Far from the Madding Crowd*: the plot is enjoyable, there are beautiful scenes of rural life, and the ideas are interesting.

17. Robert Louis Stevenson

Stevenson is remembered chiefly for the children's classic, *Treasure Island*. Though the popularity of *Treasure Island* is fading, Stevenson's reputation may rise as the mystical element, the Zen element, in his work is better appreciated. One of the chief writers on Zen, R. H. Blyth, never tires of quoting Stevenson's *Fables*. Stevenson's high spirits and playful attitude should not cause us to take him lightly—rather, they should make us respect him all the more.

One of the themes of Stevenson's work is moral ambiguity, "the co-presence of good and evil qualities in the same person."[2] Long John Silver, for example, one of the main characters in *Treasure Island*, is initially good, then evil, then good again. But the most famous example of moral ambiguity in Stevenson's work is the protagonist of *The Strange Case of Dr Jekyll and Mr Hyde*.

Stevenson is classified as a neo-Romantic. He doesn't focus on the nitty-gritty of modern life (as Émile Zola did), but instead writes about earlier times (as Walter Scott did). Perhaps his best works are *The Master of Ballantrae* and *Weir of Hermiston* (though *Weir* is unfinished). In addition to writing fiction, Stevenson wrote travel narratives and essays about literature.

Stevenson died at 44, and was buried in the Samoan Islands. He wrote his own epitaph—a poem with an affirmative, Zennish tone, a poem that affirms both life and death:

Under the wide and starry sky,
Dig the grave and let me lie.

---

1 Ch. 29

2 "The Sea Cook: A Study in the Art of Robert Louis Stevenson," by W. W. Robson, in *On the Novel*, edited by B. S. Benedikz

Glad did I live and gladly die,
And I laid me down with a will.
This be the verse you grave for me:
Here he lies where he longed to be;
Home is the sailor, home from sea,
And the hunter home from the hill.

Has a writer ever achieved more with such simple language?

18. Conrad

Joseph Conrad was born into the Polish aristocracy, but lived most of his life in England, and wrote in English. Conrad spent his early adulthood as a sailor, rising to the rank of captain, and many of his novels are sea stories. Just as Proust wrote about the dying world of the French aristocracy, so Conrad wrote about the dying world of the sailing ship. While Proust's works appeal to literary people, Conrad's works have broad appeal; Conrad is a favorite among un-literary people. Though his prose is sometimes flowery, it's always clear.

One of Conrad's best-known works is the novella *Heart of Darkness*. There are some excellent critical studies of *Heart of Darkness*, such as an essay that compares it to Joseph Campbell's theory of the mythical hero.[1] *Conrad the Novelist*, by Albert Guerard, contains valuable essays not only on *Heart of Darkness*, but on all of Conrad's works.

Another popular Conrad novella is *The Secret Sharer*. Among his novels, *Nostromo* and *Lord Jim* are especially well-regarded, while *The Secret Agent* and *Under Western Eyes* are praised for their depiction of Russian psychology, and for their depiction of anarchist/terrorist psychology.

19. Rudyard Kipling

Kipling was born in India in 1905, and spent his early years there. His father was an artist, an art teacher, and a museum curator who illustrated several of Kipling's books. His mother's maiden name was MacDonald (the family was Scottish); one of her sisters married the

---

[1] "Myth and Archetype in *Heart of Darkness*," by James Mellard, *Tennessee Studies in Literature*, 13 (1968): pp. 1-15

painter Edward Burne-Jones, another sister was the mother of Stanley Baldwin, a British prime minister.

When Kipling was five, his parents sent him and his sister to board with strangers in England, while they remained in India. Gone were the obedient servants who had surrounded him in India, gone the loving parents. Kipling later dubbed his domicile The House of Desolation. He spent seven unhappy years there, then spent four happier years at an English boarding school; his school years were the basis of a book called *Stalky & Co.*

When he was 16, Kipling moved back to India, where his father had found him a job on a newspaper. He published a volume of poems when he was 20, and a volume of stories when he was 22. The volume of stories was called *Plain Tales From the Hills*, and was soon followed by more story-collections (Kipling was always a prolific writer). His reputation in India was growing, and he was even becoming known in England.

After seven years in India, Kipling decided to pursue a literary career in England. He travelled from India to England via Burma, Hong Kong, Japan, and the U.S.; he later described his travels in *From Sea to Sea*. In 1889, at the age of 23, he arrived in London, where he was hailed as the new genius. At 24, he was churning out stories and poems at a rapid rate, prompting Robert Louis Stevenson to say, "At this rate his works will soon fill the habitable globe.... Kipling is by far the most promising young man to appear since—ahem—I appeared."[1]

Kipling decided to try his hand at novel-writing, and wrote four novels in the next twelve years, while continuing to write stories and poems. His first novel was *The Light That Failed*, about a successful painter who becomes gradually blind. His second was *The Naulahka*, which he co-wrote with an American publisher, Wolcott Balestier (he became close friends with Balestier, and when Balestier died suddenly in 1891, Kipling married Balestier's sister, Carrie). The third was *Captains Courageous*, about cod fishing in New England ("It seems very

---

[1] Letter to Henry James, Dec. 29, 1890; quoted in *Kipling: The Critical Heritage*, ch. 10, p. 65. Flushed with success, Kipling cabled his parents in India, "Genesis 45:9," which reads, "Haste ye, and go up to my father, and say unto him, Thus saith thy son Joseph [Kipling's real name was Joseph Rudyard Kipling], God hath made me lord of all Egypt: come down unto me, tarry not." One reason Kipling travelled from India to England via the Pacific was to meet Robert Louis Stevenson in Samoa, but Kipling didn't make it to Samoa, and never met Stevenson.

odd to me," Oscar Wilde said, "that a man should write a whole novel about cod-fishing—but then I suppose that is because I do not like cod"[1]. His fourth novel was *Kim* (1901), often called his best novel; *Kim* is about a boy travelling through India who becomes involved with English espionage and Tibetan Buddhism. Kipling's novels didn't arouse as much public enthusiasm as his poems and stories, and he finally decided that the novel wasn't for him.

As Andrew Lang said, few writers have succeeded in both the short story and the novel; Maupassant succeeded in the short story, but his novels are mediocre. Poe succeeded in the short story, but didn't attempt a novel. Chekhov succeeded with stories and plays, but didn't attempt a novel. Hawthorne is one of the few who succeeded with both stories and novels.[2] Perhaps we should compare Kipling to Maupassant: both were masters of the short story, less successful with the novel. But while Maupassant wrote only prose, Kipling was known for his poetry as much as his prose.

When Kipling was 41, he received the Nobel Prize; he was the first English-language writer to receive it, and to this day, he's the youngest person ever to receive it. Henry James said, "Kipling strikes me personally as the most complete man of genius (as distinct from fine intelligence) that I have ever known." Kipling's poems and stories were so widely read that many of their phrases passed into everyday speech (such as "white man's burden" and "somewhere east of Suez"), or became book titles (such as *The God That Failed* and *A Savage War of Peace*). His children's books—such as *Just So Stories* and *The Jungle Book*—were especially popular. When he was in France during World War I, a French soldier who was under fire asked him to explain how the idea for the *Jungle Book* came to him.[3] In 1899, when he was seriously ill, the world waited for news, and even the Kaiser sent him a telegram.

Journalists were constantly trying to interview him, so he learned to maintain a stony silence. When he was living in Vermont, and saw journalists approaching, he hid in a neighbor's barn. "Why don't you tell them to go to hell?" his neighbor asked. "Can't do that, they would write

---

[1] Lord Birkenhead, *Rudyard Kipling*, Ch. 11, "The End in Vermont," p. 164

[2] See Lang's essay in *Kipling: The Critical Heritage*, ch. 12

[3] Lord Birkenhead, *Rudyard Kipling*, Ch. 17, p. 267

it all up in their papers."[1] He disliked biographers even more than journalists, and called biography "higher cannibalism." He wrote,

Seek not to question other than
The books I leave behind.

He had a substantial income, and built himself a large house in Dummerston, Vermont (near Brattleboro), which he called Naulahka; he lived in Vermont for four years.[2] Later he bought an old English mansion, Bateman's, where he spent the last thirty years of his life. At Bateman's, he had his own brook, which he used to generate his own electricity. He received farming advice from Rider Haggard, an agriculture expert and the author of *King Solomon's Mines*, *She*, and other novels. Kipling and his family enjoyed Haggard's stories about his years in Africa. Like Kipling, Haggard had experienced the death of a child, and never fully recovered. In his later years, Haggard said that he and Kipling were "in supreme sympathy.... A long talk with Kipling is now one of the greatest pleasures I have left in life."[3]

Kipling was interested in practical matters, and began driving a car in 1897, when cars had 6 horsepower, and travelled 15 miles per hour.[4] He often interrogated tradesmen and engineers, then put his knowledge to use in his stories. His curiosity was described as "insatiable," and his memory as "prodigious."[5] Like his contemporary H. G. Wells, Kipling wrote stories about future technologies: in 1903, he wrote "Wireless," about using radio to communicate with a past century; in 1904, he wrote "With the Night Mail," about flying across the Atlantic in a plane that almost flew itself; and in 1907, he wrote "As Easy as A.B.C." in which a broadcasting company governs the world. Kipling was as interested in the past as the future, and wrote two books that put English history into fictional form: *Puck of Pook's Hill*, and *Rewards and Fairies*.

---

[1] Ibid, ch. 10, p. 148. Birkenhead says that Kipling's "desire for privacy... has so often been referred to as neurotic and unnatural."(p. 148)

[2] The word "Naulahka" comes from a building in Lahore Fort in Pakistan. The correct spelling seems to be "Naulakha."

[3] *The Age of Kipling*, edited by John Gross, "A Matter of Vision," pp. 131, 134

[4] Lord Birkenhead, *Rudyard Kipling*, Ch. 16, p. 236

[5] Lord Birkenhead, pp. 326, 327; see also p. 206, where his memory is described as "astounding."

In his later years, Kipling's popularity declined. He seemed out of touch with modern taste. He was a staunch defender of the British Empire, and believed that the British could govern India better than the Indians themselves.[1] He also opposed Home Rule for Ireland. Kipling was scornful of democracy, and thought the strong man should rule alone. He complained that the British wasted their time with soccer and cricket; he thought they should train for war instead, by fighting mock battles, etc.[2] His days were darkened by the deaths of his son and daughter, by his unhappy marriage, and by illness.

In a 1942 essay, Orwell called Kipling a "jingo imperialist," and said that "during five literary generations every enlightened person has despised him." In a period that was preoccupied with darkness and evil, Kipling's "bouncing vulgar vitality" was unfashionable. Kipling was a champion of empire at a time when empire was viewed with disfavor. While most intellectuals were starting to question Western civilization, Kipling thought that Western societies had an obligation to rule, educate, and civilize non-Western societies:

Take up the White Man's burden—
Send forth the best ye breed—
Go bind your sons to exile
To serve your captives' need;
To wait in heavy harness,
On fluttered folk and wild—
Your new-caught, sullen peoples,
Half-devil and half-child.

Kipling lamented democratic trends in countries like Japan and India, and defended non-democratic countries like Russia.

He had shaken his head ruefully over Japan, "the second oriental country which has made it impossible for a strong man to govern alone" [the first probably being

---

[1] Birkenhead, p. 218. Kipling believed that "the conditions of modern life had grown to such complexity as to make it impossible for any government whatever to fulfill its task perfectly, and that the Indian Civil Service with its long tradition of the leadership of 'a strong man governing alone' [was] as good an administrative organization as the world had ever known."(Birkenhead, p. 222)

[2] Birkenhead, p. 224. Kipling's optimism about the British Empire was undermined by the Boer War, by "the spectacle of this mighty Empire struggling desperately to defeat a handful of Boer farmers."(p. 229) A great power frustrated by guerrilla warfare.

India]. He had regarded the shrill chatter of the Congress Party in India with contempt, and the vulgarity of Congress in the USA with horror. In the future, he was to be one of the many who at first sight genuflected before the unlovely shrine of Mussolini.[1]

In defense of Kipling, however, it should be noted that he always opposed Marxism and Nazism. And he had a knack for anticipating future developments; for example, he anticipated the world wars.

Kipling never relaxed his fears of Germany [Birkenhead writes]. In 1908: "You are dead right about the Teuton and I fear the time shorter even than we think." Two years later: "We in England are just camping comfortably on the edge of a volcano, and telling each other that the danger of a German explosion is over.... Meanwhile the Teuton is angry, and is taking measures and steps as fast and as hard as he can."[2]

Around 1930, Kipling "spoke always about the coming war, the advent of which he clearly predicted."[3]

The advent of Hitler placed beyond doubt his long-held and brilliantly perceptive convictions of Germany's aggressive intentions: "The Were-Wolf has got tired. He's been a man for twelve years, and has got all out of mankind that he needs. At least he can't get any more—so it is time for him to change shape. In less than a year he will be clamoring for the return of his Colonies, as 'necessary for his self-respect.' You wait and see!"[4]

There's an excellent biography of Kipling by Lord Birkenhead; the longer biography by Charles Carrington also deserves mention. Kipling wrote an autobiography, *Something of Myself*.[5] The Kipling Society's website is an excellent resource (www.kipling.org.uk).

---

[1] Ch. 15, pp. 217, 218

[2] Ch. 16, p. 252. Birkenhead says that, as Kipling grew older, he developed a "malignant hatred of the Germans, which produced such murderous stories as 'Mary Postgate'.... His mistrust of them had begun long before, when he first realized that an assault on civilization was coming."(p. 227)

[3] Ch. 22, p. 325

[4] Ch. 25, pp. 342, 343

[5] If you want to read Kipling's autobiography, consider the version edited by Thomas Pinney, *Something of Myself and Other Autobiographical Writings*, Cambridge: Cambridge University Press, 1990

20. E. M. Forster

Along with D. H. Lawrence and Virginia Woolf, E. M. Forster is one of the key figures in early-twentieth-century English fiction. Born in 1879, Forster began writing novels at an early age, and also stopped writing novels at an early age. By the time he was 31, he had published four novels: *Where Angels Fear To Tread*, *The Longest Journey*, *A Room With A View*, and *Howards End*. During the remainder of his long life, he wrote only two novels: *A Passage to India*, one of his most highly-regarded works, and *Maurice*, which dealt with homosexual themes, and wasn't published until after Forster's death.

Perhaps Forster stopped writing fiction because, being homosexual, he couldn't empathize with heterosexual characters, and he couldn't express his homosexual feelings publicly. Perhaps he stopped writing fiction because astute critics, like Virginia Woolf, argued that his fiction was a failure—though it had lively scenes and deep thoughts, it didn't form an artistic whole. Forster is a fine essayist and critic, and wrote a book called *Aspects of the Novel*. Was he too great a thinker to be a great artist? Did he understand the machinery of fiction too well to believe in fiction?

Forster was one of the first English writers to appreciate D. H. Lawrence's genius, and sing his praises, at a time when Lawrence was controversial. Like Lawrence, Forster wrote several travel books, drawing on his experiences in India and Alexandria.

As Forster appreciated Lawrence, so Forster himself was appreciated and praised by the great American critic, Lionel Trilling. When Forster met Trilling in the U.S., Forster said, "So this is the man who made me famous."[1]

Forster admired Jane Austen for her lively humor, and Walt Whitman for his profound mysticism. Forster's fans (of whom I'm one) believe that his fiction is a marvelous combination of humor and profundity. Forster did what every great intellectual must do: he respected culture, he made culture enjoyable, and he pursued spiritual growth.

21. D. H. Lawrence

---

[1] I recommend a critic named Laurence Brander, who wrote studies of Forster, Aldous Huxley, Somerset Maugham, George Orwell, etc.

David Herbert Lawrence was born in 1885, and died in 1930. He's one of the brightest stars in modern literature, but doesn't enjoy the reputation he deserves. Compared to the fiction of Kafka, Proust, and Joyce, the fiction of Lawrence is more traditional and readable, less quirky and eccentric.

If ever there were a prolific writer, it was Lawrence: he wrote short stories, novels, poetry, plays, translations, travel books, literary criticism, philosophical works, and countless letters. One of his best novels is an early work, *Sons and Lovers*, which describes his coming-of-age as a miner's son. Critics who look askance at autobiographical fiction say that Lawrence's best novels are *The Rainbow* and *Women in Love*.

When Lawrence was 27, he met Frieda Weekley, a professor's wife. Frieda was then 33, and had three young children. She came from an aristocratic German family; her maiden name was Frieda von Richthofen (she was related to the famous ace Baron von Richthofen, "The Red Baron"). Frieda abandoned her children, and eloped with Lawrence to Germany. They stayed together until Lawrence's death about twenty years later. One of Lawrence's best-known novels, *Lady Chatterley's Lover*, is about an affair between an upper-class woman and a working-class man.

In England, Lawrence's fiction was lambasted and suppressed as pornographic. He and Frieda spent most of their time abroad; Lawrence spoke of his 'savage pilgrimage.' Lawrence and Frieda honeymooned in southern Germany, and then walked over the Alps to Italy; this trip was the basis for Lawrence's first travel book, *Twilight in Italy*. Later they lived in and around Sicily, where Lawrence wrote a travel book called *Sea and Sardinia*. Then they left Europe, stopping in Sri Lanka and Australia before settling in Taos, New Mexico. (Their sojourn in Australia provided Lawrence with material for his novel *Kangaroo*.) After some visits to Mexico, Lawrence wrote *Mornings in Mexico*. Health problems prompted Lawrence to return to Italy, where he wrote his last travel book, *Sketches of Etruscan Places*.

The main theme of his work is that we should listen to our body:

> My great religion [Lawrence wrote] is a belief in the blood, the flesh. We can go wrong in our minds. But what our blood feels... is always true. The intellect is only a bit and a bridle. What do I care about knowledge? All I want is to answer to my blood, direct, without the fribbling intervention of mind, or moral, or what not.[1]

---

[1] Letter to Earnest Collings, January 17, 1913

Lawrence isn't merely an advocate of uninhibited sex; he wasn't a champion of the body for its own sake. He urges us to listen to the body in order to satisfy psychological needs and foster spiritual growth, in order to develop the whole person and reach our full potential. Lawrence was a harsh critic of modern, Western society, which he accused of stifling human nature. He admired primitive societies—societies that were close to nature and close to the body, like Etruscan society and Aztec society. Lawrence aspired to be a prophet-artist, and to present a new view of man, of love, etc. He even urged his friends to join him, and create a community. He rebelled against Victorian mores, and also against the ornate style of Victorian writers; his short, simple sentences remind one of Forster.

Lawrence understood the occult as well as any writer, as is evident from his novella, *The Fox*. A good way to approach Lawrence is by reading *The Fox*, in combination with a book edited by Harold Bloom, *Bloom's Major Short Story Writers: D. H. Lawrence*. The English critic F. R. Leavis wrote a book called *D. H. Lawrence: Novelist*, which is one of the best studies of Lawrence's work.

I strongly recommend *D. H. Lawrence: A Personal Record*, a moving and readable memoir by Jessie Chambers Wood, a close friend of Lawrence in his early years. A friend from his later years, Catherine Carswell, wrote *Savage Pilgrimage: A Narrative of D. H. Lawrence*; Leavis called Carswell's biography, "admirable and indispensable."[1] If you want a more modern biography, consider *D. H. Lawrence: A Biography*, by Jeffrey Meyers. (Meyers also wrote biographies of Hemingway, Fitzgerald, Conrad, etc.)

Harold Bloom said that, among 20th-century English poets, Lawrence is second only to Hardy.[2] Lawrence's travel writings have been ranked among the best in the English language. Edmund Wilson said that Lawrence's study of American literature is "one of the few first-rate books that have ever been written on the subject." E. M. Forster called Lawrence, "the greatest imaginative novelist of our generation." Lawrence is a remarkable blend of wide learning and bold originality, deep thinking and exuberant creativity.

---

[1] *D. H. Lawrence: Novelist*, "Introduction," footnote 3, p. ix

[2] See the Introduction to *Bloom's Major Short Story Writers: D. H. Lawrence*

22. Shaw and Wells

George Bernard Shaw was raised in a musical household in Dublin. After moving to London, he became a music critic, and was caught up in the Wagner craze that swept Europe in the 1880's. Shaw then turned from music criticism to drama criticism, and became an enthusiastic admirer of Ibsen. In his forties, Shaw emerged as a dramatist and political activist. Shaw believed that playwrights should follow Ibsen's example, and use drama as an instrument for social reform. Shaw expressed his ideas in plays, and also in essays and prefaces to his plays. Shaw was the antithesis of a pure artist; he used art as a vehicle for philosophy and politics.

Shaw believed that political problems couldn't be solved by the reform of institutions, but only by the evolution of man; "our only hope," he wrote, "is in evolution. We must replace the Man by the Superman." Shaw believed in eugenics, in trying to improve mankind by selective breeding; he dreamed of a society of supermen, "an England in which every man is a Cromwell, a France in which every man is a Napoleon, a Rome in which every man is a Caesar."

Shaw believed that democracy was a failure, just as monarchy had been a failure. Democracy is only popular, Shaw argued, among people who haven't experienced it, that is, among people who live in despotisms and oligarchies; once democracy is actually tried, people lose faith in it. Shaw believed that criminals shouldn't be imprisoned, since their nature led them to criminal behavior, and their nature can't be changed. He believed that criminals should be executed, and he called execution "quite reasonable and very necessary." He believed that people should have to earn the right to live in a civilized community; "the right to live is abused," he said, "whenever it is not constantly challenged."[1] Being an atheist, Shaw rejected the idea that human life is sacred; he viewed man from the standpoint of biology, not religion.

Next to Shakespeare, Shaw is the most popular English-language playwright. His plays are witty and light-hearted, lacking in passion and lacking in deep emotions. Shaw was more at home with comedy than tragedy. Shaw's style is as light and flippant as his content. Shaw tried to create lively, popular dramas that would express serious ideas.

---

[1] See *Man and Superman*, "The Revolutionist's Handbook and Pocket Companion" and *On the Rocks*, preface. "Shaw's Man and Superman," by J. Stamm (*American Imago*, winter 1965) is an interesting sketch of Shaw.

H. G. Wells, a contemporary of Shaw's, was a popular and prolific writer; Wells wrote both fiction and non-fiction. Wells was a pioneer in the field of science fiction. Like Shaw, Wells rejected Christianity and embraced a religion based on social progress. Like Shaw, Wells believed that progress was impossible without government control of reproduction:

> To prevent the multiplication of people below a certain standard, and to encourage the multiplication of exceptionally superior people [is] the only real and permanent way of mending the ills of the world.... In that way man has risen from the beasts, and in that way men will rise to be over-men.[1]

Wells believed that nations should be combined into larger nations, and that eventually the whole world should be one nation.

23. Chesterton and Belloc

While Shaw and Wells represent the secular school, G. K. Chesterton and Hilaire Belloc represent the Catholic perspective. While Shaw and Wells tried to make man new and better, Chesterton and Belloc thought we should take man as he is, a flawed sinner. Chesterton and Belloc often engaged in public debates with Shaw and Wells (Wells complained that "debating Mr. Belloc is like arguing with a hailstorm"). Shaw referred to the duo as "Chesterbelloc." Chesterton and Belloc advocated an economic theory called distributism, that is, broad-based ownership, in opposition to capitalism (ownership by a few) and socialism (ownership by the state). Chesterton and Belloc were busy journalists as well as prolific authors.

Chesterton wrote defenses of Christianity (such as *Orthodoxy* and *The Everlasting Man*) that were intended for a broad audience. He was admired by C. S. Lewis, a later defender of Christianity. Chesterton wrote short stories featuring a detective, Father Brown, who understands that evil is universal, and tries to put himself in the shoes of the criminal. Chesterton's study of Dickens helped spark a Dickens revival.

Belloc was born in France to a French father and an English mother; his father died when he was 2, and he grew up in England. Belloc wrote numerous biographies (Richelieu, Cromwell, Napoleon, etc.) in which

---

[1] *Mankind In the Making*, "The Problem of the Birth Supply." Those interested in Wells should read the last third of his *Anticipations*; also the introduction and chapter eight of his *Experiment in Autobiography*.

he champions the Catholic faith; he also wrote several books about military history. A tireless walker, Belloc described his walk from central France to Rome in a book called *The Path to Rome*; he also wrote other travel books, such as *The Cruise of the Nona* (about sailing around England) and *The Pyrenees*.

24. Evelyn Waugh and Graham Greene

In the next generation, other Catholic writers rose to prominence, including Evelyn Waugh and Graham Greene. Waugh's early novels were humorous and satirical. In 1930, Waugh converted to Catholicism, and his religious beliefs are evident in his novel *Brideshead Revisited*, and in his trilogy *Sword of Honour*, which draws on Waugh's experiences as a soldier in World War II. Waugh wrote a biography of the Catholic martyr Edmund Campion, and a biography of Ronald Knox (like Waugh, Knox converted to Catholicism; Knox was the author of religious works and crime novels). Waugh also wrote a historical novel about the Empress Helena, a Catholic saint and the mother of Constantine. Waugh was a favorite of the American conservative William F. Buckley, himself a Catholic. The critic Edmund Wilson called Waugh "the only first-rate comic genius that has appeared in English since Bernard Shaw."[1] Waugh's travel books are highly-regarded; several of his travel books (and two of his novels) deal with Africa. Among Waugh's relatives were many writers: his father (Arthur), his brother (Alec), his son (Auberon), and his grandson (Alexander).

Graham Greene's long life spans most of the 20th century: he lived from 1904 to 1991. Greene converted to Catholicism early (age 22), and drifted away from Catholicism in his later years. In the 1950s, he stopped attending Mass. Political themes became important in his fiction; he was critical of American foreign policy, and sympathetic toward Castro's Communism. Greene travelled widely, and was employed by the British secret service; many of his novels are set in foreign countries. For example, *The Heart of the Matter* is set in Sierra Leone, and deals with espionage as well as religious themes. If you want to learn more about Greene (and Waugh and Chesterton and Belloc), consider Ian Ker's book, *The Catholic Revival in English Literature, 1845-1961*.

---

[1] Wikipedia, quoting *Classics and Commercials, A Literary Chronicle of the Forties*, by Edmund Wilson, page 140, Vintage Books, New York, 1962

25. Somerset Maugham

Another prominent English writer, older than Greene, is W. Somerset Maugham, best known for his novel *Of Human Bondage*. Early in his career, Maugham achieved success both as a novelist and as a playwright. In 1908, "he had four plays running simultaneously in London, and Punch published a cartoon of Shakespeare biting his fingernails nervously as he looked at the billboards." But despite his popularity, Maugham was never regarded by critics as one of the great writers of his time; Maugham himself said he was "in the very first row of the second-raters."

Like Greene, Maugham served in the British secret service, and drew on his experiences in his writings; Maugham's novel *Ashenden* influenced later spy novels, such as the James Bond series (as Poe's detective stories influenced later detective fiction). Maugham's commercial success enabled him to travel widely—visiting outposts of the British Empire, listening to stories, gathering material; it is said that he left behind a string of angry hosts, who didn't like the way he portrayed them. Maugham travelled to the Pacific to research his novel about Gauguin, *The Moon and Sixpence*.

Maugham's short stories are wonderful; I strongly recommend "The Outstation," "The Unconquered," "Rain," "The Letter," etc. Maugham's prose is clear, and his work is highly readable; not for him is the experimental, the avant-garde, and the obscure. George Orwell said, "The modern writer who has influenced me most is Somerset Maugham, whom I admire immensely for his power of telling a story straightforwardly and without frills." If you want to read about Maugham himself, consider Ted Morgan's biography, or Maugham's own work *The Summing Up*.

26. Wodehouse and Christie

Perhaps the most popular British writers of the 20th century were P. G. Wodehouse and Agatha Christie. Both were born in the late 1800's, and both continued producing bestsellers until the late 1900's. Both wrote to entertain the reader, not to change him or enlighten him.

Wodehouse wrote in a comic vein. His father was a judge in Hong Kong, and during his early years, Wodehouse rarely saw his parents. He reminds one of a child who has been left alone, and has no goal except to have fun. Wodehouse has enormous literary talent, and considerable culture. As a stylist, he has few equals. His writing is so light-hearted that one of his critics called him "the performing flea" of English letters. His style seems to poke fun at style, his culture seems to poke fun at culture. He's best known for a series of stories and novels about a valet named Jeeves and his boss, Bertie Wooster; among the titles in this series are *The Inimitable Jeeves* (1923), and *Carry On, Jeeves* (1925).

Agatha Christie achieved enormous popularity with her mysteries. Christie began her career with *The Mysterious Affair at Styles* (1920). Her early work was influenced by the Sherlock Holmes stories, as those stories were influenced by Poe's "Murders in the Rue Morgue." Among her best-known works are *Murder on the Orient Express* (1934) and *Curtain* (1975), in which her detective, Hercule Poirot, leaves the stage.

Christie grabs your attention on the first page, and holds your attention to the last page; you want to learn the solution to the puzzle, you want to know who did it. There are no wasted words, no flowery language, no digressions; as they say in politics, Christie "stays on message." Every page is a pleasure, an effortless pleasure. The author uses an astonishing amount of cleverness, reasoning; one might compare the author to a chess player. Christie gives us very little Christie, she reveals very little about herself; her writing is objective, not subjective.

Since Christie's work is so concise, it's suitable for reading aloud, and since it's so clear, it's suitable for young readers, and for foreigners who are trying to learn English. It could persuade youngsters that reading is pleasurable.

Christie's writing has dignity, courtesy, taste. She doesn't use the vulgar device, popular in Hollywood, of ridiculing the nobility.

The weaknesses of Christie's fiction are obvious: the characters aren't three-dimensional and life-like, the story is utterly unrealistic. There are no deep feelings or thoughts; the reader is neither moved nor enlightened, merely entertained. The author doesn't create a world; she merely creates a puzzle.

Many other mystery writers became popular, including the English writer Dorothy Sayers, and the American writers Dashiell Hammett and Raymond Chandler. Among the more contemporary writers in this genre are the Americans John D. MacDonald and Donald Westlake; in these writers, one often finds a comic strain that reminds one of Wodehouse. Instead of trying to arouse the reader's curiosity, as Christie did, these writers try to make the reader laugh.

And then there are writers of thrillers who try to create suspense. The Scottish writer John Buchan is known for novels like *The Thirty-Nine Steps*; Buchan also wrote an acclaimed biography of the Scottish hero Montrose, and an autobiography called *Memory Hold-the-Door* (also known as *Pilgrim's Way*). Ian Fleming wrote popular spy novels featuring James Bond; Fleming himself was an intelligence officer in World War II. Alistair MacLean wrote popular action novels, such as *Ice Station Zebra*; some of MacLean's works draw on his experiences in the British Navy.

27. Anatole France

Anatole France was preoccupied with romantic affairs rather than with utopian plans or religious beliefs. France had numerous mistresses. In France's opinion, love made life rich and exciting; amending Descartes's formula, France said, "I love, therefore I am." But France's amorous adventures didn't bring him happiness. In his old age, France complained that he had never been happy for a single day, for a single hour. He was always discontent, always striving for something beyond his grasp.[1]

Unlike Shaw and Wells, France respected style, and polished his sentences carefully. He revised his work over and over. "I insist on as many as eight proofs," he said; "my most valuable working tools are the pastepot and the scissors." Unlike Proust, France wrote short sentences and short books; France's work is easy to read, and enjoyed wide popularity between 1890 and 1930.

France believed that the best French stylists were Montaigne, Rabelais, Racine, and other older writers. Compared to these older writers, nineteenth-century French writers, like Chateaubriand and Flaubert, were, in France's opinion, artificial and affected. France thought that the best stylists were the writers who didn't try to be great stylists, the writers who wrote freely and naturally. France thought that nineteenth-century writers "have 'effort' written all over them.... They strain after effect... they aim at being stylists."[2]

---

[1] See Brousson, *Anatole France Himself*. The aged Goethe also felt that he had experienced little happiness. "There has been nothing but toil and care," Goethe said; "in all my seventy-five years, I have never had a month of genuine comfort."

[2] See N. Ségur, *Conversations With Anatole France*, "Versailles and the Romantic Spirit." France's view of French prose agrees with that of Tocqueville. Tocqueville thought that the golden age of French prose was the seventeenth century, when "style [was] the mere vehicle of

In addition to short stories and novels, France wrote numerous critical essays and a biography of Joan of Arc. France believed that neither literature nor literary criticism should aspire to be objective and impersonal. All artistic works, in France's view, reflect the soul of their creator. "What do we admire in the *Divine Comedy*," France asked, "unless it be the great soul of Dante?" In his critical essays, France set forth his own feelings and opinions, with no attempt at objectivity. "The good critic," France wrote, "is he who relates the adventures of his own soul among masterpieces. Objective criticism has no more existence than has objective art."[1]

France's imaginative works are generally light-hearted and ironic. Many are set in distant times and places, and rest on a foundation of historical knowledge. For example, his novel *The Gods Are Athirst* is based on his long study of the French Revolution. France believed that literature should idealize life, and avoid the ugly; he pointed out that Greek art idealized life. France hated the grim realism of Zola, and wrote, "I will not, certainly, deny [Zola's] detestable fame. No one before him had raised so lofty a pile of ordure."[2]

France's imaginative work is large in quantity, uneven in quality. An excellent book could be made from France's best short stories, but some of his short stories are second rate. Some of his novels are also second rate—for example, *The Crime of Sylvestre Bonnard* and *Penguin Island*. I recommend Brousson's *Anatole France Himself*, a witty and enjoyable book containing France's remarks on various subjects. Tylden-Wright's biography, *Anatole France*, is concise and interesting.

28. Maupassant

Like Anatole France, Maupassant was a story-teller whose works are light-hearted in tone, and whose style is simple and direct. France

---

thought." Later French writers were interested in style for its own sake. The best French writers, according to Tocqueville, aimed at clarity and brevity. (See *Correspondence and Conversations of Alexis de Tocqueville With N. W. Senior*, 8/26/50.)

[1] See *On Life and Letters*, vol. 1, preface, and *The Crime of Sylvester Bonnard*, "May"

[2] See *On Life and Letters*, vol. 1, "*La Terre*" and "George Sand and Idealism in Art"

loved Maupassant's stories, and said that Maupassant "possesses the three great qualities of the French writer, first, clearness, then again, clearness, and lastly, clearness."[1] Maupassant's stories have less scholarship, and more life, than France's stories. While France's stories are often set in distant times and places, Maupassant's stories are set in his own time, and his own country.

Maupassant's mother was a close friend of Flaubert; in fact, Maupassant may have been the natural son of Flaubert. When Maupassant was in his twenties, Flaubert spent several years teaching him the art of fiction; rarely has one writer had such a direct influence on another. Flaubert taught Maupassant to be a careful observer, to find the distinctive features in whatever he saw, to find what other people had overlooked. Finally, in 1880, when Maupassant was thirty, he published "Boule de Suif," which showed that he had indeed learned the art of fiction. Flaubert said, "'Boule de Suif,' the story by my disciple [is] a masterpiece of writing, comedy and observation." After the success of "Boule de Suif," Maupassant quit his civil service job, devoted himself to writing, and produced about three hundred short stories, before falling victim to syphilis and dying at forty-two.

Maupassant's stories aren't as consistent in quality as Joyce's stories. While Joyce aspired to rival the greatest names in literature, Maupassant had more modest ambitions. Maupassant wrote too hastily, he didn't have enough respect for literature. His popularity, and his reliance on writing for income, prompted him to write too much. His stories are skillful rather than profound, entertaining rather than philosophical. He didn't explore the outer limits of human nature. Maupassant's weaknesses are especially evident in his novels—for example, in *Pierre and Jean* and *Bel-Ami*. As Joyce said, "I could not call [*Bel-Ami*] a great work. Like everything Maupassant wrote it is in miniature."[2] Maupassant's best short stories, however, are as good as any short stories ever written, and ensure that his popularity will last for a long time to come. I recommend "Boule de Suif," "Mouche," and "Madame Tellier's Establishment."

Because Maupassant is so popular, many have tried to profit by translating his works; there's no standard English translation of his works. The titles of his short stories, like the titles of Chekhov's short stories, are translated in various ways. To avoid confusion, translators

---

[1] *On Life and Letters*, vol. 1, "M. Guy de Maupassant and the French Story-Tellers"

[2] See Power, *Conversations With James Joyce*, 15

should indicate the original, French title of each story. Readers should
beware of translations that don't give the translator's name.

29. Flaubert

Flaubert is more respected by critics than Maupassant, but less
popular with readers. Flaubert is deeper than Maupassant, but less lively,
less charming. Maupassant enjoyed life, Flaubert hated it; "I have no
greater comfort," Flaubert wrote, "than the hope of leaving this world
soon and not proceeding to another, which might well be worse."
Flaubert endowed his most famous character, Madame Bovary, with his
own distaste for everyday reality; he once said, "*Madame Bovary, c'est
moi.*"[1]

Flaubert's sour, masochistic spirit led him to take extreme pains
with his writing. If Maupassant wrote too hastily, Flaubert wrote too
slowly. Flaubert would polish a single sentence for several days; "from
the day that style was first invented," he said, "I think that no one has
ever taken more pains than I."[2] Flaubert was scrupulous about content
as well as style; for example, he spent years studying ancient Carthage
in order to write *Salammbo*, and he spent years doing research for
Bouvard and Pecuchet. Now, however, both *Salammbo* and *Bouvard
and Pecuchet* are forgotten.

Flaubert's entire life was dedicated to literature. Flaubert was at
home in the world of books, a stranger in the world of practical affairs;
"there is such a chasm now between me and the rest of the world," he
wrote, "that I am sometimes astonished to hear the simplest and most
natural remarks."[3]

Flaubert's novels, with the exception of *Madame Bovary*, have little
interest for modern readers. His best works are his short story, "A Simple
Heart," his *Dictionary of Platitudes*, and his letters (edited by Rumbold).
Flaubert and Madame Bovary, by Steegmuller, is an excellent

---

[1] See *Selected Letters*, letter to George Sand, #98, and Steegmuller,
Flaubert and Madame Bovary: A Double Portrait, III, 4.

[2] Steegmuller, *Flaubert and Madame Bovary: A Double Portrait*, III, 2.

[3] See *Dictionary of Platitudes*, p. 179 (Rodale Press, London, 1954), and
Selected Letters, 9/45.

biography. *Intimate Remembrances*, by Flaubert's niece, Caroline Commanville, is an excellent biographical sketch, a work that shows how good a short biography can be.[1]

30. Other French Writers

Stendhal's novels, *The Red and the Black* and *The Charterhouse of Parma*, once enjoyed a high reputation. Like other early novelists, however, Stendhal is gradually sinking into oblivion. Even in the nineteenth century, some readers—such as Flaubert—doubted the quality of Stendhal's works. But despite his shortcomings, Stendhal is far more profound and interesting than other early novelists, such as Scott and Hugo; Nietzsche admired Stendhal, but took a dim view of Hugo. Of greater interest than Stendhal's novels are his treatise, *On Love*, and his autobiographical works.[2]

Balzac's reputation, which was never as high as Stendhal's, has fallen lower than Stendhal's. Balzac depicted certain types of people: the farmer, the doctor, the aristocrat, etc. Balzac didn't depict the universal features of human nature, as the best writers do. As Gide said, "It is good to read Balzac before the age of twenty-five; afterward it becomes too difficult. How much hodge-podge one has to go through in order to find nourishment."[3] Some of Balzac's short works, such as *Droll Stories*, are still enjoyable to read.

Balzac had a deep interest in the occult, Swedenborg, mesmerism, phrenology, etc., and he discusses these subjects in his novels *Louis Lambert*, *The Magic Skin*, and *Seraphita*. Balzac discusses mesmerism and the power of will in a wonderful short story, "A Passion in the Desert"; this story may be the best introduction to Balzac. If you want to

---

[1] *Intimate Remembrances* can be found in *The Complete Works of Flaubert,* vol. 2, (M. W. Dunne, 1904). Those interested in Flaubert should read his *Selected Letters* (edited by R. Rumbold).

[2] See Steegmuller, *Flaubert and Madame Bovary: A Double Portrait*, III, 3. Anatole France also doubted the quality of Stendhal's works (see Brousson, *Anatole France Himself*, "Oh, Gobineau!").

[3] *Pretexts*, "The Ten French Novels..." (edited by J. O'Brien; Dell Publishing Co., Inc., 1959)

read a short study of Balzac, I suggest the Balzac chapter of Stefan Zweig's *Three Masters: Balzac, Dickens, Dostoyevsky.*[1]

Before the novel became an important genre, France produced several first-rate dramatists. Corneille and Racine wrote stately and dignified dramas that appealed to an aristocratic audience; they specialized in tragedy. The tragedies of Corneille and Racine have little appeal to modern readers who read them in translation. On the other hand, the comedies of Molière are still fresh and alive. One of Molière's comedies, *The Misanthrope*, is more successful than any other literary work at depicting an ideal man. Like many of Molière's comedies, *The Misanthrope* has an underlying seriousness. "Molière is so great," said Goethe, "that one is astonished anew every time one reads him. He is a man by himself—his pieces border on tragedy."[2]

31. Three Spanish Writers

Three writers from Spain's Golden Age deserve special mention: Cervantes, Calderon, and Gracian. Cervantes' *Don Quixote* is one of the most popular and respected works in Western literature. Though its fame has dimmed somewhat in recent times, *Don Quixote* is still enjoyable to read. In addition to *Don Quixote*, Cervantes wrote plays and stories; his story "The Colloquy of the Dogs" has been called a harbinger of psychoanalysis. Calderon, though not as well known as Cervantes, is always mentioned when people speak of outstanding dramatists; Calderon's masterpiece, *Life Is A Dream*, is still an impressive work today. Gracian wrote an allegorical novel, *El Criticon*, but his most popular work is a collection of 300 aphorisms; in English, this collection is usually called *The Art of Worldly Wisdom*. Gracian's pessimistic view of human affairs struck a chord with Schopenhauer, who translated him into German.

---

[1] The best critical essay on Balzac that I've found is an essay that compares Balzac's *Seraphita* to Melville's *Billy Budd*: "Melville's Seraphita: Billy Budd, Sailor," by John S. Haydock, originally published in Melville Society *Extracts* (No. 104, March 1996, pp. 2-13)

[2] *Conversations With Eckermann,* 5/12/25

32. Washington Irving

Washington Irving was one of the first American writers to acquire an international reputation. He was born and raised in New York City, and when he was 26, he published a satirical *History of New York*. He popularized terms like "Gotham" (a nickname for New York City) and "Knickerbocker" (a nickname for New Yorkers).

His best-known work is *The Sketch Book*, published in 1820, which included the short stories "Rip van Winkle" and "The Legend of Sleepy Hollow." Several pieces in *The Sketch Book* deal with Christmas traditions, and Irving shaped how Americans celebrate Christmas. While many of the pieces in *The Sketch Book* are charming, some are sugary; Irving's writing is graceful and elegant, but lacks intellectual or emotional depth.

Irving wrote historical works, including biographies of George Washington and Columbus, and travel books, including a book about the Alhambra. Irving held several diplomatic posts; in the 1840s, he served as U.S. minister to Spain. He travelled throughout Europe, and was acquainted with Walter Scott, Dickens, Poe, and other writers. Irving was known for his conversational skill, and was "one of the world's most in-demand guests."[1]

When he finally returned to the U.S. in 1832, Irving wrote three books on the American West, including *A Tour on the Prairies*. He bought a house on the Hudson River, Sunnyside, where he lived for many years; it's now a museum.

33. James Fenimore Cooper

Like Irving, Cooper had an international reputation in the early 1800s. Cooper is often described as a Romantic novelist, the American Scott. His father was a Congressman and the founder of Cooperstown, New York, where James grew up. Though we associate him with Indian fights, he was also a pioneer of the sea novel (Robert Louis Stevenson referred to him as "Cooper of the wood and wave"). Like Melville, Cooper went to sea while still a teenager, serving on both a merchant ship and a naval ship.

Cooper's most famous novel, *The Last of the Mohicans*, was published in 1826, when Cooper was 37; it was part of a series called the

---

[1] Wikipedia article on Irving

Leatherstocking novels, which feature the frontiersman Natty Bumppo and his Indian friend, Chingachgook. Cooper often wrote about political topics; he became embroiled in quarrels, and sued several critics for libel. He lived in Europe for several years, and wrote three novels about Europe, including *The Bravo*, which was based in Venice, and took a dim view of Venice's aristocratic government.

Cooper's works were admired by Hugo, Balzac, Conrad, and many others. When the composer Schubert was on his death-bed, his chief wish was to read more Cooper novels. Like Scott, Cooper has few readers today, and fewer fans.

34. Hawthorne

Nathaniel Hawthorne was from a prominent New England family; one of his ancestors had been a judge at the Salem Witch Trials. Hawthorne published two volumes of short stories: *Twice-Told Tales* and *Mosses from an Old Manse*. He also wrote two books that re-told Greek myths: *A Wonder-Book for Girls and Boys*, and *Tanglewood Tales*. His most popular work was *The Scarlet Letter*, which he followed with three other novels, *The House of the Seven Gables*, *The Blithedale Romance*, and *The Marble Faun*. All four of his novels are set in Massachusetts, except for *The Marble Faun*, which is set in Italy.

Hawthorne called these four books "romances" rather than "novels" because they don't aim at verisimilitude; his work is sometimes classified as "dark romanticism." Melville said that Hawthorne's stories were "shrouded in blackness, ten times black." Hawthorne's preoccupation with sin and guilt put him at odds with the sunny Transcendentalists; Emerson said, "his writing is not good for anything."

Hawthorne's prose is elegant and graceful; as Poe put it, Hawthorne's style is "purity itself."

Though he was on friendly terms with Longfellow, Melville, Emerson, Thoreau and others, Hawthorne wasn't gregarious; according to Wikipedia, "Hawthorne was almost pathologically shy and stayed silent when at gatherings." When Hawthorne died in 1864, at the age of 59, Emerson spoke of, "the painful solitude of the man, which, I suppose, could no longer be endured, and he died of it." Hawthorne was happily married, and had three children, but his wife said, "he hates to be touched more than anyone I ever knew."

Hawthorne worked as a customs official—first in Boston, later in Salem, and finally in Liverpool, England. The Liverpool post was especially well-paid, and enabled Hawthorne and his wife to travel in Italy (these travels inspired *The Marble Faun*). He obtained the Liverpool post through President Franklin Pierce, whom he had known at Bowdoin College, and for whom he wrote a campaign biography.

35. Longfellow

Henry Wadsworth Longfellow was born in Portland, Maine, in 1807. His maternal grandfather, Peleg Wadsworth, had been a general in the Revolutionary War, and his father was a trustee of Bowdoin College. Longfellow himself attended Bowdoin, where he met Hawthorne. When he was a college senior, he wrote his father thus:

> I most eagerly aspire after future eminence in literature, my whole soul burns most ardently after it, and every earthly thought centers in it... If I can ever rise in the world it must be by the exercise of my talents in the wide field of literature.[1]

After graduating from Bowdoin, Longfellow spent three years in Europe, studying modern languages. In Madrid, he met Washington Irving. When he returned to the U.S., he became a professor of modern languages at Bowdoin, but the work didn't satisfy his lofty ambitions.

He made another trip to Europe, where he studied Scandinavian languages, and then became a professor at Harvard. "As a professor, Longfellow was well-liked, though he disliked being 'constantly a playmate for boys' rather than 'stretching out and grappling with men's minds.'"

Like Irving, Longfellow often wrote in a sweet, sentimental vein. Longfellow was considered one of the "Fireside Poets," along with William Cullen Bryant, John Greenleaf Whittier, James Russell Lowell, and Oliver Wendell Holmes. Longfellow's works were extremely popular in his time; many Americans knew his poems by heart (such as "Paul Revere's Ride"). He was popular in Europe, too; "It was reported that 10,000 copies of *The Courtship of Miles Standish* sold in London in a single day." One of his most popular works is *The Song of Hiawatha*, a narrative poem based on Indian legends. Jung discussed the psychological significance of *Hiawatha* in his *Symbols of Transformation*. Longfellow spent many years on a translation of Dante, and he also

---

[1] Wikipedia article on Longfellow

translated Michelangelo's poetry. He was married twice, and both his wives died prematurely; he suffered from recurrent depression.

Longfellow's poetry was so popular that his 70th birthday, in 1877, was celebrated as a kind of national holiday. "In 1879, a female admirer traveled to Longfellow's house in Cambridge and, unaware to whom she was speaking, asked Longfellow: 'Is this the house where Longfellow was born?' Longfellow told her it was not. The visitor then asked if he had died here. 'Not yet,' he replied."[1] Longfellow died in 1882.

36. Poe

Edgar Allan Poe is a great writer because he writes from his heart, from his experience; he's true to himself. His writing has energy, vivacity, originality. He doesn't imitate, he is imitated. He inspired the detective fiction of Arthur Conan Doyle, and he inspired science-fiction writers like Jules Verne and H. G. Wells. In his day, Poe was a well-known critic, one of the first critics to recognize Hawthorne's talent. James Russell Lowell called Poe "the most discriminating, philosophical, and fearless critic upon imaginative works who has written in America."[2] Poe's poems, such as "The Raven" and "Annabel Lee," have won more popular favor than critical favor (Emerson called Poe "the jingle man," and Harold Bloom spoke of Poe's "dreadful poems"[3]).

Poe is remembered today more for his short stories than for his criticism or his poetry. Poe's stories can be divided into "tales of terror" and "tales of ratiocination." D. H. Lawrence (whom Harold Bloom called "Poe's best critic"[4]) preferred the tales of terror to the tales of ratiocination. Among the tales of terror, Lawrence was particularly interested in "The Fall of The House of Usher" (often called Poe's best story) and "Ligeia." Lawrence dismissed the tales of ratiocination (such as "The Murders in the Rue Morgue" and "The Gold-Bug") as "mechanical."

---

[1] Wikipedia article on Longfellow

[2] Quinn, Arthur Hobson (1941), *Edgar Allan Poe: A Critical Biography*, p. 432; cited in Wikipedia article on Poe

[3] *Bloom's Major Short Story Writers: Edgar Allan Poe*, Introduction, p. 9

[4] *Bloom's Major Short Story Writers: Edgar Allan Poe*, Editor's Note, p. 8

Poe had a gift for ratiocination, for puzzle-solving. When the first installments of Dickens' *Barnaby Rudge* appeared in the U.S., Poe quickly identified the murderer, prompting Dickens to exclaim "That man must be the devil!"[1] Poe prided himself on being able to unravel any system of coded writing; he challenged "the universe" to send a code to his magazine that he couldn't break. "The Gold-Bug" deals with codes, and it inspired William Friedman, who helped to break the Japanese code in World War II.

Poe wasn't content with small puzzles, he tried to solve the biggest puzzle of all: the universe itself. Even as a youngster, he had observed the stars from his porch through a telescope, and as he grew older, he kept up with developments in astronomy. He also studied the philosophical writings of Coleridge and others. In his last years, he wrote *Eureka*, which mixes philosophy and cosmology. Poe chose the title *Eureka* because he thought he had solved the puzzle of the universe: "What I have propounded," he wrote, "will (in good time) revolutionize the world of Physical and Metaphysical Science. I say this calmly—but I say it."[2] Poe was indeed capable of deep philosophical insights, and some of his astronomical theories were ahead of their time (for example, he anticipated the Big Bang theory).

D. H. Lawrence devotes a chapter to Poe in his *Studies in Classic American Literature*. Lawrence argues that Poe depicts the collapse of personality, the loss of self, that results from excessive love or excessive hate. Poe's characters lose themselves in passion, they don't find themselves, they don't find their center. Poe fails to achieve the detachment that comes with maturity, he fails to offer a vision of spiritual growth. In his poem "Annabel Lee," Poe describes a love that is excessive, immature, and unrealistic:

It was many and many a year ago,
In a kingdom by the sea,
That a maiden there lived whom you may know
By the name of Annabel Lee;
And this maiden she lived with no other thought
Than to love and be loved by me.

I was a child and *she* was a child,

---

[1] Marie Bonaparte, *The Life and Works of Edgar Allan Poe*, ch. 17, p. 100

[2] Marie Bonaparte, *The Life and Works of Edgar Allan Poe*, ch. 20, p. 155

In this kingdom by the sea;
But we loved with a love that was more than love—
I and my Annabel Lee....

Poe depicts a love that is immoderate and unhealthy, a love that ends in early death. Poe's characters "kill the thing they love."

Proust depicts excessive attachment, love carried to the point of obsession, but unlike Poe, Proust also points the way to wisdom, maturity, detachment. Proust depicts spiritual growth, Poe doesn't. Proust suffers and overcomes suffering, Poe just suffers.

Poe could depict terror because he experienced it, and he could depict mental instability because he experienced it. He dreaded being alone, especially at night, and if he was writing at night, his aunt would sit up with him to keep him company.[1] In his last years, lucid periods alternated with spells of madness. The traumas that Poe experienced in early childhood—his father left the family when Poe was two, and his mother died when he was three—left a lasting mark on him.

Marie Bonaparte, a descendant of Napoleon Bonaparte and a disciple of Freud, wrote a lengthy study of Poe's life and work. Her book can serve as an introduction to Freud's ideas. I suggest that one start by reading Poe's story "The Murders in the Rue Morgue," and then read Bonaparte's analysis of that story. Another way to approach Poe is by reading "The Black Cat," then reading James Gargano's essay, "'The Black Cat': Perverseness Reconsidered."[2]

Perhaps Poe's most famous student was Baudelaire, who translated Poe into French, and helped make Poe popular in Europe. Poe's morbid streak struck a responsive chord in Baudelaire; Baudelaire said that he was fond of Poe "because he resembled me."[3] Readers are often fond of writers to whom they feel akin.

Poe's mental instability and alcoholism brought him to an early grave; he died in 1849, at the age of 40. Shortly before his death, he spent an afternoon with friends in Richmond. A meteor passed over his head, prompting a joke about omens; after he died, his friends felt that the

---

[1] Marie Bonaparte, *The Life and Works of Edgar Allan Poe*, ch. 20, p. 154

[2] *Texas Studies in Literature and Language*, Vol. 2, No. 2 (Summer 1960), pp. 172-178

[3] See Louis Untermeyer, *Makers of the Modern World*, "Baudelaire"

meteor had indeed been an omen.[1] Perhaps the meteor was an example of a linkage between the human world and the inanimate world, the sort of linkage that Poe had depicted in works like "The Fall of The House of Usher."

37. Whitman

Walt Whitman is one of the most gifted American writers, with a unique, original style and a profound, mystical worldview. His magnum opus, *Leaves of Grass*, began as a short work, and gradually grew into a long work. I recommend the original, 1855 edition of *Leaves of Grass*, edited by Malcolm Cowley and published by Penguin Classics. But even this short book is often obscure and somewhat difficult to read. At his best, Whitman is superb, but his ecstatic moments don't add up to a coherent philosophy, and his flights of genius don't add up to an artistic whole.

Whitman is considered the quintessential American writer, the writer in whom American literature first found its own voice. But like Nietzsche, Schopenhauer and others, Whitman wasn't appreciated as much in his native land as he was abroad. Many of Whitman's prominent 19th-century fans were English—Rossetti, Swinburne, etc. Perhaps the distinctively American character of Whitman's work made it more appealing, more fresh, more different in England than in America. But there were a few of Whitman's American contemporaries who appreciated his work, including Emerson and Thoreau. Emerson was the first to recognize Whitman's genius, calling *Leaves of Grass* "the most extraordinary piece of wit and wisdom that America has yet contributed....[I] have felt much like striking my tasks, and visiting New York to pay you my respects."

Whitman didn't attend any college. At age 10, Whitman became a printer's apprentice, and at 12, he began working in printing shops. Whitman's parents were neither educated nor wealthy. In short, Whitman was what some people think (wrongly, in my view) that Shakespeare was: a great writer with little formal education, a great writer nourished by his own genius and by his experience of the world, a great writer whose creativity was enhanced by his lack of formal education.

---

[1] Marie Bonaparte, *The Life and Works of Edgar Allan Poe*, ch. 22, p. 200

Perhaps it's this lack of education that gives Whitman his naive tone. His relationship with the reader is like that of no other writer. In his poem, "Crossing Brooklyn Ferry," Whitman addresses readers in future generations as if author and reader were in the same room:

Just as you feel when you look on the river and sky, so I felt;
Just as any of you is one of a living crowd, I was one of a crowd;
Just as you are refreshed by the gladness of the river and the bright flow, I was refreshed;
Just as you stand and lean on the rail, yet hurry with the swift current, I stood, yet was hurried;
Just as you look on the numberless masts of ships, and the thick-stemmed pipes of steamboats, I looked.

Whitman is the poet of New York City, as Melville is the poet of the open sea, and Twain is the poet of the half-civilized frontier, and the Mississippi River.

38. Melville

Herman Melville came from an old, established family. His maternal grandfather was one of the heroes of the Battle of Saratoga, while his paternal grandfather was involved in the Boston Tea Party. When Melville was a boy, his family's fortunes declined, prompting Melville to go to sea. After a stint in the merchant marine, and a stint as a teacher, Melville joined a whaling voyage in 1841, when he was 21. When the ship docked at an island in the Pacific, Melville deserted, and lived briefly among the natives. Eventually he returned to the U.S. on a warship.

Living with the natives provided him with material for his first book, *Typee*, which was popular, and made Melville a well-known writer. His second book, *Omoo*, continued the story of his Pacific adventures, but wasn't as popular as *Typee* (both books were classed as novels, but drew heavily on Melville's own experiences).

Melville had acquired a reputation as "the man who had lived among cannibals," but he wasn't satisfied, he wanted to be regarded as a serious writer, he had literary ambitions. In his third book, *Mardi*, the characters go to sea, and then begin to philosophize. Critics grumbled, Melville's popularity waned.

In his next two books, *Redburn* and *White-Jacket*, Melville put his lofty ambitions on hold, and tried to revive his popularity. He referred to these books as "two *jobs* which I have done for money—being forced to it as other men are to sawing wood." *Redburn* drew on his experiences in the merchant marine (Melville said that it was "trash," and that he "wrote it to buy some tobacco with"). *White-Jacket* drew on his experiences on a warship.

His sixth book, *Moby-Dick*, written when Melville was 31, drew on his experiences on a whale ship. With *Moby-Dick*, Melville ignored contemporary taste, and staked his claim to immortality. *Moby-Dick* is Melville's masterpiece—a blend of character, drama, symbolism, and philosophy. Perhaps he was inspired by his friendship with Hawthorne, perhaps by his close reading of Shakespeare. The influence of Shakespeare is evident in Melville's preoccupation with evil, fate, and prophecy.

Even in *Moby-Dick*, though, Melville's philosophizing is somewhat heavy-handed, and his prose is somewhat wordy and obscure. Leonard Woolf said that Melville wrote "the most execrable English," and Bernard DeVoto said, "Though Melville could write great prose, his book frequently escapes into a passionately swooning rhetoric."[1]

The public responded coolly to *Moby-Dick*, as it had to *Mardi*. Melville's next novel, *Pierre*, had an even chillier reception, and at the age of 32, Melville's literary career was on the rocks. Though he wrote two more novels (*Israel Potter* and *The Confidence Man*), most of his later work is poetry and short stories.

Perhaps his best-known story is "Bartleby, the Scrivener." Melville was hurt by criticism of his writings, and in "Bartleby," he described a clerk who refuses to write.

When Melville died at 72, he left a manuscript in his desk—the novella *Billy Budd*, one of his most highly-regarded works. At the time of his death, he was forgotten in the U.S., but he had some admirers in England. Melville's reputation in the U.S. grew in the 1920s, when the U.S. was becoming aware of itself as a distinct civilization, American literature was beginning to be taught at American colleges, and scholars began looking for writers who represented American civilization.

I strongly recommend Edward Edinger's Jungian study of *Moby Dick*; it's a great literary analysis and also a great introduction to psychology. If you want to read a biography of Melville, consider *Melville: His World and Work*, by Andrew Delbanco.

---

[1] See DeVoto's essay in *Twentieth Century Interpretations of* Adventures of Huckleberry Finn.

In his last years, Melville kept a Schiller quotation on his desk: "Stay true to the dreams of thy youth." The young Melville had dreamed of literary immortality, and had striven to achieve it, and now he has the immortality that he strove for. Many readers today enjoy Melville's wit, wisdom, and vitality.

39. Mark Twain

Mark Twain is the most popular of American writers; everyone enjoys novels like *Tom Sawyer*, *Huck Finn*, and *Pudd'nhead Wilson*. In addition to writing novels, Twain wrote many delightful short stories, and many travel books. Twain appeals to adults who want to re-capture the spirit of boyhood, and he appeals to civilized readers who want to re-capture the spirit of an uncivilized world. Twain is so light-hearted and humorous that we're apt to take him lightly, and forget that he had vast ambitions and vast talents.

Twain was born in 1835, and grew up in Hannibal, Missouri, on the Mississippi River (Hannibal was the setting for Twain's best-known works, *Tom Sawyer* and *Huck Finn*). His father was a small-town lawyer and judge. His older brother published a newspaper, the *Hannibal Journal*, and Twain began writing for this newspaper at the age of 12. Like Whitman, Twain learned the craft of typesetting and printing. From age 18 to 22, Twain worked as a printer in New York, Philadelphia, St. Louis, and Cincinnati.

When he returned to Missouri, he met a steamboat pilot, and decided to become a pilot himself. "Twain studied 2,000 miles of the Mississippi for more than two years before he received his steamboat pilot license in 1859."[1] His river experiences were the basis for his book *Life on the Mississippi*.

Twain persuaded his younger brother to learn piloting, too. His brother was killed in a steamboat explosion. A month before his death, Twain had a prophetic dream. He developed a strong interest in the occult, was inclined to believe in life-after-death, and was an early member of the Society for Psychical Research (among the members of this society were William James, Arthur Conan Doyle, Yeats, and Jung).

When the Civil War broke out, river traffic declined, and so did the demand for pilots. So at age 26, Twain headed west with his older brother. He tried his hand as a miner, and wrote stories and travel pieces

---

[1] Wikipedia article on Twain

for various newspapers. His Western adventures inspired the book *Roughing It*. His first big success was the short story "The Jumping Frog of Calaveras County" (1865).

In 1866, a California newspaper sent him to Hawaii. Soon he began lecturing about his travels. In 1867, a newspaper funded a trip to Europe and the Middle East, a trip that was the basis for *Innocents Abroad* (a second trip to Europe was the basis for *A Tramp Abroad*). In 1870, he married, and spent two years working on a newspaper in Buffalo, New York, before moving to Hartford; he and his family lived in Hartford for 17 years (his Hartford house is now a museum).

Twain was more than a humorist. He was interested in history, read Carlyle's *French Revolution* countless times, and wrote a serious book about Joan of Arc, which he regarded as his best book (it's called *Personal Recollections of Joan of Arc*). He had a keen interest in the Shakespeare controversy, and like Whitman, he was convinced that the man from Stratford wasn't the real author. He was interested in science, and often visited the lab of Nikola Tesla. In his novel *A Connecticut Yankee in King Arthur's Court*, he depicts a time-traveler introducing modern science to a medieval society. He patented several inventions; "most commercially successful was a self-pasting scrapbook; a dried adhesive on the pages only needed to be moistened before use."

Twain's attempt to market an automatic typesetter was an abysmal failure, and left him deeply indebted. He also lost money in a publishing venture (as did Walter Scott). To pay his debts, he gave lectures around the world (Freud heard him speak in Vienna). This lecture tour was the basis for another travel book, *Following the Equator*.

His political views became more radical as he grew older. He was critical of missionaries and imperialists, and defended the rights of indigenous peoples. He criticized American policy in the Philippines, and supported violent revolution in Russia. He also supported women's rights, and labor unions.

In 1909, Twain said, "I came in with Halley's Comet in 1835. It is coming again next year, and I expect to go out with it. It will be the greatest disappointment of my life if I don't go out with Halley's Comet. The Almighty has said, no doubt: 'Now here are these two unaccountable freaks; they came in together, they must go out together.'" He died in 1910, one day after the comet passed. Two of his novels (*The Prince and the Pauper* and *Pudd'nhead Wilson*) deal with the "mystic connection" between people born on the same day. A volume of autobiography was published in 2010, 100 years after Twain's death (as he had stipulated), and became a bestseller.

His real name was Samuel Clemens; the pen name "Mark Twain" was a common riverboat expression, meaning that the water was a safe depth—at the second mark on the sounding line (the second mark was two fathoms, or 12 feet). Twain's grave in Elmira, New York has a 12-foot monument.

40. Henry Adams

Henry Adams was born into an illustrious family of Presidents and ambassadors, and became one of the foremost men-of-letters that America has produced. He moved in political circles, intellectual circles, social circles; he was familiar with the levers of power, had much experience as a journalist, and was widely traveled. He achieved distinction in several different literary genres. His history of the U.S. in the early 1800s is highly regarded, he wrote two novels (*Democracy* and *Esther*), and he wrote a study of medieval culture called *Mont Saint Michel and Chartres*. But the work for which he's chiefly remembered is his autobiography, *The Education of Henry Adams*. The great sorrow of his life was the suicide of his wife, Clover, at age 42 (she had become depressed after her father's death). Clover charmed many people. In a letter to Adams, John Hay described her as,

> That bright, intrepid spirit, that keen, fine intellect, that lofty scorn for all that was mean, that social charm which made your house such a one as Washington never knew before and made hundreds of people love her as much as they admired her.

Apparently Henry James was also charmed by Clover, and used her as the model for the heroines of *Daisy Miller* and *Portrait of a Lady*.

41. Henry James

Like Henry Adams, Henry James was born into a prominent, wealthy, American family. As Adams' brother, Brooks, was a distinguished intellectual, so James' brother, William, was a famous philosopher/psychologist. Henry James is more popular with critics than with readers. Critics praise three novels from his later years: *The Golden Bowl*, *The Ambassadors*, and *The Wings of the Dove*. Readers, on the other hand, are more fond of early works like *Washington Square* and *Daisy Miller*. The style of these early works is more clear and readable than the style of his late works. Perhaps James' best novel is a product of his middle years, *Portrait of a Lady*, which is a favorite of both critics and readers. James spent most of his adult life in England, and a recurrent theme of his fiction is Americans encountering Europe.

During James' lifetime, his works had a mixed reception. In 1890, his novel *The Tragic Muse* fell flat. He vowed to quit writing novels, and he began writing plays. But in 1895, when his play *Guy Domville* fell flat, he returned to novel-writing. James was also a prolific non-fiction writer, trying his hand at autobiography (he wrote three volumes of autobiography), travel narrative (his *Italian Hours* is still popular), and literary criticism (his *Art of Fiction* is frequently quoted, and he wrote a book-length study of Hawthorne).

42. Jack London

Jack London was an American adventurer who was born in California in 1876. He spent much of his life on the fringe of civilization, and many of his books deal with Alaska and Hawaii. He concentrates on the contest between man and animal, between man and the elements—the struggle for survival. His fast-moving, hard-charging fiction struck a chord with contemporary readers, and he became rich by writing for magazines. As he grew older, he began to write for money, he stole material from other writers, and the quality of his work declined. He died at age 40. London's critics insist that his fiction is just a series of episodes, not an organic whole. Among his best-known works are *The Call of the Wild*, *The Sea-Wolf*, *White Fang*, and the autobiographical *Martin Eden*. He was interested in the occult, and his novel *Star Rover* (sometimes called *The Jacket*) deals with reincarnation and out-of-body experiences.

43. Hemingway

Perhaps the last great generation of American writers was the generation of Hemingway, Faulkner, and Wolfe (some people add to this trio the names of F. Scott Fitzgerald and John Dos Passos). Hemingway was a celebrity while still in his 20s. His spare style appealed to his contemporaries, and his adventurous life captured the imagination of the public. But the novelty of his style wore off, the despairing tone of his work left some readers cold, and some of his later works, like *Across the*

River and Into the Trees, were panned by the critics. It became fashionable to say "I don't like Hemingway."

But Hemingway's reputation will doubtless make a comeback, when people focus on his best works rather than his worst, on his strengths rather than his weaknesses. He was a great literary artist, a great reporter of places, experiences, feelings. T. S. Eliot said he had "considerable respect" for Hemingway's work because "he seems to me to tell the truth about his own feelings at the moment when they exist."[1] And Joyce had high praise for Hemingway's story "A Clean, Well-Lighted Place," calling it one of the best short stories ever written.

Hemingway's *Old Man and the Sea* is a great novella, perhaps better than *Moby Dick*. Hemingway's prose is simpler, more sublime than Melville's, and his story is more touching than Melville's. Hemingway's old man, Santiago, loves and respects the giant fish. Thus, *Old Man* is the opposite of *Moby Dick*, in which Ahab is consumed with hatred for the white whale. Santiago has a humble love for the sea creatures that he calls his "brothers," while Ahab pits his titanic hatred against the universe. Hemingway's novella is a perfect blend of the realistic and the mythic. Melville, however, may be a more profound writer—better at psychological subtlety, better at the occult dimension. Hemingway's hero is a hero for our time: he doesn't have high birth or great natural gifts; he's an average man, a working man, who achieves greatness through persistence, through his indomitable spirit, through his acceptance of suffering. Both Hemingway and Melville built their story from an actual event, both stretched the facts to the breaking point, but both created stories that "ring true." Hemingway admired Conrad, and his *Old Man and the Sea* may have been inspired by Conrad's story, "Youth".

As a stylist, Hemingway aims at simplicity and truth. His style is typical of modern style insofar as it lacks structure, grammatical structure, grammatical clarity. As long as his words are clear and truthful, he doesn't care how he throws them in, or how they function grammatically. One might trace this to the decline of Latin study, or to the influence of journalism (Hemingway himself was a journalist). As an example, let's look at Hemingway's description of Mr. and Mrs. Macomber riding with their guide, Wilson: "She was sitting far back in the seat and Macomber was sitting forward talking to Wilson who turned sideways talking over the back of the front seat." Notice how the words

---

[1] Quoted in *Hemingway and Faulkner in Their Time*, by Earl H. Rovit and Arthur Waldhorn

are jumbled up without regard to grammatical structure, yet the overall effect is clear and vivid. It would be difficult to diagram that sentence, and say what grammatical function each word plays, but it's not a difficult sentence to read. Hemingway was so fond of simplicity that he criticized Melville and Thoreau for being literary.

Hemingway didn't write from his imagination, as Kafka did. He wrote about his experiences; he wrote about the summers he spent in Michigan as a boy, about his experiences on the Italian front in World War I, about his years in Paris (where he knew Gertrude Stein, Ezra Pound, and other writers), about Spain and the Spanish Civil War, about safaris in Africa, about the Florida Keys and Cuba. Hemingway was preoccupied with death and violence, and often wrote about war, bullfighting, and hunting. In 1961, at the age of 62, when his body was injured and his memory declining, Hemingway shot himself.

If you want to read about Hemingway, consider the works of Princeton professor Carlos Baker, who wrote a biography of Hemingway, critical studies, and Selected Letters. The most detailed Hemingway biography is the five-volume work by Michael Reynolds. The leading American critics all wrote about Hemingway; for example, Alfred Kazin wrote about Hemingway in *On Native Grounds*, Edmund Wilson in *The Wound and the Bow*, and Leslie Fiedler in *Love and Death in the American Novel*.

If you want a quick introduction to Hemingway, read his short story "The Killers" and the critical essay on "The Killers" by Robert Penn Warren and Cleanth Brooks. Both the story and the critical essay can be found in *Understanding Fiction*, an excellent anthology of stories and critical essays put together by Warren and Brooks. *Understanding Poetry* is another noteworthy anthology by Warren and Brooks. Warren was a fine poet and novelist in his own right, best known for his novel *All the King's Men*, which deals with the Louisiana politician, Huey Long. Brooks was a prominent critic, who wrote several well-regarded studies of poetry.

44. Thomas Wolfe

Wolfe's early death seemed to hang over his life like a dark fate, and he lived with a wild urgency; he died in 1938, at age 37. While Hemingway's style is spare, prosaic, Wolfe's is romantic, poetic. While Hemingway aims to tell the truth, Wolfe has a penchant for exaggeration. The city that Wolfe wrote about most was a city that Hemingway disliked: New York. Despite his untimely death, Wolfe's work has a more affirmative tone than that of Hemingway or Faulkner. Hemingway sometimes despaired, but Wolfe didn't have time for despair; Wolfe loved the world like one who has to leave it soon. He even loved death, as mystics sometimes do. Wolfe said Yes to the whole world.

What strikes one about Wolfe is his subjectivity, his preoccupation with the motions of his own soul. But he also has a sure sense of the external world, and created many memorable characters and scenes. Faulkner called Wolfe the best American novelist of his time. Nobody surpasses Wolfe at depicting the wonder of being alive. Critics, however, are often cool toward Wolfe, perhaps because his work has more passion than structure.

If you want to try Wolfe, I recommend his first and most famous novel, *Look Homeward, Angel*, which deals with his early years in Asheville, North Carolina, and his college years at the University of North Carolina. Wolfe also wrote some excellent short works, such as "The Lost Boy" and "The Web of Earth." If you want to read a biography of Wolfe, consider *Look Homeward*, by the famous Lincoln biographer David Herbert Donald. Also consider Wolfe's own autobiographical writings, such as "God's Lonely Man" and *The Story of a Novel*. If you want to read a good critical essay about Wolfe, I suggest "Thomas Wolfe and Death."[1]

Wolfe anticipated his early death: "Something has spoken to me in the night, burning the tapers of the waning year; something has spoken in the night, and told me I must die.... A wind is rising, and the rivers flow."

45. Faulkner

Faulkner is more obscure, more difficult to read, than Hemingway or Wolfe. He didn't become popular as quickly as Hemingway and Wolfe did, but his style appeals to modern taste, and his reputation is at least as high today as that of Hemingway or Wolfe. Faulkner's reputation extended to Europe; among his fans was Sartre, the French philosopher. Sartre said that the dominant note of Faulkner's work was hopelessness—a preoccupation with the past, an inability to look to the

---

[1] *Thomas Wolfe: Three Decades of Criticism*, edited by Leslie A. Field, "Thomas Wolfe and Death," by J. Russell Reaver and Robert I. Strozier

future. Sartre described Faulkner as "a lost man," just as Gertrude Stein told Hemingway that his was "a lost generation."

While Wolfe focused on his own soul, Faulkner turned to the outside world, and tried to depict the people he knew in his native Mississippi. His early works and late works aren't highly-regarded. His best works are those written during his middle period, such as *The Sound and the Fury*, *Light in August*, and *Absalom, Absalom!*

Faulkner was in ecstasy while writing *The Sound and the Fury*, and the reader can get much pleasure from it, too, if he can overcome the initial hurdles. I recommend the Norton Critical Edition, and also Volpe's book, *A Reader's Guide to William Faulkner*. With the help of books like these, the difficulties of *The Sound and the Fury* will melt away. Faulkner describes everyday life so vividly that his characters are more real than real people.

46. Flannery O'Connor

Like Faulkner, Flannery O'Connor was from the South, and wrote about the South. O'Connor was an Irish Catholic with deep religious convictions. But she has a lively sense of humor, and a readable style; she's both a genuine artist and a sincere believer. O'Connor uses violence and imminent death to rouse her characters—and perhaps her readers, too—from their spiritual slumbers. O'Connor herself lived with the threat of death: she suffered from lupus, and died at 39.

Though she wrote two novels, O'Connor is best known for her short stories, and her *Complete Stories* won a National Book Award in 1972. Her best-known story is "A Good Man Is Hard To Find." But perhaps the best way to approach O'Connor is to read "The Artificial Nigger," then the fine critical essay on it by Joyce Carol Oates.[1]

47. Lovecraft & Co.

H. P. Lovecraft was an only child, and a sickly child; his mother often kept him home, and he rarely went to school. He never finished high school, and had no career besides story-writing. "The adult

---

[1] "The Action of Mercy," Joyce Carol Oates, *The Kenyon Review*, Winter, 1998, pp. 157-160

Lovecraft was gaunt with dark eyes set in a very pale face (he rarely went abroad before nightfall)."[1] He read widely; one of his favorites was Poe, and he also read Nietzsche. He spent most of his life in Providence, Rhode Island. His life was largely solitary, but he had a network of correspondents, many of whom were fellow writers of horror and fantasy. It is said that he wrote more letters than anyone in history, with the exception of Voltaire.

A Lovecraft scholar named S. T. Joshi created a book from Lovecraft's letters, *Lord of a Visible World: An Autobiography in Letters*. Joshi also edited a book called *Caverns Measureless to Man: 18 Memoirs of Lovecraft*. And Joshi wrote a two-volume Lovecraft biography, *I Am Providence: The Life and Times of H. P. Lovecraft* (originally published in one volume under the title *H. P. Lovecraft: A Life*; also published in abridged form as *A Dreamer & A Visionary: H. P. Lovecraft in His Time*).

Older writers like Cervantes, Fielding, and Dickens wrote for a general audience, but modern fiction has become split between high-brow and low-brow. High-brow writers like Proust and Joyce make many demands on the reader, while low-brow writers like Lovecraft and Robert E. Howard can be enjoyed even by youngsters. Lovecraft never wrote a full-length novel; he wrote stories and novellas for pulp magazines like *Weird Tales* and *Amazing Stories*.

Lovecraft's stories were inspired by earlier horror writers, such as Poe, and also by his own inner demons. He was

> overwhelmed by feelings of anxiety by 8 years old.... Beginning in his early life, Lovecraft is believed to have suffered from night terrors... he believed himself to be assaulted at night by horrific "night gaunts." Much of his later work is thought to have been directly inspired by these terrors.[2]

Lovecraft had a deep connection to Providence, a strong sense of place, history, and architecture, he writes superb prose, and his stories hold your attention. Like Ruskin, Lovecraft had a fondness for the old and an aversion for the new. Sometimes he called himself an "antiquarian." He published 13 issues of his own magazine, which he called *The Conservative*. Lovecraft agreed with Spengler that the modern West was decadent; Wikipedia speaks of his "anti-modern worldview."

Lovecraft died of cancer in 1937 at the age of 46. "In accordance with his lifelong scientific curiosity, he kept a diary of his illness until

---

1 Wikipedia article on Lovecraft
2 Wikipedia article on Lovecraft

close to the moment of his death." His scientific bent is apparent in his stories, which often scoff at "popular superstition," and try to provide a material explanation for ghosts and other occult phenomena.

Lovecraft corresponded with two prominent horror/fantasy writers, Robert E. Howard and Clark Ashton Smith. They never met, perhaps because Lovecraft lived in Providence, Howard in Texas, and Smith in California. Howard is best known for stories about Conan the Barbarian.

L. Sprague de Camp wrote biographies of Lovecraft and Howard, and he continued Howard's work in books like *Conan the Adventurer*. De Camp wrote several historical novels, such as *The Dragon of the Ishtar Gate*. Many of his books were written in collaboration with his wife, Catherine Crook de Camp.

Lovecraft wrote an essay called "Supernatural Horror in Literature," which surveyed the development of the genre. Edmund Wilson said that Lovecraft's essay was "a really able piece of work... He had read comprehensively in this field—he was strong on the Gothic novelists— and writes about it with much intelligence." Lovecraft begins his essay thus:

> The oldest and strongest emotion of mankind is fear, and the oldest and strongest kind of fear is fear of the unknown. These facts few psychologists will dispute, and their admitted truth must establish for all time the genuineness and dignity of the weirdly horrible tale as a literary form.

Lovecraft discusses four "modern masters" of the ghost story: Lord Dunsany, M. R. James, Arthur Machen, and Algernon Blackwood.

48. Dunsany, Tolkien, etc.

Dunsany was perhaps the only writer who influenced Lovecraft as much as Poe did. Lovecraft wrote modestly, "There are my 'Poe' pieces and my 'Dunsany' pieces—but alas—where are my Lovecraft pieces?" Dunsany was born into the Irish aristocracy, and spent much of his life at Ireland's oldest castle, Dunsany Castle, which dates back to 1080. He was part of the Irish Literary Revival, he donated to the Abbey Theater, and he was friends with Yeats, Lady Gregory, Padraic Colum, George William Russell ("A.E."), Oliver St. John Gogarty ("Buck Mulligan"), etc. His youth was divided between England and Ireland; some of his relatives were English. In his later years, Dunsany spent most of his time in England, where he was friends with Kipling. Dunsany was an avid hunter and athlete, and he fought in both the Boer War and World War I.

One of Dunsany's novels is called *The King of Elfland's Daughter*; according to Wikipedia, it's "considered by many to be Dunsany's finest novel and a classic in the realm of fantasy writing." Jorge Luis Borges, who's sometimes classed as a fantasy writer, compared Dunsany to Kafka. Lovecraft heard Dunsany lecture, and was much impressed. Robert E. Howard was also a Dunsany fan. Dunsany developed the "club tale"—tall tales told at a gentleman's club, collected in *The Travel Tales of Mr. Joseph Jorkens* and other volumes. The science-fiction writer Arthur C. Clarke wrote Dunsany-inspired "club tales," which were collected in *Tales from the White Hart*. L. Sprague de Camp collaborated with Fletcher Pratt on a book of club tales called *Tales from Gavagan's Bar*.

Perhaps the most popular of all fantasy writers is J. R. R. Tolkien, best known for his trilogy *The Lord of the Rings*. Tolkien was an Oxford professor of Anglo-Saxon literature; his students said that hearing him recite *Beowulf* was an "unforgettable experience." He was a close friend of C. S. Lewis, who was also an Oxford professor and fantasy writer. Both Tolkien and Lewis were devout Christians; Tolkien was Catholic, Lewis Anglican. Much of Tolkien's *Lord of the Rings* was written during World War II; Tolkien said it was "quickened to full life by war," and he called his book "a history of the Great War of the Ring." In Tolkien's trilogy, The Shire battles Mordor, as England battled Nazi Germany.

An older fantasy writer, who influenced both Tolkien and C. S. Lewis, is George MacDonald. MacDonald was friends with Mark Twain, John Ruskin, Walt Whitman, and other eminent writers; he was also a mentor to Lewis Carroll. MacDonald was well-known in his day for fantasies and fairy tales that have spiritual import. For a time, MacDonald worked as a minister, and some of his books deal with Christian themes. MacDonald said, "I write, not for children, but for the child-like, whether they be of five, or fifty, or seventy-five." Two of his best-known stories are "The Golden Key" and "The Wise Woman"; two of his best-known novels are *Lilith* and *The Princess and the Goblin*.

Lewis Carroll's work is popular with both children and adults. Carroll's famous stories, *Alice's Adventures in Wonderland* and *Through the Looking Glass*, combine wild fantasy with clever wit. I recommend *The Annotated Alice*, with notes by Martin Gardner, or the Norton Critical Edition of *Alice*.

49. Clarke and Heinlein

Arthur C. Clarke was influenced by Dunsany's fantasy fiction and by H. G. Wells' science fiction. Clarke was born and raised in England, but spent much of his adult life in Sri Lanka, to which his love of scuba diving drew him. Among Clarke's most admired novels are *Childhood's End* and *Rendezvous with Rama*. In his fiction, Clarke speculates about the evolution of a higher race, as a result of contact with an advanced, alien civilization. Clarke also wrote some non-fiction books, such as *The Promise of Space*. Clarke was interested in Buddhism, and in the paranormal.

Another well-known writer of science fiction is Robert Heinlein. Heinlein grew up in Missouri, and spent most of his adult life in California. Among his best-known works are *Stranger in a Strange Land, The Moon Is a Harsh Mistress*, and *Time Enough For Love*. Heinlein was a nudist and an advocate of free love; his work was popular with the hippies of the 1960s. He was a pioneer of "social science fiction," which mixed social theories with hard science. Like Clarke, Heinlein had a knack for anticipating the impact of technology on society; he "foresaw Interstate Highways (*The Roads Must Roll*), concern over nuclear power generation (*Blowups Happen*), international nuclear stalemate (*Solution Unsatisfactory*—i.e., the Cold War) as well as numerous other lesser examples." Heinlein wrote many books for young readers. Some American astronauts read Heinlein as youngsters, and quoted him when they were on the moon.

50. Arthur Machen and Algernon Blackwood

One of Lovecraft's favorite writers was Arthur Machen; Lovecraft called Machen, "master of an exquisitely lyrical and expressive prose style." Lovecraft's story "The Dunwich Horror" was influenced by Machen's novella *The Great God Pan*. Stephen King called Machen's novella "Maybe the best [horror story] in the English language." Among Machen's other admirers were Wilde, Yeats, Arthur Conan Doyle, Aleister Crowley, and Borges. Through Borges, Machen influenced Magical Realism.

Machen's autobiographical novel *The Hill of Dreams* is often called his masterpiece. In this novel, a young dreamer imagines Wales in Roman times; later he goes to London to seek his fortune as a writer.

Machen was from Wales (Monmouthshire), had a deep connection to the area, and often set his fiction there.

Machen was receptive to the occult, and contemptuous of rationalism and materialism. He was a member of The Hermetic Order of the Golden Dawn, which grew out of the Freemasons and the Rosicrucians. Other members of this Order included Yeats, Bram Stoker, and Algernon Blackwood.

Lovecraft was a fan of Blackwood's fiction, and spoke of, "Algernon Blackwood, amidst whose voluminous and uneven work may be found some of the finest spectral literature of this or any age." Blackwood was an avid outdoorsman, fond of skiing, mountain-climbing, etc. One of his most famous stories, "The Willows," is about a canoe trip on the Danube. He was especially fond of the Swiss Alps, and after his death, his ashes were scattered there.

Like Poe and Schopenhauer, Blackwood believed that the occult revealed a new aspect of reality, leading to a new worldview and a revolution in human culture. Blackwood wrote,

> My fundamental interest, I suppose, is signs and proofs of other powers that lie hidden in us all; the extension, in other words, of human faculty....
> I believe it possible for our consciousness to change and grow, and that with this change we may become aware of a new universe.

According to Wikipedia, Blackwood's novels *Julius LeVallon* and *The Bright Messenger* "deal with reincarnation and the possibility of a new, mystical evolution in human consciousness." Henry Miller said that *The Bright Messenger* is "the most extraordinary novel on psychoanalysis, one that dwarfs the subject." Blackwood is a deep thinker who can throw light on human nature and on the occult.

51. J. D. Salinger and John Williams

An imaginative writer who lives in the reader's own time and place has a charm that writers from a different time and place, however great they may be, can't have. A writer who lives in the reader's own time and place can relate to the reader's own experience, can depict a world that is familiar to the reader, and can speak the reader's own language. One of the best imaginative writers in the modern U.S. is J. D. Salinger. Salinger's early work (*Nine Stories* and *The Catcher in the Rye*) is consistently high in quality, but his later work (such as *Hapworth 16, 1924*) is disappointing.

Some of Salinger's early work was written while he was a soldier in World War II. The same is true of Salinger's contemporary, John Williams, author of the acclaimed novel *Stoner*. While Salinger used colloquial language, Williams used simple, straightforward language. While Salinger was a product of Eastern cities and Eastern prep schools, Williams grew up in Texas, and *Stoner* has the air of The Plains. While Salinger was a recluse, Williams was an English professor at the University of Denver, and the protagonist of *Stoner* is an academic. While Salinger's work is rich in humor, Williams' work lacks humor, and has little action. Nonetheless, Williams' work is entertaining, readable, and moving. While reading *Stoner*, one forgets that it's a novel; it seems more true than real life, one connects with his characters as if they were real people. One critic, Morris Dickstein, said that *Stoner* was, "Something rarer than a great novel—it is a perfect novel, so well told and beautifully written, so deeply moving, it takes your breath away." In addition to *Stoner*, Williams wrote an historical novel, *Augustus*, which was the co-winner of the National Book Award in 1973, and *Butcher's Crossing*, which is set in Kansas in frontier times.

52. American Critics

Norman Podhoretz is an American critic and essayist. Podhoretz wrote a book called *Bloody Crossroads: Where Literature and Politics Meet*, which contains some fine essays on contemporary writers such as Solzhenitsyn, Kundera and Kissinger. Podhoretz is one of the few American writers who can be called "a man of letters"; he writes for the general reader, not the scholar, and he's conscious of style—both as a writer and as a reader. He was one of the original neo-conservatives, and he sometimes lets his politics affect his literature; in his book on the Hebrew prophets, for example, he makes remarks on contemporary politics. In our time, culture is often politicized—by the Right as well as the Left. The politicization of intellectual life has been called "the treason of the intellectuals."

Podhoretz borrowed the phrase "bloody crossroads" from Lionel Trilling, one of the leaders of the so-called New York Intellectuals. Trilling respects literary values as few American writers ever have, and he tries to point the way to a healthy literary culture. He wrote some fine essays, which were collected in books like *The Liberal Imagination*.

For many years, Trilling taught at Columbia, and one of his colleagues there was Jacques Barzun. Barzun was born into a cultured

French family, then came to the U.S. and attended Columbia. Barzun's specialty is cultural history; he's at home with visual art, music, literature, philosophy, etc. He's particularly interested in the French composer Berlioz, and the American philosopher William James. He often wrote about higher education, and he helped design Columbia's curriculum, which was wide-ranging and classics-oriented—like Barzun himself. Barzun was often critical of modern culture. One of his most popular books is a tome called *From Dawn to Decadence: 500 Years of Western Cultural Life, 1500 to the Present.*

Simon Schama is an English-born Columbia professor. Though not as wide-ranging as Barzun, Schama writes both history and art history. He made a popular documentary called *A History of Britain*, and another documentary called *Simon Schama's Power of Art.* He has written books about Rembrandt, the French Revolution, the Golden Age of Dutch culture, and other subjects.

Perhaps the most famous American literary critic of the 20th century was Edmund Wilson. Wilson was a layman's critic, not a professor's critic; he thought criticism should be literature, not science. He published critical essays in periodicals, later collecting them in books. One of his best-known essay-collections is *Axel's Castle*, which discusses modern writers like Joyce and Proust. He also published a study of socialism called *To the Finland Station*, and numerous autobiographical volumes. Wilson's private life was stormy, and he was married four times. It is said that when he quarreled with one of his wives, the critic Mary McCarthy, he would go to his study and lock the door, and she would stuff burning papers under the door.

When Isaiah Berlin met Wilson, he was surprised to find "a thick-set, red-faced, pot-bellied figure not unlike President Hoover."[1] When people meet great writers, they're often surprised to find that they don't look like great writers, they look like ordinary mortals. One who met Tolstoy, for example, expected to find an imposing prophet, and was surprised to find a stooped old man who supported himself with a cane. And when Proust met Anatole France, he was amazed to find an ordinary mortal with a goatee, and a nose that curled like a snail shell. The literary self and the everyday self aren't the same; the literary self is six inches taller than the ordinary self. If we're familiar with the literary self, the everyday self surprises us. Conversely, if we're familiar with the everyday self, the literary self surprises us; as Proust put it, we can't

---

[1] Quoted in "Missionary: Edmund Wilson and American culture," by Louis Menand, *New Yorker*, August 8, 2005

believe in the genius of a person with whom we went to the opera last night.

After the death of his friend F. Scott Fitzgerald, Wilson seemed to lose faith in American literature, in the potential of American literature. The great generation was fading away. The only American writer who interested Wilson was Salinger.

A contemporary of Wilson's, F. R. Leavis, was perhaps the leading English critic of his generation. Leavis began his career with poetry-criticism (*New Bearings in English Poetry*), then turned to the English novel (*The Great Tradition*). Leavis approached English literature with a kind of religious seriousness; he had little use for playful, witty writers like Sterne. One of his favorite novelists was D. H. Lawrence; according to Podhoretz, Leavis' writing about Lawrence "sounds more like prayer than criticism."[1] Leavis admired the American-turned-English writer T. S. Eliot, who taught Leavis to appreciate the Metaphysical Poets, and to castigate Romantic Poets like Shelley. Eliot's critical essays are among the most respected in modern times. Following Eliot's hints, Leavis tried to draw a map of English literature (as I'm attempting to draw a literary map). Leavis was studied closely by New York Intellectuals like Trilling, Podhoretz, and Philip Rahv.[2]

53. Kundera, etc.

The Czech writer Milan Kundera is certainly one of the best writers that the 20th century has produced. Since moving to France in 1975, Kundera has written several works in French. He also has a firm grasp of English, and he polished the English translations of his own books. The son of a musician, Kundera has a deep knowledge of music, and often discusses music in his works. Kundera's works often depict life in a Communist society, and often include explicit sexuality. Kundera is as profound as Solzhenitsyn, and more entertaining than Solzhenitsyn. Kundera's work is often harsh and brutal, but his harshness isn't carried to an extreme, as Solzhenitsyn's is, and it doesn't prevent him from being highly entertaining and highly readable. Kundera has taste. Kundera's

---

[1] *The Bloody Crossroads*, "F. R. Leavis: A Revaluation," p. 87

[2] Rahv's essays are almost as good as Trilling's; I recommend Rahv's *Literature and the Sixth Sense* (which doesn't deal with the occult, though the title implies that).

novels might be described as "thought novels" or "idea novels," in the tradition of the Austrian novelists Robert Musil and Hermann Broch.

Musil is best-known for his huge, unfinished work, *The Man Without Qualities*. Though never popular in the English-speaking world, Musil is highly esteemed elsewhere. When Thomas Mann was asked "Who are the best writers of our time?" Mann named only Musil.

Broch is best known for his trilogy *The Sleepwalkers* and for his *Death of Vergil*. *The Sleepwalkers* deals with the loss of faith in modern Europe, and the rise of nihilism. *The Death of Vergil* deals with the last hours of the Roman poet—his concern that his poetry hasn't been faithful to grim reality, etc. Broch himself seemed to question the value of literature in his final years, and he preferred to spend his time writing non-fiction, and helping Jewish refugees. Broch himself was Jewish, and barely escaped Nazi camps. Like Musil, Broch is little known in the English-speaking world, but regarded by many as one of the 20th century's great novelists.

Stefan Zweig was born into a wealthy, assimilated Jewish family, and grew up in Vienna. He had a cosmopolitan attitude, and was critical of Zionism, though friendly with Theodor Herzl, the father of Zionism. A champion of European culture in a broad sense, Zweig said that his biography of Erasmus was a concealed autobiography. When Hitler came to power, Zweig left Austria, eventually settling in Brazil. In 1942, depressed by Nazi conquests and the apparent collapse of European civilization, Zweig committed suicide with his wife. One might say that Broch turned against literature because it didn't match reality, and Zweig turned against reality because it didn't match literature. It's difficult for the modern writer to affirm both reality and literature; Erich Heller said that Goethe was "the last great poet who lived and worked in a continual effort to save the life of poetry *and* the poetry of life."[1]

Though best known for his fiction, Zweig also wrote biographies of Magellan, Mary Queen of Scots, etc. (Earlier I mentioned Zweig's *Three Masters: Balzac, Dickens, Dostoyevsky*.) Just before his death, Zweig completed an autobiography, *The World of Yesterday*.

54. Middle-Eastern and Indian Poets

Kabir has been called the most quoted writer in India. A weaver by trade, Kabir lived in northern India in the 1400s. His poems have been

---

[1] *The Disinherited Mind*, p. 32

translated into English by Tagore and (more recently) by the American poet Robert Bly. Kabir has a mystical outlook, shunning religious formalities, finding the true spirit of religion in the here and now:

O servant, where dost thou seek Me?
Lo! I am beside thee.
I am neither in temple nor in mosque: I am neither in Kaaba nor in Kailash:
Neither am I in rites and ceremonies, nor in Yoga and renunciation.
If thou art a true seeker, thou shalt at once see Me: thou shalt meet Me in a moment of time.
Kabir says, "O Sadhu! God is the breath of all breath."

Another poet with a mystical outlook is Rumi, who lived in the 1200s. Rumi is often described as a Sufi (Sufism is Islam's brand of mysticism). Sufism sometimes spurned religious law, and clashed with orthodox Moslems. Like other brands of mysticism, Sufism says that God is within you, that God and the universe and you are one. Sufism believes that the essence of all religions is the same. Rumi reached out to Jews, Christians, etc., and people of all faiths came to his funeral.

Rumi spent most of his life in Konya, Turkey, and he wrote in Persian. One of the chief events of Rumi's life was his close friendship with a mystic named Shams. The most well-known translator of Rumi into English is Coleman Barks. Rumi strikes a chord with modern readers; he has been called the most popular poet in the U.S.

Hafiz also wrote in Persian. Hafiz lived in Iran in the 1300s. His poetry has long been known in the West, and inspired Goethe's *West-östlicher Diwan*. The most popular Hafiz translator today is Daniel Ladinsky. Like Kabir and Rumi, Hafiz has a mystical outlook that unites disparate creeds.

Another popular poet from Iran is Omar Khayyam, who lived around 1075. An accomplished mathematician and astronomer, Omar is best known today for a poetic work called the *Rubaiyat*. The most famous translation of the *Rubaiyat* is Edward Fitzgerald's (it was also translated by Richard Le Gallienne).

Rabindranath Tagore, who translated Kabir into English, won the Nobel Prize in 1913. Though Tagore wrote some fiction, he's best known for his poetic works, such as *Gitanjali*. *Gitanjali* is somewhat obscure, but it contains passages of extraordinary beauty and depth; especially remarkable is the way it treats the subject of death:

I know that the day will come when my sight of this earth shall be lost,
and life will take its leave in silence, drawing the last curtain over
my eyes.
Yet stars will watch at night, and morning rise as before, and hours heave
like sea waves casting up pleasures and pains.
When I think of this end of my moments, the barrier of the moments
breaks and I see by the light of death thy world with its careless
treasures. Rare is its lowliest seat, rare is its meanest of lives.
Things that I longed for in vain and things that I got—let them pass. Let
me but truly possess the things that I ever spurned and overlooked.

Tagore was acclaimed by his contemporaries, including Yeats and Gide,
and even today he's extremely popular in India. Tagore was not only a
poet, he was also a gifted musician and painter.

55. Lorca

Like Tagore, the Spanish poet Federico García Lorca was a musician and artist as well as poet. As a young man, Lorca was best known
for his musical talents, and as he grew older, his drawings were sometimes exhibited, but now his fame rests on his literary works, his poems
and plays. Lorca is one of the major figures in 20th-century poetry, but
his work isn't well-known in the English-speaking world, perhaps
because poetry is so difficult to translate.

Some languages—English, French, etc.—seem to be old and tired,
producing little poetry, and less poetic drama. When one looks at Lorca's
work, one is struck by how much energy and vigor, how much music, is
still in the Spanish language; Lorca wrote not only poetry, but also poetic
drama. Tagore's language (Bengali) also seems to have a musical energy
that isn't found in English, French, etc.; Tagore's songs were sung by all
classes of people.

Maybe it isn't the language that becomes old and tired, maybe it's
the soul that becomes old and tired. The creative energy of the Spanish
soul is evident not only in poetry (Lorca) but also in philosophy (Ortega)
and visual art (Picasso). In the 20th century, when the heart of Europe
seemed weak and weary, the periphery of Europe seemed to still possess
creative energy: Spain's contribution to modern culture is considerable,
Ireland's contribution to modern culture, especially literature, is also
considerable, and the writers of Central and Eastern Europe, such as

Kundera and Solzhenitsyn, seem to have a power not found in the old centers of European civilization.

In 1919, at the age of 21, Lorca entered the University of Madrid. Though he published almost nothing, he gained a wide reputation through his public readings. "Verse is made to be recited," Lorca said; "in a book it is dead." When he was 24, Lorca collaborated with the composer Manuel de Falla, writing *Gypsy Ballads* and other works.

At the age of 30, Lorca was internationally famous, but displeased with "the myth of my gypsy-hood." Suffering from an emotional crisis, he sought relief in America and Cuba. The trip inspired a book of poems called *Poet in New York*, which expressed Lorca's horror at modern, urban civilization. Like Goethe, Lorca had a passion for puppets since his childhood days, and when he was 33, Lorca wrote two puppet plays. But even these puppet plays were overcast with melancholy.

At 34, Lorca founded a drama troupe, and during the next three years, his troupe performed classical Spanish drama (Lope de Vega, Calderón, Cervantes, etc.) for all classes of the Spanish population. (When one hears about puppets, plays and poetry readings, one is struck anew at how different things were before the advent of TV, movies, etc.)

At 35, having learned from his stage experience, Lorca wrote a dramatic trilogy, which is perhaps his best-known work. When Lorca was 38, the Spanish Civil War broke out, and Lorca was shot by the Nationalists, fulfilling the premonition of violent death that is found in his works.

56. Pessoa

Like Lorca, the Portuguese writer Fernando Pessoa is a major 20th-century writer who's little-known in the English-speaking world. The American poet Edwin Honig translated both Lorca and Pessoa into English. Another important author of Pessoa translations and Pessoa studies is Richard Zenith. One of Pessoa's best-known works is *The Book of Disquiet*.

Pessoa spent part of his childhood in South Africa, where he learned English. Some of his literary works are in Portuguese, some in English. During his lifetime, Pessoa published in England as well as in Portugal. He spent his adult years in Lisbon, making a living by translating business letters between Portuguese and English.

Pessoa frequented the cafés and restaurants of Lisbon, jotting down poems and reflections on scraps of paper, or on menus. When he returned home, he stuffed these barely-legible scraps in a drawer. When he died in 1935, at the age of 47, Pessoa left behind about 25,000 literary scraps. Much of his work is fragmentary, incomplete. Pessoa was at home with both poetry and short prose reflections.

Pessoa admired Whitman, and Pessoa's work contains mystical elements, Zennish elements, as Whitman's does. In Pessoa's work, however, one also finds dark streaks of pessimism that remind one more of Kafka than Whitman. One might say that Pessoa was better at writing Zen than at living it. In a chronology of Pessoa's life, one finds entries such as "1933: experiences severe depression." Pessoa's life was loveless and lonely; he never married. He said that he belonged to a generation that had "lost all respect for the past and all belief or hope in the future."[1]

Pessoa viewed literature not as an expression of life, but as a substitute for life, a release from life. Richard Zenith describes him as "relentlessly detached from physical life."[2] Pessoa had a rich imagination, and he created several imaginary characters or "heteronyms," furnishing them not only with biographies but also with literary works. Much of Pessoa's work is written under the name of one of his various heteronyms; in this respect, Pessoa reminds one of Kierkegaard, who also created imaginary writers.

Pessoa was interested in the occult, translated some works on occult matters into Portuguese, practiced astrology, and corresponded with Aleister Crowley, a prominent English occultist.

Pessoa's prose works contain some impressive philosophical passages, such as this passage:

> Since the second half of the eighteenth century, a terrible, progressive illness has fallen on our civilization.... The ruin of aristocratic influence created an atmosphere of brutality and indifference to the arts.... The ruin of classical ideals made everyone into potential artists—bad artists.... The horror of action, which has to be vile in a vile society, sullied our spirit. The soul's higher activity sickened; only its lower activity, because it was more vital, did not decay; with the other inert, it assumed control over the world.... The only recourse for souls born to command was abstention.[3]

One is reminded of Yeats' famous lines: "The best lack all conviction, while the worst are full of passionate intensity."

---

[1] Richard Zenith, *Fernando Pessoa & Co.: Selected Poems*, Introduction
[2] ibid
[3] *The Book of Disquiet*, translated by Alfred Mac Adam, #470

In one essay, Pessoa predicted Portugal would soon produce a great poet, a poet who would make an important contribution to European literature. Perhaps this feeling of a great destiny, great potential, inspired Pessoa to create great literature himself.

There are many striking passages in Pessoa's works. Though you may not find the content of his work attractive, Pessoa grabs your attention with his style. You know you're in the presence of a great literary talent. Like most great literary talents, Pessoa was completely immersed in literature. "My destiny," he wrote to a secretary named Ophelia, "belongs to another law whose existence you do not even sense."[1]

57. Isaac Bashevis Singer

Singer was born and raised in Poland's Jewish community. In 1935, when he was 33, Singer moved from Poland to the U.S. But even when he lived in the U.S., Singer continued to write in Yiddish. Many of his writings were first published in newspapers and magazines; later they were translated from Yiddish to English, and published in book form. Singer sometimes translated his own works into English.

Singer had a keen interest in Polish-Jewish history. His first novel, *Satan in Goray*, deals with a pogrom that took place in 1648, and one of his later novels, *The Slave*, also deals with this period.   Though   he wrote numerous novels, Singer's fame rests chiefly on his short stories. He was a student of the short-story form, and read Maupassant, Chekhov, etc.

One of Singer's best-known stories is "The Spinoza of Market Street." It has everything one could wish for in a short story: a sense of history, depth of thought, lively characters, humorous touches. It can be found in a volume called *The Collected Stories of Isaac Bashevis Singer*; Singer himself chose the stories for this volume.

Singer's most famous story is "Gimpel the Fool," which depicts a saintly character who is mistreated but loves the world anyway. Even when dealing with a serious theme, Singer is witty and gritty and lively. Gimpel is aware of death and prepared for death:

At the door of the hovel where I lie, there stands the plank on which the dead are taken away. The grave-digger Jew has his spade ready. The grave waits and the

---

1 *The Keeper of Sheep*, translated by Edwin Honig, Introduction

worms are hungry; the shrouds are prepared—I carry them in my beggar's sack.... When the time comes I will go joyfully.

Gimpel's joyful acceptance of death is typical of sages in all cultures.

Singer's father was a rabbi, and Singer was steeped in Judaism. In his early 20s, though, he broke with his father's world, and "he stopped attending Jewish religious services of any kind, even on the High Holy Days."[1] He had some connections in the Polish-Jewish literary world—two of his older siblings were writers—and he acquired a literary reputation at an early age. In his later years, two of his works were made into movies: the novel *Enemies, a Love Story*, and the short story "Yentl."

Singer was a passionate vegetarian. "In relation to [animals]," he wrote, "all people are Nazis; for the animals, it is an eternal Treblinka.... If there would come a voice from God saying, 'I'm against vegetarianism!' I would say, 'Well, I am for it!' This is how strongly I feel in this regard."[2]

58. Ancient Writers

One can't appreciate ancient poetry if one reads it in translation. In order to appreciate ancient poetry, one must read it in the original, and to do that requires that one spend years studying ancient languages. Before the twentieth century, Western education consisted largely of studying ancient languages. Those who knew Greek and Latin were educated; those who didn't, weren't educated. Now, however, only a few scholars know Greek and Latin. Ancient poetry is therefore gradually sinking into oblivion.

One of the few ancient poets who isn't sinking into oblivion is Homer. Homer engages the reader's attention in a way that other epic poets, such as Vergil and Milton, fail to do. Homer's works are enjoyable to read in almost any translation. An Irish writer, Padraic Colum, has made an excellent abridgment of Homer; though the title of Colum's work is *The Children's Homer*, it will interest adults as well as children. If you want to read Homer in unabridged form, the Robert Fagles translation is highly regarded.

---

[1] Wikipedia article on Singer
[2] Wikipedia article on Singer

Poetry is derived from primitive religious rites, hence poetry emerges early in the history of literature; poetry precedes prose. As civilization matures, the best writers turn increasingly to prose. Prose fiction became popular during the latter days of ancient civilization. *Daphnis and Chloe*, by Longus, is a delightful love story in a pastoral setting; Goethe said, "one would do well to read [*Daphnis and Chloe*] every year... and to receive anew the impression of its great beauty."[1] The *Satyricon* of Petronius, one of Nietzsche's favorite books, is a light-hearted, bawdy work. *The Golden Ass* of Apuleius, one of Flaubert's favorite books, resembles the *Satyricon* in its loose form and earthy humor. Apuleius was receptive to Hermetic ideas; the Jungian writer Marie-Louise von Franz found much spiritual wisdom in *The Golden Ass*, and devoted an entire volume to it. While Longus wrote in Greek, Petronius and Apuleius wrote in Latin.

---

[1] *Conversations With Eckermann*, 3/20/31

IV. History

1. General History

I recommend *A Little History of the World*, by the renowned art historian, Ernst Gombrich. It's a concise summary of world history, it's highly readable, and it provides enough detail/anecdote to enliven the narrative. It's intended for youngsters, but it has much to offer adults, too. It has been approved by a *consensus gentium*; it has been a world-wide bestseller since its publication in 1936. Gombrich didn't work on an English translation of *Little History* until his last years. He laid aside this English translation after the September 11, 2001 attacks, which destroyed his faith in civilization. (His granddaughter completed the translation.)

Gombrich's *Story of Art* is also intended for young people, and has also been very popular; it's probably the best one-volume history of art. Students of art history should also consider Gombrich's *Art and Illusion*.

I recommend *The Human Web: A Bird's-Eye View of World History*, by William McNeill and his son, J. R. McNeill. It's a top-notch book, learned yet readable, concise yet detailed. Gombrich's *Little History* deals with Socrates, Shakespeare, Copernicus, etc. *The Human Web* is utterly different: it deals with practical matters like the development of corn, rice, and other crops, the spread of disease, the use of fossil fuels, etc. *The Human Web* is longer and requires more patience than Gombrich's book, but it gives you a better understanding of human history. *The Human Web* is strong where *A Little History* is weak, and vice versa; the two books complement each other.

William McNeill was a professor at the University of Chicago, best known for his 1963 book *The Rise of the West: A History of the Human Community*. Among his other books are *Venice: The Hinge of Europe*, and *History of Western Civilization: A Handbook*. McNeill also wrote a biography of Toynbee that Elie Kedourie described as "a solid and felicitously written, indeed outstanding work." J. R. McNeill is an environmental historian, best known for *Something New Under the Sun: An Environmental History of the Twentieth-century World*. One might describe both McNeills as writers of "big history."

2. Burckhardt

Jacob Burckhardt was one of the leading historians of the nineteenth century. Burckhardt was born in Switzerland, and became a teacher at Basel, where he was a colleague and friend of Nietzsche. Burckhardt is known as the father of cultural history. While earlier historians had concentrated on political and military history, Burckhardt discussed the total life of the people, including religion, art and literature.

Burckhardt's most famous book is *The Civilization of the Renaissance in Italy*; the Dutch historian Huizinga called it, "that transcendent masterpiece." A rare meeting between the perfect author and the perfect subject has produced an extraordinary work. The first three parts of the book are especially good—readable and interesting, profound and philosophical. The two pages on Leon Battista Alberti are unforgettable.

Alberti was a "Renaissance man": he was interested in everything. After describing how Alberti studied music, law, physics, math, painting and literature, Burckhardt says "he acquired every sort of accomplishment and dexterity, cross-examining artists, scholars, and artisans of all descriptions, down to the cobblers, about the secrets and peculiarities of their craft."[1] Alberti had an extraordinary appetite for life; Burckhardt speaks of, "the sympathetic intensity with which he entered into the whole life around him. At the sight of noble trees and waving cornfields he shed tears; handsome and dignified old men he honored as a 'delight of nature', and could never look at them enough."[2] Such an appetite for life, such an attitude of wonder in the face of reality, is the essence of the Renaissance.

According to Burckhardt, during the Middle Ages "man was conscious of himself only as a member of a race, people, party, family, or corporation," but during the Italian Renaissance, "man became a

---

[1] *The Civilization of the Renaissance in Italy*, II, 2
[2] ibid

spiritual *individual*."[1] Individuality reached its zenith, according to
Burckhardt, in the Renaissance humanists, who turned their backs on
Christianity, revered the ancients, and tried to live and write like the
ancients.

Burckhardt's *History of Greek Culture*, which is as interesting as his
work on the Italian Renaissance, also deals with individuality.
Burckhardt argues that the Greeks had a highly developed individuality,
while other societies of the time crushed individuality beneath the weight
of group, caste and morality.[2]

In addition to his works on the Greeks and the Italian Renaissance,
Burckhardt wrote *The Age of Constantine*, which deals with a decadent
phase of Roman history.

3. Huizinga

Johan Huizinga was one of the leading historians of the twentieth
century. Huizinga described himself as a cultural historian, as one who
worked within the tradition that Burckhardt had begun. Huizinga
concentrated on a period to which Burckhardt had paid little attention:
the Middle Ages. Huizinga's most famous work is *The Waning of the
Middle Ages*, in which he argues that the late Middle Ages were a period
of weariness, pessimism and decadence. *The Waning of the Middle Ages*
is a superb historical work—profound, readable and well-written.
Though it isn't a long book, it discusses many aspects of medieval life:
philosophy, literature, painting, chivalry, love, etc. Huizinga describes
how medieval piety often found expression in rituals and external forms.
Medieval man had considerable respect for saints, and for relics of saints:
"In 1392, King Charles VI of France, on the occasion of a solemn feast,
was seen to distribute ribs of his ancestor, Saint Louis; to Pierre d'Ailly
and to his uncles Berry and Burgundy he gave entire ribs; to the prelates
one bone to divide between them, which they proceeded to do after the
meal."[3]

Huizinga also discusses the Middle Ages in *Men and Ideas*, a
collection of essays. Most of the essays in *Men and Ideas* are excellent.

---

[1] *The Civilization of the Renaissance in Italy*, II, 1
[2] Frederick Ungar Publishing Co., New York, 1963; translated from the
abridged version (1958) of the two-volume German edition
[3] *The Waning of the Middle Ages*, ch. 12

In an essay called, "The Task of Cultural History," Huizinga describes the type of history that he and Burckhardt wrote. Huizinga argues that history should resurrect the past, and should give the reader a sense of what it was like to be alive during a particular period. Huizinga deplores the modern tendency to write romanticized history and romanticized biography, to try to make history entertaining and amusing: "No literary effect in the world," writes Huizinga, "can compare to the pure, sober taste of history."[1]

Other essays by Huizinga are collected in a volume called *Dutch Civilization in the Seventeenth Century and Other Essays*. Much of this book is written not for the general reader, but for Huizinga's fellow Dutchmen and contemporaries. Huizinga's preoccupation with the Netherlands reminds one of Ortega's preoccupation with Spain. In an essay called, "The Aesthetic Element in Historical Thought," Huizinga declares that he has "faith in the importance of the aesthetic element in historical thinking," and that he opposes the idea that history should attempt to be scientific. "The historian," says Huizinga, "tries to re-experience what was once experienced by men like ourselves....The true study of history involves our imagination and conjures up conceptions, pictures, visions."[2]

Huizinga's *In the Shadow of Tomorrow* isn't a historical work, but rather an analysis of Western civilization. It discusses the problems besetting the West, from moral anarchy to artistic decadence. Though it sometimes reminds one of Ortega's *Revolt of the Masses*, it's less pertinent to our time than Ortega's work since much of it is a criticism of Fascism. It is, however, an interesting, brief and readable book. Huizinga notes that modern education and the mass media both have harmful effects on culture: "Our time [is] faced by the discouraging fact that two highly vaunted achievements of civilization, universal education and modern publicity, instead of raising the level of culture, appear ultimately to produce certain symptoms of cultural devitalisation and degeneration."[3]

In looking at modern art, Huizinga finds a trend toward the irrational in both modern literature and modern painting. Literature and painting have become increasingly unintelligible. Throughout history, says Huizinga, poetry has always maintained "a certain connection with

---

[1] *Men and Ideas*, "The Task of Cultural History"

[2] *Dutch Civilization in the Seventeenth Century and Other Essays*, "Two Wrestlers With the Angel"

[3] *In the Shadow of Tomorrow*, ch. 7

rational expression.... It is not until the closing years of the [nineteenth] century that one sees poetry purposely steering its course away from reason."[1]

Huizinga had a special interest in America and American history. He wrote *Man and the Masses in America* and also *Life and Thought in America*; these two books are sometimes published together in one volume. These books look at American history before 1925, and they also look at modern society in general, including newspapers, movies and literature. Huizinga pays special attention to the economic forces that have shaped American history.

In many of Huizinga's works, he discusses the play element in culture. Finally, when his life was drawing to a close, and he was a prisoner of the Nazis, he collected his thoughts on this subject into a book called *Homo Ludens: A Study of the Play-Element in Culture*. *Homo Ludens* contains some very interesting ideas, but it presents these ideas in a rather dry and scholarly manner. Huizinga argues that play is one of fundamental facts of human life, and is at the root of poetry, music, philosophy—even jurisprudence and war. Anyone interested in plumbing the depths of human nature, anyone interested in the question of why people fight wars, create culture, etc., should take Huizinga's ideas into account. Huizinga is discussing more than play, he's discussing human nature, the fundamental drives within human nature.

> The spirit of playful competition [writes Huizinga] is, as a social impulse, older than culture itself and pervades all life like a veritable ferment. Ritual grew up in sacred play; poetry was born in play and nourished on play; music and dancing were pure play.... We have to conclude, therefore, that civilization is, in its earliest phases, played. It does not come *from* play... it arises *in* and *as* play, and never leaves it.[2]

Huizinga's book on Erasmus is an uninspired work, perhaps because Erasmus himself was uninspiring.

4. Toynbee

Arnold Toynbee was born in England during the late nineteenth century, and did most of his writing during the twentieth century. Toynbee is best known for his multi-volume work, *A Study of History*,

---

[1] *In the Shadow of Tomorrow*, ch. 18
[2] *Homo Ludens: A Study of the Play-Element in Culture*, ch. 11

in which he argues that civilizations decline when the ruling elite can no longer control the rebellious working classes. According to Toynbee, the ruling elite tries to restore order by imposing a universal state, but this measure can only succeed temporarily. Meanwhile, the working classes develop a new religion within the universal state, and this new religion gradually takes the form of a universal church, which survives when the universal state disintegrates. The universal church becomes the seed of a new civilization. Toynbee's theory is based on the decline of Rome and the rise of Christianity, though he insists that it's a universal historical law. Toynbee is an ardent Christian, and his historical theories often reflect his piety. Like Hegel, Toynbee thinks there's a divine plan in history.

Many of Toynbee's books are about current events. Even if one has no interest in the theory that Toynbee sets forth in his *Study of History*, Toynbee's other books will still be of interest. Toynbee's best work is *Civilization On Trial*, a collection of essays. Toynbee's prose is learned and poetic, his ideas broad and profound.

Toynbee was struck by the change in the role of Europe that occurred during his lifetime: during his youth, Europe was on top of the world, and had colonies on every continent, but by the end of World War II, Europe had lost most of its colonies, and no longer dominated the world. But Western influence is still strong, even though the West doesn't dominate the world as it used to; Toynbee foresaw "a radical Westernization of the entire world."[1] But as Western culture, once the possession of a small elite, is gradually dispersed through all social classes and all nations, its quality is lowered; the wider its dispersion, the lower its quality.

Non-Western nations are faced with a dilemma: to imitate the West, adopt a low form of Western culture, and lose their spiritual vitality and creativity, or to isolate themselves from the West. Toynbee points out that Japan tried first one approach then the other, first isolation then imitation. While Japan has attained material success, this success has come at the cost of spiritual vitality and creativity. Toynbee argues that even nations that succeed in imitating the West, as Japan has, can't accomplish anything except "to enlarge the quantity of the machine-made products of the imitated society instead of releasing new creative energies in human souls."[2] Thus, while the Western world is in a difficult

---

[1] *Civilization On Trial*, ch. 6
[2] *Civilization On Trial*, ch. 10

predicament, a spiritual crisis, so too the non-Western world is in a difficult predicament.

Toynbee thinks it's imperative that the power of the United Nations be increased, so that it will gradually become a world government. The best hope for civilization is, in Toynbee's view, to develop a world government and to build a world civilization on a religious foundation, a Christian foundation.

In addition to *A Study of History* and *Civilization On Trial*, Toynbee wrote *Hellenism: The History of a Civilization*, which is a clear and concise summary of ancient civilization, from Homer's time to the fall of the Roman Empire; it emphasizes economics and military affairs. Toynbee also wrote—or rather, edited—*Half the World: The History and Culture of China and Japan*, which is an excellent introduction to China and Japan.

5. Chinese History

Ray Huang's book *1587, A Year of No Significance* is a classic in the field of Chinese history. Huang was born in China in 1918, and fought against the Japanese in World War II. Later he studied at the University of Michigan, and became an assistant to the famous Sinologists Joseph Needham and John K. Fairbank. Huang liked to take a broad view; one of his books is called *China: A Macro History*.[1]

Another classic in the field of Chinese history is *Daily Life in China on the Eve of the Mongol Invasion, 1250-1276*, by Jacques Gernet. Gernet also wrote the 800-page *History of Chinese Civilization* (originally published in French as *Le Monde chinois*).

For a quick look at old China, consider L. Carrington Goodrich's *Short History of the Chinese People*, which was published in 1943 and reprinted in 2002. One reader said it's "still a very useful book because of its concise and precise descriptions, great illustrations and excellent maps.... The best introduction I know to Chinese history."

For a more detailed look at old China, consider a 1,000-page book called *Imperial China: 900-1800*, by Frederick W. Mote. Mote worked for years on the *Cambridge History of China*, then summarized his work in *Imperial China: 900-1800*. Born in Nebraska in 1922, Mote spent his

---

[1] Huang is sometimes classed as a writer of "big history" (see Wikipedia's article, "Big History").

long career at Princeton. Like Ray Huang, Mote was a student of John K. Fairbank.

6. Ancient History

A study of ancient history should begin with the Russian historian Rostovtzeff, who wrote a two-volume *History of the Ancient World*. The first volume deals with Mesopotamia, Egypt and Greece, and is entitled *The Orient and Greece*. The second volume, which deals with Rome, is even more interesting than the first. Rostovtzeff's work is well-written, well-organized and profound. Not satisfied with literary sources, Rostovtzeff drew on archaeology, and his books contain photographs of artifacts.

Though Rostovtzeff isn't famous, he has a high reputation among scholars. Arnaldo Momigliano, who knew the man and the work, said that Rostovtzeff had an "uncanny gift of calling ancient things to life." Momigliano described Rostovtzeff as

> a man of great physical strength and exceptional memory, passionate and egotistic, capable of lecturing in six different languages and of quarreling in as many.[1]

His Wisconsin students called him "Rough Stuff."
Huizinga quotes Rostovtzeff respectfully.

> The oppressing question [wrote Huizinga] with which Rostovtzeff concludes his *Social and Economic History of the Roman Empire* is still unanswered: "Is it possible to extend a higher civilization to the lower classes without debasing its standard and diluting its quality to the vanishing point? Is not every civilization bound to decay as soon as it begins to penetrate the masses?"[2]

Beware of Rostovtzeff's *Social and Economic History of the Roman Empire*. Though it's a good book and his best-known book, it's dry and difficult to read; it has no anecdotes and no personalities. It's written for professional scholars, not for laymen.

Though I'm a fan of Rostovtzeff's two-volume *History of the Ancient World*, some readers may want more detail. Such readers should consider *A History of Greece to 322 B.C.*, by Nicholas Hammond (also

---

[1] Momigliano, *Studies On Modern Scholarship*
[2] *Men and Ideas*, "The Task of Cultural History"

known as N.G.L. Hammond). During World War II, Hammond was a guerrilla fighter in Greece, and he later wrote *Venture into Greece: With the Guerrillas, 1943-44.* Hammond had a special interest in Macedonia, and wrote much about Philip, Alexander, etc.

Another noteworthy Hammond is Mason Hammond, author of *The Antonine Monarchy, The City in The Ancient World*, etc. During World War II, Mason Hammond was one of the "Monuments Men" who tried to find art works stolen by the Nazis.

A popular book about the discovery and excavation of ancient cities is *Gods, Graves & Scholars: The Story of Archaeology*, by C. W. Ceram. If you want to look at the practical side of antiquity, consider *Ancient Engineers*, by L. Sprague de Camp.

The Ancient City, by Fustel de Coulanges, looks at the Greeks and Romans from the standpoint of cultural anthropology; it describes the primitive religious ideas that were the foundation of ancient society. *The Ancient City* is clear and readable, and throws light not only on the Greeks and Romans, but on primitive man in general. It describes how primitive man worshipped his ancestors, how each primitive family had its own religion, how the individual was submerged in the family, and how the eldest son carried on the family religion. It also describes how the ancient city-state developed out of the primitive family, and how the ancient statesman was both ruler and priest, just as the primitive father had been both ruler and priest.

No essay on the Western classics would be complete if it failed to mention the eighteenth-century English historian, Edward Gibbon, and his famous work, *The Decline and Fall of the Roman Empire*. Gibbon is known for his prose style and for his irreverent attitude toward religion. Gibbon's prose is ponderous and precious, but it can teach one much about the English language. If you want a taste of Gibbon, read Chapter 15 of his *Decline and Fall*, a chapter which deals with the early Christians.

Herodotus, a Greek historian, is often called the father of history. Herodotus's *Histories* deals with the wars between the Persians and the Greeks, and with other topics in ancient history. It's a readable and entertaining work, sprinkled with stories and legends.

Thucydides wrote history in a more serious, sober and factual way than Herodotus did. Thucydides is the author of *The Peloponessian War*, which describes the war between Athens and Sparta (and their allies), a war in which Thucydides himself participated. Thucydides's reputation is higher than that of any other ancient historian, with the possible exception of Tacitus. His work is profound and philosophical, as well as lively and readable. Thucydides views human affairs in a cold, unemotional way that reminds one of Machiavelli. Thucydides notes the changes in the Greek spirit that took place during the Peloponessian War:

> There was a general deterioration of character throughout the Greek world. The simple way of looking at things, which is so much the mark of a noble nature, was regarded as a ridiculous quality and soon ceased to exist.[1]

The Peloponessian War lasted about thirty years. Though Thucydides lived through the entire war, his account of the war stops about five years before its end. So another writer, Xenophon, wrote about the last years of the war, and its aftermath, in a book called *Hellenica*. (I mentioned above that Xenophon also wrote several works about Socrates.) Perhaps Xenophon's best-known work is *Anabasis*, which describes a march into Mesopotamia, and a retreat back to the coast; Will Durant called this march and retreat "one of the great adventures in human history." One might compare it to the "Long March" of the Chinese Communists.

Livy is one of the earliest and most famous Roman historians. Livy is the author of a multi-volume work that begins with the founding of Rome and goes all the way to the end of the Roman Republic; only part of Livy's work is still extant.

Julius Caesar is another early Roman historian, best known for his *Gallic Wars*, which describes Caesar's own campaigns in Gaul. Caesar's work is famous for the simplicity and clarity of its style.

Tacitus lived several generations after Livy and Caesar, and his work is more sophisticated and refined than the work of Livy and Caesar. Tacitus is the only Roman historian who rivals Thucydides in philosophical profundity and psychological subtlety. "One object only," wrote Tacitus, "is to be pursued insatiably: the applauding voice of posterity. For by despising fame, the virtues that acquire it are despised."[2] Tacitus has long enjoyed a high reputation; Montaigne, Gibbon, and many others revered Tacitus as one of the greatest writers of ancient times. Tacitus is best known for his *Histories* and his *Annals*, both of which deal with the Roman Empire. Tacitus also wrote brief works on oratory, on the natives of Germany, and on his father-in-law, the general and governor Agricola. Much of Tacitus's work has not survived. Tacitus's work is famous for its dense, complex style, and for its bitterness toward the tyranny of the Roman emperors.

---

[1] *The Peloponessian War*, 3
[2] *Annals*, IV, 38

Suetonius lived a generation or two after Tacitus, when Roman civilization was sinking into decadence. Suetonius is the author of *The Lives of the Caesars*, a collection of biographies of Roman emperors. Suetonius writes bedroom history; his work contains much gossip and rumor. In fairness to Suetonius, however, it should be said that his work is readable and lively—more so than Tacitus's—and it can teach one much about later Roman history.

In more recent times, one of the most well-known historians of antiquity is J. B. Bury, who wrote a multi-volume history of Greece, a biography of St. Patrick, a study of the barbarian invasions in late antiquity, and other books. A product of the Victorian age, Bury had the vast erudition and wide range that is rarely found in the historians of our time. Bury even learned Russian and Hungarian in order to research the Eastern Roman Empire, and his works on Byzantine civilization are highly regarded.

As Bury is known for his history of Greece, and Gibbon for his history of the Roman Empire, so Theodor Mommsen is known for his multi-volume history of the Roman Republic. Mommsen's work is still respected today—more respected than Bury's, though not as respected as Gibbon's. If you want to read a historian who's more contemporary than Mommsen, and who wrote in English, try H. H. Scullard, who wrote about both the Roman Republic and the Roman Empire. Scullard collaborated with Max Cary on *A History of Rome*, a respected work often used in college classes. Scullard wrote a biography of Scipio Africanus the Elder, a study of Roman Britain, a book about the elephant in antiquity, and other works.

One of Scullard's most eminent contemporaries in the field of ancient history was Arnaldo Momigliano. It would be difficult to identify Momigliano's *magnum opus*, perhaps because he focused on teaching rather than writing, perhaps because he wrote mostly articles rather than books, perhaps because he had such high standards that he hesitated to write anything. Momigliano had a special interest in the writing of history (historiography)—how the ancients wrote history, how Gibbon wrote history, etc. At the end of his life, when his health was failing, Momigliano saw students in his own quarters, an oxygen tank next to him.[1]

Like Momigliano, Ronald Syme was interested in ancient historiography, and wrote biographies of Tacitus and Sallust. But while

---

[1] See Edward Shils, *Portraits: A Gallery of Intellectuals*, "Introduction" by Joseph Epstein

Momigliano was content to study ancient historians, Syme tried to follow in their footsteps, and write like they wrote; with Syme, admiration became emulation. Syme's fame rests on *The Roman Revolution*, a book whose style and tone reminded many readers of Tacitus. *The Roman Revolution* discusses the demise of the Republic, and the rise of the Empire.

If we move forward to our own time, we find two eminent historians who specialize in late antiquity: Peter Brown and Glen Bowersock. Brown wrote (among other books) a biography of St. Augustine, Bowersock wrote (among other books) a biography of Julian the Apostate.

Harold Lamb wrote popular history for a wide audience. Lamb wrote a biography of Hannibal, the Carthaginian general who fought against Rome. Lamb had a special interest in Asia, and wrote a biography of Genghis Khan, and two books on Russian history. His only book about the Western hemisphere is *New Found World: How North America Was Discovered and Explored*. (Harold Lamb shouldn't be confused with Charles Lamb, an English essayist and a friend of Coleridge, Wordsworth, etc.)

Donald Kagan focuses on Greek history in the time of Pericles. He wrote a four-volume history of the Peloponnesian War, a one-volume work on the same war, a biography of Pericles, and a more general historical work called *On the Origins of War and the Preservation of Peace*. He's also the co-author of an excellent textbook called *The Western Heritage* (and a more comprehensive textbook called *The Heritage of World Civilizations*). Donald Kagan's two sons, Robert and Frederick, are prominent conservatives, and have written numerous books about international affairs and military matters.

If you want ancient history in fictional form, consider the fiction of Robert Graves, such as *I, Claudius*. Graves was an English man-of-letters, known for his numerous translations of ancient literature, and for his World War I memoir, *Good-bye to All That*. Graves prided himself on his poetry, and had a certain disdain for his prose works.

Graves translated Suetonius' *Twelve Caesars*. He said that, after reading Suetonius' life of Claudius, Claudius appeared to him in a dream, and "demanded that his real story be told." So *I, Claudius* was inspired by a dream.

Marguerite Yourcenar wrote a highly-regarded novel about Roman history, *Memoirs of Hadrian*. In 1980, Yourcenar became the first woman elected to the Académie française.

Ancient Rome has long been a popular subject with novelists. Three of the most popular novels of the 19th century were set in ancient Rome:

- Lew Wallace, an American, wrote *Ben-Hur* (1880), which sold even more copies than *Gone with the Wind*
- The Polish novelist Henryk Sienkiewicz wrote *Quo Vadis* (1895), which has been translated into more than 50 languages. Like *Ben-Hur*, *Quo Vadis* takes a favorable view of Christianity
- The English novelist Edward Bulwer-Lytton wrote *The Last Days of Pompeii* (1834). One character in this novel, the Witch of Vesuvius, shows Bulwer-Lytton's interest in the occult. Later he wrote *Vril, the Power of the Coming Race* (sometimes called *The Coming Race*), which explores occult themes further.

7. Medieval History

There are two criteria by which books can be judged. The first is Quality, or what a book is in itself. The second is Effect, or what a book can do for you, the pleasure and knowledge that a book can give you. The ideal book combines Quality and Effect, the worst books lack both.

An example of a book that ranks high in Effect, but is somewhat lacking in Quality, is *The Year 1000: What Life Was Like At The Turn Of The First Millennium: An Englishman's World*. The authors of *The Year 1000* (Robert Lacey and Danny Danziger) are experienced writers, journalists, people who make a living with their pen. They've succeeded in writing a readable, entertaining, interesting book; one is sorry when it ends. They haven't succeeded, however, in writing a classic; their work is directed at the contemporary reader, not at posterity. Their knowledge of their subject is somewhat thin, and they lack the ability to reach general concepts, large ideas. But they've done a good job of collecting anecdotes, and weaving them into a narrative.

Another popular book about the Middle Ages is Thomas Cahill's *How the Irish Saved Civilization: The Untold Story of Ireland's Heroic Role from the Fall of Rome to the Rise of Medieval Europe*. Cahill followed this bestseller with books about the Jews and the Greeks.

The American scholar Norman Cantor wrote about medieval history in a way that was accessible to the layman. One of Cantor's books is called *Medieval Lives: Eight Charismatic Men and Women of the Middle Ages*. Cantor wrote about other medievalists in *Inventing the Middle Ages: The Lives, Works and Ideas of the Great Medievalists of the*

Twentieth Century. Cantor wrote a textbook called *The Civilization of the Middle Ages* (1993), and he edited *The Encyclopedia of the Middle Ages.*

One of the most eminent English medievalists is David Knowles, who specialized in English monasteries. Knowles was a monk himself, as well as a Cambridge professor. Among his books are *Saints and Scholars: Twenty-Five Medieval Portraits*, and biographies of Thomas Becket.

Another eminent English medievalist is Steven Runciman. Runciman started out as a student of J. B. Bury at Cambridge, and later wrote numerous books on medieval and Byzantine civilization, notably a 3-volume work on the Crusades.

Ernst Kantorowicz was a leading German medievalist. After Hitler came to power, Kantorowicz left Germany, ending up at Princeton's Institute for Advanced Study, where he was a colleague of such luminaries as Einstein, Panofsky, and Kennan. (In his memoirs, Kennan has left us a vivid portrait of Kantorowicz.) Kantorowicz wasn't a prolific writer, and his fame rests on just two books: his biography of Frederick II, and his study of the medieval cult of royalty, *The King's Two Bodies.*

One of the most respected historians of modern times was Owen Chadwick, who wrote a history of Christianity, a study of the Reformation, etc. In his youth, Chadwick was a star rugby player. He was an Anglican priest, he taught at Cambridge for many years, and in 1981, he won the Wolfson History Prize. His brother Henry Chadwick was also a distinguished historian.

8. G. M. Trevelyan

One of Chadwick's acquaintances at Cambridge was historian G. M. Trevelyan (George Macaulay Trevelyan). Trevelyan was related to the famous 19th-century historian Thomas Babington Macaulay. Trevelyan's writings have been called accessible, literate, openly biased, and out of fashion. One scholar said Trevelyan was once "probably the most widely read historian in the world; perhaps in the history of the world."

Trevelyan's disciple, J. H. Plumb, also took a popular approach. Plumb, in turn, inspired a younger group of popular historians, a group that included Simon Schama. So the next time you enjoy a Schama documentary, you should thank Trevelyan, who was Schama's intellectual grandfather.

Plumb praised Trevelyan for "the skill of his literary craftsmanship. Trevelyan [was] a natural storyteller.... He is the poet of English history." Among Trevelyan's books are *British History in the Nineteenth Century*, *England Under the Stuarts*, *English Social History*, and *History of England*. Trevelyan was active in the Youth Hostel movement, and tried to preserve historic sites through the National Trust.

9. Renaissance History

If you want to read about Michelangelo, a classic in the field is the biography by John Addington Symonds. Symonds also wrote a multi-volume work on the Italian Renaissance, and biographies of various English poets (Shelley, Philip Sidney, and Ben Jonson).

Walter Pater is another 19th-century English writer who wrote a classic study of the Italian Renaissance. Pater's book is shorter than Symonds', and focuses on individual writers and artists, rather than the Italian Renaissance in general.

The Medici, by G. F. Young, covers a broad span of Italian history, and discusses both politics and culture. Young has the literary flair that was once common among historians, and is now rare. (G. F. Young should not be confused with G. M. Young, who is best known for his study of the Victorian period, *Portrait of an Age*, which Simon Schama called, "the greatest long essay ever written.")

A talented and prolific Russian writer, Dmitry Merezhkovsky, wrote a historical novel about Leonardo called *The Romance of Leonardo da Vinci*. Merezhkovsky wasn't a cool scholar, he was a passionate mystic, and his books reflect his passionate nature. Later I'll discuss his fascinating book on Napoleon.

There are countless studies of Elizabeth I. I recommend J. E. Neale's biography, *Queen Elizabeth I*, and Mandell Creighton's *Age of Elizabeth*. If you want a more contemporary work on Elizabeth, consider *Elizabeth I and Mary Stuart: The Perils of Marriage*, by Anka Muhlstein. (Muhlstein has also written about her ancestor, James Rothschild, about the French explorer La Salle, etc. Twice Muhlstein won the French Academy's prize for history.) Antonia Fraser wrote a well-regarded biography of Mary Queen of Scots, as well as biographies of other monarchs.

Anthony Grafton specializes in Renaissance intellectual life. Among his works are studies of the Renaissance scholar Joseph Scaliger, the Renaissance astrologer Cardano, and the Renaissance architect Leon

Battista Alberti. Grafton also wrote *The Footnote: A Curious History*. Another highly-regarded specialist in Renaissance intellectual life is Paul Kristeller.

If you're interested in how ordinary people lived at this time, try Steven Ozment's book, *Magdalena and Balthasar: An Intimate Portrait of Life in 16th Century Europe Revealed in the Letters of a Nuremberg Husband and Wife.*

10. American History

American history begins with Native Americans. Charles Mann wrote about Native Americans in a book called *1491: New Revelations of the Americas Before Columbus*. Mann is neither an academic nor a specialist; he writes for the general reader.

Paul Radin wrote about the philosophy and mythology of Native Americans. Unlike Charles Mann, Radin devoted his whole career to the study of Native Americans. Around 1910, Radin lived for several years among the Winnebago Indians of the upper Midwest.

One of the most highly-regarded books on immigrating to America is Oscar Handlin's *The Uprooted: The Epic Story of the Great Migrations That Made the American People*; Handlin's book won a Pulitzer Prize in 1952. One of Handlin's students at Harvard, Bernard Bailyn, wrote several books about early immigrants to America; Bailyn called these books "The Peopling of British North America." Bailyn is a leader in the field of early American history, and his books have won two Pulitzer Prizes. One of Bailyn's most well-known students was Gordon Wood, who also focused on early American history. Wood won a Pulitzer Prize for *The Radicalism of the American Revolution*; Wood also wrote a study of Benjamin Franklin, a brief history of the American Revolution, etc.

Perhaps the best short biography of Washington is Marcus Cunliffe's *George Washington: Man and Monument*. The best long biography of Washington is James Flexner's four-volume work. Flexner condensed his four-volume work into a popular one-volume biography, *Washington: The Indispensable Man*. Flexner was a friend of the art historian Bernard Berenson, and he wrote numerous books about American painting. Flexner wasn't an academic; rather, he was a wide-ranging man-of-letters.

Joseph Ellis wrote acclaimed biographies of Washington, Adams, and Jefferson, and he won a Pulitzer Prize for *Founding Brothers: The*

Revolutionary Generation. Ellis' work is both scholarly and popular; his biographies are relatively short.

Joseph Ellis' teacher at Yale was Edmund Morgan, a highly-respected historian who specialized in early American history. Among Morgan's books are *The Birth of the Republic: 1763-89*, *The Gentle Puritan: A Life of Ezra Stiles, 1727-1795*, and studies of Franklin and Washington.

A good book about colonial Boston is *Paul Revere and the World He Lived In*, by Esther Forbes; Forbes also wrote *Johnny Tremain*, a novel about colonial Boston intended for younger readers. David Hackett Fischer wrote *Paul Revere's Ride*, and the Pulitzer-Prize-winning *Washington's Crossing*. If you want to learn how average people lived in early America, consider *A Midwife's Tale*, by Laurel Ulrich.

For the period between the Revolution and the Civil War, consider *Inheriting the Revolution: The First Generation of Americans*, by Joyce Appleby. Also consider *Andrew Jackson: His Life and Times*, by H. W. Brands. Brands tries to tell entertaining stories, and make history enjoyable. He narrated the history of the U.S. in a series of biographies.

Perhaps the most famous study of the Civil War is Shelby Foote's three-volume work, *The Civil War: A Narrative*. Foote was a novelist, and he takes a literary approach to writing history; he prides himself on his lack of footnotes. Two short books were excerpted from Foote's work: *Stars in Their Courses: The Gettysburg Campaign*, and *The Beleaguered City: The Vicksburg Campaign*. Foote also wrote *Shiloh: A Novel*, which deals with one of the Civil War's major battles. Foote edited an anthology called *Chickamauga And Other Civil War Stories* (previously published as *The Night Before Chancellorsville*); this anthology has stories by Faulkner, Eudora Welty, Thomas Wolfe, etc. And Foote wrote an introduction to Stephen Crane's famous CivilWar novella, *The Red Badge of Courage*.

The most popular CivilWar book may be *Killer Angels*, by Michael Shaara. *Killer Angels* is a short historical novel about the Battle of Gettysburg. It's based on memoirs of participants; it might be called a hybrid of history and fiction, or it might be called a new type of historical fiction.

If you want a comprehensive, one-volume history of the Civil War, consider James McPherson's *Battle Cry of Freedom*, which won a Pulitzer Prize in 1989. McPherson's scholarly credentials are impeccable, and he tries to appeal to the layman as well as the scholar. Consider also a book by T. Harry Williams called *Lincoln and His*

Generals. Williams also wrote *The History of American Wars*, and he contributed a chapter to a book called *Why the North Won the Civil War.* Two Southern men-of-letters, Allen Tate and Robert Penn Warren, wrote books about the Civil War.

There are many good CivilWar memoirs. One of the best is Ulysses Grant's, published by Penguin with an introduction and notes by James McPherson; consider also the LibraryOfAmerica edition of Grant's memoirs, which has numerous letters written by Grant. Frank Haskell, a Union officer, wrote a memoir of Gettysburg, which has been edited by historian Bruce Catton.

As for Confederate memoirs, a private named Sam Watkins wrote *Company Aytch*, which describes the life of the common soldier; it's lively and entertaining, a superb memoir. Moxley Sorrel, an aide to Longstreet, wrote *Recollections Of A Confederate Staff Officer*, which is as entertaining as *Company Aytch*. George Eggleston, who fought in Jeb Stuart's cavalry, wrote a charming memoir called *A Rebel's Recollections.* Douglas Southall Freeman, who wrote multi-volume works on Robert E. Lee and George Washington, has high praise for a memoir called *Destruction and Reconstruction*, by Richard Taylor, son of President Zachary Taylor. Freeman says that Richard Taylor is "the one Confederate general who possessed literary art that approached first rank."[1] Freeman was especially fond of the early part of Taylor's book, which deals with his service under Stonewall Jackson. *Recollections and Letters of General Robert E. Lee* is a highly-regarded book by Lee's son. *Mary Chesnut's Civil War* is a diary edited by C. Vann Woodward; it won the Pulitzer Prize for History.

If you want to read a biography of Lincoln, a good choice would be David Herbert Donald's *Lincoln*. If you want a shorter biography, consider *Abraham Lincoln and Civil War America*, by William Gienapp. A longer biography is Carl Sandburg's four-volume work *Abraham Lincoln: The War Years*; Sandburg was a renowned poet, so his work is literary rather than scholarly. If you want a first-hand look at Lincoln, consider *Inside Lincoln's White House: The Complete Civil War Diary of John Hay*, edited by Burlingame and Ettlinger. *Team of Rivals* is a book about Lincoln's cabinet by Doris Kearns Goodwin; Goodwin has also written acclaimed books about the Roosevelts, Kennedys, etc.

---

[1] This quote probably comes from Freeman's book *The South to Posterity: An Introduction to the Writings of Confederate History.*

In the early 1900s, Charles Beard was a leading American historian. Beard wrote *An Economic Interpretation of the Constitution*, which argued that the Founding Fathers were motivated by economic interests, not philosophical principles. Beard wrote many other books, including a three-volume survey of American history (*The Rise of American Civilization, America in Midpassage*, and *The American Spirit*). Beard's wife, Mary, was a supporter of women's rights and labor unions; she collaborated with her husband on several books.

Among the younger historians who were influenced by Beard was Richard Hofstadter. In his early work, Hofstadter stressed conflicts between economic interests; his book *Social Darwinism in American Thought, 1860-1915* was critical of American capitalists. Later in his career, however, Hofstadter broke with Beard, and moderated his Leftist views; he emphasized consensus in the American polity, rather than conflict. One of his best-known books is *The American Political Tradition and the Men Who Made It*, which consists of 12 biographical sketches of American statesmen. Hofstadter was a widely-read historian, a public intellectual; he won Pulitzer Prizes for *Anti-intellectualism in American Life* and *The Age of Reform: From Bryan to F.D.R.* Hofstadter respected literary values, and was a friend of the literary critic Alfred Kazin. (Richard Hofstadter should not be confused with Douglas Hofstadter, best known as the author of *Gödel, Escher, Bach*.)

Richard Hofstadter taught at Columbia, where one of his students was Mike Wallace, co-author (with Edwin Burrows) of a two-volume, Pulitzer Prize-winning history of New York City (as of 2011, volume two hasn't been finished; Wallace is writing volume two by himself).

Another prominent historian in the mid-20th century was Arthur M. Schlesinger, Jr. He wrote books on the Presidencies of Franklin Roosevelt and John Kennedy, and he won a Pulitzer Prize for *The Age of Jackson*. His father (Arthur M. Schlesinger) was also a well-known historian.

Geoffrey Ward has written several acclaimed books about Franklin Roosevelt. Ward also wrote the script for *The Civil War* and other KenBurns documentaries.[1] Joseph P. Lash won many awards for *Eleanor and Franklin*; Lash also wrote about Eleanor Roosevelt's later years, and about Franklin Roosevelt's partnership with Winston Churchill.

---

[1] The script for *The Civil War* was co-written by Geoffrey Ward and Ric Burns.

Ken Burns' *CivilWar* documentary was narrated by David McCullough, one of the most popular historians of recent decades. McCullough is known for his biographies of John Adams and Harry Truman, and for his books about the Panama Canal, the American Revolution (*1776*), Teddy Roosevelt (*Mornings on Horseback*), the Wright Brothers, and other subjects.

One of the most popular books on American history is Eric Goldman's *Rendezvous With Destiny: A History of Modern American Reform.* "For decades it was a staple of the undergraduate curriculum in history, highly regarded for its style and its exposition of modern American liberalism."[1] *Rendezvous With Destiny* won the Bancroft Prize in 1953. One scholar described it thus: "lively, well-written, and highly readable, it provided an overview of eight decades of reformers, complete with arresting vignettes of numerous individuals." Goldman was a professor at Princeton for many years.

The history of a town can provide a fresh and valuable perspective on the history of a nation. I recommend a history of Concord, Massachusetts called *Concord: American Town*, by Townsend Scudder. It's written in a sugary, cute style (the style that Huizinga excoriated), but it illustrates the major themes of American history, and it does so in a readable, entertaining way.

If you want a one-volume history of the U.S., a good choice might be *The Oxford History of the American People*, by Samuel Eliot Morison (it was also published as three separate paperback volumes). Morison collaborated with Henry Steele Commager on a popular textbook called *The Growth of the American Republic*. Morison had a special interest in the sea, and won Pulitzer Prizes for his biographies of Columbus and John Paul Jones. He wrote a 15-volume history of the U.S. Navy in World War II. A native of Boston, and a professor at Harvard, Morison was interested in local history, and wrote several books about Massachusetts and Harvard.

11. Napoleon and Hitler

Philosophers and psychologists will never tire of studying Napoleon and Hitler. The similarities between their careers have often been remarked: both were born outside the nations over which they ruled (Napoleon was born in Corsica, Hitler in Austria); both had genius; both

---

[1] en.wikipedia.org/wiki/Eric_F._Goldman

rose from lowly positions to positions of absolute power; both created extensive empires; both were defeated in Russia, then attacked by a coalition of enemies, and eventually destroyed.

Many interesting works have been written about Napoleon. *Napoleon: A Pictorial Biography*, by André Maurois, is an excellent introduction to Napoleon. It's as lively and readable as Maurois's work on Voltaire.

Napoleon the Man, by Merezhkovsky, is a brief and fascinating work. The quotations from those who were acquainted with Napoleon are the most interesting part of this book, much more interesting than the author's own remarks. One who reads this book will want to read the primary sources from which Merezhkovsky gleans his quotations. But these primary sources are voluminous, and require far more patience from the reader than Merezhkovsky's work requires. (Earlier I mentioned Merezhkovsky's work on Leonardo.)

As a boy, Napoleon was enthusiastic and idealistic. He was inspired by ancient history, by Plutarch's stories of Greek and Roman heroes, and by French tragedies. He was determined to emulate the heroes of history and drama, and to do great things. He couldn't understand why the people around him had no desire to be heroes. He turned his back on society; he was solitary and morose.

Napoleon combined a knack for practical affairs with dreamy romanticism; one person who knew him said that he was

> fond of everything which inclined towards reverie: the poems of Ossian,
> subdued light, melancholy music.... Listening to subdued and slow music,
> he would fall into a kind of trance which none of us dared interrupt by the
> slightest movement.[1]

The Personality of Napoleon, by J. H. Rose, is the opposite of Merezhkovsky's *Napoleon the Man*: while Merezhkovsky deals with the soul of Napoleon, Rose deals with the policies of Napoleon—his legal, economic, political and military policies. Though it's different from Merezhkovsky's work, Rose's work is well-written and interesting. Another interesting work about Napoleon is Herold's *The Mind of Napoleon*, a collection of Napoleon's remarks. Bourrienne, Napoleon's schoolmate and secretary, wrote a multi-volume memoir of Napoleon.[2]

---

[1] *Napoleon the Man*, ch. 8

[2] I recommend the English edition edited by R. W. Phipps (New York: Scribner's, 1895). Phipps has improved on the original; he has inserted numerous interesting footnotes, many of which consist of quotations

The contemporary historian Andrew Roberts wrote a biography of Napoleon, and several other Napoleon-related books. Roberts has also written extensively about the World War II era.

Adventures in the Rifle Brigade is a popular memoir by a British soldier, John Kincaid, who fought in the Napoleonic Wars. The English novelist C. S. Forester wrote a popular series of novels about the Royal Navy in the Napoleonic Wars; this series features a character named Horatio Hornblower.

My favorite book about Hitler is Steven Sage's *Ibsen and Hitler*, which presents a startling new theory about Hitler, and contains much information about his life and personality, all in a short and readable volume. The best Hitler biographies are those by Alan Bullock, Joachim Fest, and Ian Kershaw. Of the three, Bullock's is the earliest and the shortest, Kershaw's the latest and the longest. There are many books by people who knew Hitler, such as *The Young Hitler I Knew* by August Kubizek, *Hitler Was My Friend* by Hitler's photographer Heinrich Hoffman, and *Inside the Third Reich* by Albert Speer. Hitler's conversations were published as *Hitler's Table Talk*. Hitler's autobiography, *Mein Kampf*, is occasionally interesting, as is Mussolini's autobiography. Those interested in Mussolini should read Emil Ludwig's *Talks With Mussolini*.

12. Kedourie, etc.

In the field of history, one of the best contemporary scholars is Elie Kedourie, who specialized in nationalism and in Middle Eastern affairs. Though Kedourie was Jewish, he was critical of Jewish nationalism. Kedourie's political views were conservative. One liberal intellectual of whom Kedourie is especially critical is Toynbee; Kedourie's essay, "The Chatham House Version," is a scathing attack on Toynbee.[1]

Paul Johnson is another contemporary historian with a conservative orientation. Johnson's book, *Modern Times*, is a survey of twentieth-century history. While Kedourie's work is scholarly, serious and

---

from other memoirs of the period. He has also deleted certain passages of the original. But even with some passages deleted, the book is still four volumes in length, and each volume consists of about four hundred pages.

[1] This essay can be found in Kedourie's book, *The Chatham House Version and Other Middle Eastern Studies.*

profound, Johnson's work is anecdotal and journalistic. Johnson's anecdotes often shock the reader, as when he describes a politician in India who began each day by drinking a glass of his own urine. But a great historical work is more than a string of anecdotes, it's a serious commentary on the human condition. Unfortunately, modern historians have discovered that their books will be bestsellers if they're crammed with spicy anecdotes.

Kedourie was a student of Michael Oakeshott, a conservative theorist best known for his essay-collection, *Rationalism in Politics*. Like Kedourie, Oakeshott was critical of utopian political plans. According to Oakeshott, the ship of state has neither starting-point nor destination; its goal is to stay afloat.

Another well-known historian of the Middle East is Bernard Lewis. Like Kedourie, Lewis had a high reputation within academia, and like Kedourie, Lewis was conservative in his politics (Lewis supported the effort to topple Saddam Hussein). But while Kedourie was little known outside academia, Lewis burst into prominence after the September 11 attacks. He came as close as any scholar to anticipating those attacks, and in the wake of the attacks, every TV channel wanted to interview him. Lewis is the author of numerous books, including *The Middle East: A Brief History of the Last 2,000 Years* and *What Went Wrong?*

13. Goitein and Grunebaum

While Kedourie and Lewis often wrote about the modern Middle East, Goitein and Grunebaum are known for their studies of the medieval Middle East. S. D. Goitein specialized in Jewish studies, Gustave E. Von Grunebaum in Islamic studies. Both wrote in a scholarly, somewhat dry fashion; their works were never bestsellers. I recommend Goitein's book, *Jews and Arabs: Their Contacts Through The Ages*. Though it requires some patience from the reader, it can teach one much about both Jews and Arabs. Goitein discusses the close connections between Jewish and Arab civilization. For example, he says that Muhammad was heavily influenced by the Jewish religion, while Jewish writers like Yehuda Halevi were heavily influenced by Arab culture. Goitein's deep appreciation for literature is shown in remarks such as,

[When] Yehuda Halevi describes how, while rising from his sleep at midnight, he was overcome by the majestic beauty of the starlit sky, we believe with all our hearts that he has actually had that experience.[1]

Goitein is best known for *A Mediterranean Society*, his five-volume study of medieval Jewish life. These five volumes are based on Goitein's study of documents in a Cairo synagogue (actually the documents were in the archive or "geniza" of the synagogue). Goitein died in 1985, on the very day that he sent the last volume to the publisher.

Grunebaum is best known as the author of *Medieval Islam*. Grunebaum's comments on Islamic literature are as perceptive as Goitein's on Jewish literature. Grunebaum says that around the year 1000 A.D., Islamic civilization began to decline, and Islamic writers became preoccupied with style:

> The writer no longer cares for the incident he describes; he cares only for his description. The facts are degraded to occasions for display—display, that is, of his literary skill, his wit, his erudition.[2]

Grunebaum's comments on Islamic literature and Islamic religion are so profound that they reach beyond Islam, and throw light on literature in general, and religion in general. He quotes a Muslim saint on sainthood:

> The true saint goes in and out among the people and eats and sleeps with them and buys and sells in the market and marries and takes part in social intercourse, and never forgets God for a single moment.[3]

One of Goitein's friends was Gershom Scholem, the leading authority on Jewish mysticism and the Kabbalah.

14. Kennan

One of the most famous literary works created in the U.S. is Melville's *Moby Dick*. Melville wrote *Moby Dick* when he was about 30, then, when it was coolly received, Melville lost interest in writing novels. Public appreciation motivates writers and artists; if their work is ignored, writers and artists sometimes cease creating. Conversely, if their work is appreciated, they may be inspired to put forth their best effort.

---

[1] S. D. Goitein, *Jews and Arabs: Their Contacts Through The Ages*, 7, v

[2] Gustave E. von Grunebaum, *Medieval Islam: A Study in Cultural Orientation*, VII, 1

[3] ibid, IV, 5

The American diplomat and historian George Kennan is a writer whose works were widely read and widely praised. Kennan is one of the few writers who have created enduring literary works based on 20th-century history. Kennan's remarkable literary achievements may be due, in part, to public appreciation. Kennan was internationally famous even before he wrote his first literary work, *Russia Leaves the War* (an account of Russia's departure from World War I, published in 1956). Kennan's specialty was foreign affairs in general and Russia in particular. In Kennan's time, these subjects seemed important and relevant, and Kennan himself seemed to be at the center of world affairs. While other intellectuals may have felt that they were outside American society, irrelevant and ignored, Kennan was at the hub of the wheel, and this may explain why Kennan produced a body of literary work such as few American writers have ever produced.

Fame is a threat to solitude, and Kennan noted that, in the modern U.S., "success brought down upon the head of him who achieved it so appalling a flood of publicity and commercial pressures that he had only two choices: to emigrate and live abroad or never again to write anything worthwhile at all." Kennan says he was besieged by "people who wanted jobs, people who wanted me to read their manuscripts," people who wanted him to deliver a commencement speech, etc. On the other hand, Kennan seemed to sympathize with intellectuals who weren't famous: "to have one's name not known at all is to confront a barrier that can be broken through only with much effort and luck."[1] In short, Kennan discusses the subject of fame in the same interesting and profound way that he discusses so many other subjects.

Kennan's work is full of fresh ideas and fresh insights into international affairs. Kennan is a master at weaving together an interesting narrative; Kennan is able to transport himself into the reader's shoes, and to serve up the sort of tasty and hearty fare that he himself would enjoy, if he were the reader. Kennan has taste.

Kennan is a penetrating critic of American society. He notes that, "our country bristles with imperfections—and some of them very serious ones—of which we are almost universally aware, but lack the resolution and civic vigor to correct." Kennan laments the "headlong overpopulation, industrialization, commercialization and urbanization of society." He doubts whether American democracy can cope with American problems, and wonders whether a different political system could cope with them better. Although he concentrated on foreign

---

[1] George Kennan, *Memoirs 1950-1963*, ch. 1

affairs, "the exercise seemed increasingly, with the years, an empty one; for what use was there, I had to ask, in attempting to protect in its relations to others a society that was clearly failing in its relation to itself?"[1]

John Lewis Gaddis wrote a well-regarded biography of Kennan. Gaddis is a Yale professor who specializes in the Cold War.

15. John Lukacs

One of Kennan's friends was John Lukacs, who grew up in Budapest, and later became an American historian. After Kennan died in 2005, Lukacs wrote a biography of him (*George Kennan: A Study of Character*). Lukacs also published some of his correspondence with Kennan (*George F. Kennan and the Origins of Containment, 1944-1946*). In 1961, Lukacs published a history of the Cold War, which Kennan called "a really great work of philosophical-historical analysis." Lukacs lived near Philadelphia, taught at a small Philadelphia college (Chestnut Hill College), and wrote a book called *Philadelphia: Patricians and Philistines, 1900-1950*. Lukacs is a faithful Catholic, and Chestnut Hill is a Catholic college.

Lukacs felt that, in 1900, the U.S. had a healthy culture, especially in Eastern cities like Philadelphia, but by 1950, the U.S. was sliding into vulgarity and demagoguery. Lukacs is pessimistic about Western civilization.

His hero is Churchill, whom he regards as a champion of tradition, a reactionary. Lukacs wrote much about Hitler, whom he regards as a revolutionary, the opposite of a reactionary. Lukacs often wrote about specific places/times; one of his books is *The Duel: 10 May–31 July 1940: the Eighty-Day Struggle between Churchill and Hitler*. Lukacs wrote a book about his birthplace, *Budapest 1900: A Historical Portrait of a City and Its Culture*. John Lukacs should not be confused with Georg Lukacs, a Marxist philosopher and literary critic who was also born in Budapest.

Lukacs wrote neither for a scholarly audience nor for a popular audience, he wrote for the educated layman, for posterity, but I'm not sure if his works will interest posterity. He valued style, and prided himself on his style, but unlike Kennan, Lukacs wasn't an outstanding stylist.

---

[1] ibid, ch. 4

16. Other Modern Historians

William Manchester was a Wesleyan professor and a specialist in modern history. Many of his works were popular, especially his 3-volume study of Winston Churchill, a study that discusses not only Churchill, but also the waning of the British Empire. Manchester died before his Churchill work was finished, so Paul Reid wrote the third volume.

If you want a one-volume biography of Churchill, a good choice would be Martin Gilbert's *Churchill: A Life*. Gilbert also wrote a history of the Holocaust, a history of the 20th century, histories of the two World Wars, etc. Early in his career, Gilbert assisted Churchill's son in writing an 8-volume biography of Churchill. Gilbert is known for smooth narrative rather than profound ideas.

Churchill once said, "History will be kind to me for I intend to write it." Churchill was a prolific writer, from his early days as a war correspondent until the end of his long life. *My Early Life* deals with his adventures in far-flung corners of the Empire. *Marlborough: His Life and Times* is a 4-volume study of his ancestor, John Churchill, Duke of Marlborough. When World War I ended, Churchill wrote a 6-volume history of it, and later he wrote a 6-volume history of World War II. His last major work was a 4-volume history of the English-speaking peoples. Never a great stylist, his style became rougher when he began dictating his books.

Niall Ferguson has become well-known in recent years for books that are both scholarly and popular. Ferguson is known for his grasp of economics, and he has a chair at the Harvard Business School. One of his books is called *The Cash Nexus: Money and Power in the Modern World, 1700-2000*. Perhaps his *magnum opus* is his two-volume study of the Rothschild banking family. Ferguson's *War of the World* is probably the best history of the 20th century—better than Paul Johnson's *Modern Times*. Ferguson doesn't believe in destiny; he believes that events are shaped not by grand historical laws but by individuals and their decisions. He's interested in "counter-factual history"—that is, he likes to imagine what would have happened if certain decisions hadn't been made. Ferguson's politics are generally conservative, and he often comments on contemporary affairs. He has hosted several documentaries based on his books.

Ferguson wrote a book about the British Empire, and a book about the American "empire." Another historian who wrote about the British Empire is Lawrence James, author of *The Rise and Fall of the British*

Empire. James' work is both scholarly and readable. Jan Morris wrote a 3-volume history of the British Empire (Jan was known as "James Morris" before having a sex-change operation).

Like Niall Ferguson, Ron Chernow often writes about economic history. Chernow has written about prominent business families such as Morgan, Rockefeller, and Warburg; he also wrote biographies of Hamilton and Washington. Chernow is less scholarly, less serious than Ferguson. Chernow is a former journalist, and he tries to entertain rather than enlighten; his writings are filled with anecdotes.

Daniel Yergin is a prominent economic historian and energy expert. Among his books are *The Prize: The Epic Quest for Oil, Money, and Power* and *The Commanding Heights: The Battle for the World Economy* (both these books were made into popular documentaries).[1]

If you want to read about modern European history, a classic in the field is A.J.P. Taylor's *The Struggle for Mastery in Europe, 1848-1918*. Like Niall Ferguson, Taylor didn't believe in destiny; "Nothing is inevitable," said Taylor, "until it happens." Taylor stressed the role of accident in history, and insisted that one of the chief causes of World War I was a wrong turn taken by the Archduke Franz Ferdinand's chauffeur. Taylor wrote lively prose, and delivered lively lectures; at Oxford, his lectures were so popular that the hall became over-crowded. Like Niall Ferguson, Taylor often commented on current events, and often appeared on TV.

A classic of modern history is E. H. Carr's *Twenty Years' Crisis*, which deals with the period between the world wars. Carr had a left-wing bent, and spent much of his life writing a 14-volume history of the Soviet Union. Carr is known as an exponent of realism in International Relations; he emphasized power politics rather than utopian schemes. A contemporary exponent of realism is John Mearsheimer, author of *The Tragedy of Great Power Politics* (2001).

Paul Fussell was an American professor (English Department) who fought in World War II, and wrote acclaimed books about both world wars. Fussell is best known for *The Great War and Modern Memory*, which deals with literary responses to World War I. He was also interested in travel literature, and wrote *Abroad: British Literary Travelling Between the Wars*.

Siegfried Sassoon is one of the British soldiers whom Fussell wrote about. Sassoon's *Memoirs of a Fox-Hunting Man* was acclaimed for its

---

[1] *Commanding Heights* was co-written with Joseph Stanislaw.

humor. Sassoon wrote about his World War I experiences in *Memoirs of an Infantry Officer.*

Hans Kohn was a Jewish historian who was born in Prague, fought on the Austrian-German side in World War I, spent five years in a Russian prison camp, and later became a professor in the U.S. Kohn wrote an autobiographical work called *Living in a World Revolution: My Encounters with History.* Like Elie Kedourie, Kohn had a special interest in nationalism, and wrote several books on the subject. Kohn also wrote *The Habsburg Empire, 1804–1918.*

Robert Massie is an American historian who has written about Russian history and battleship history. Massie attended Yale, won a Rhodes Scholarship, then became a journalist. His son had hemophilia, and when he learned that Nicholas II, the last Czar of Russia, had a hemophiliac son, he began reading about Nicholas II. This led to his first book, *Nicholas and Alexandra* (1967), which became very popular and launched Massie's career as a historian. In 1981, Massie won a Pulitzer Prize for his biography of Peter the Great; he also wrote a biography of Catherine the Great. Massie wrote two books about battleships: *Dreadnought*, which deals with the arms race (i.e., the battleship competition) between Britain and Germany in the decades before World War I, and *Castles of Steel*, which deals with battleships during World War I.

Another popular historian who has written about Russia is Simon Sebag Montefiore. Montefiore wrote a two-volume biography of Stalin, a history of the Romanov dynasty, and a history of Jerusalem. His brother, Hugh Sebag-Montefiore, has written about the Dunkirk evacuation and the Enigma code. The Montefiore brothers are related to Moses Montefiore, who was a prominent banker and philanthropist in the 1800s.

R. R. Palmer was an American historian best known for his textbook, *A History of the Modern World.* Palmer's study of the leaders of the French Revolution, *Twelve Who Ruled*, is a classic in the field.

If one wants to read about the dark side of twentieth-century history, one should read *Auschwitz*, by Sara Nomberg-Przytyk. It's a concise, well-written, moving memoir of the author's internment in Auschwitz. Consider also Primo Levi's famous memoir, *Survival in Auschwitz* (also called *If This Is a Man*), and Viktor Frankl's memoir, *Man's Search for Meaning* (also called *From Death-Camp to Existentialism*). Another classic from the period is the multi-volume diary of Victor Klemperer. Klemperer describes the indignities and cruelties to which Jews were subjected in Hitler's Germany. Though he was Jewish, Klemperer wasn't sent to a concentration camp because his wife was a Gentile.

Some of the most popular books about World War II are those that deal with commandos, guerrillas, escapes, etc. A British commando named W. Stanley Moss wrote two popular books: *Ill Met By Moonlight* and *A War of Shadows*. Fitzroy MacLean wrote *Eastern Approaches*, which deals with guerrilla fighting in Yugoslavia and North Africa, as well as traveling in Central Asia (MacLean also wrote *A Concise History of Scotland*, among other books). Jan Karski, a member of the Polish Resistance, wrote *Story of a Secret State* (Karski also wrote *The Great Powers and Poland: From Versailles to Yalta*). Rudolf Vrba wrote *Escape From Auschwitz*. Hampton Sides wrote *Ghost Soldiers*, about an escape from a Japanese prison.

Quartered Safe Out Here is a memoir about fighting in Burma in World War II. The author, George MacDonald Fraser, also wrote a popular series of novels featuring a character named Flashman; one might describe these novels as comic-historical. *The Railway Man*, by Eric Lomax, describes the author's experiences as a prisoner of war, forced by the Japanese to work on the Burma Railway. *Unbroken* is a bestselling book by Laura Hillenbrand about an American soldier (Louis Zamperini) imprisoned by the Japanese.

Before turning to travel literature, mention should be made of Kissinger's two volumes of memoirs. Like many modern historical works, Kissinger's memoirs are so lengthy that they're suitable only for specialists, not for general readers. But Kissinger's work has a combination of profundity and humor that sets it apart from most modern works. "It is not often," Kissinger writes of his first trip to China, "that one can recapture as an adult the quality that in one's youth made time seem to stand still; that gave every event the mystery of novelty.... This is how it was for me as the aircraft crossed the snow-capped Himalayas."[1]

17. Travel Literature

I mentioned above that Jan Morris wrote a 3-volume history of the British Empire. Morris also wrote travel literature, including studies of Oxford, Wales, Trieste, Hong Kong, Spain, the U.S., etc. Morris wrote a general study of Venice (*The World of Venice*), and also a concise history

---

[1] *White House Years*, ch. 19

of Venice (*The Venetian Empire: A Sea Voyage*). The American writer Mary McCarthy wrote *The Stones of Florence* and *Venice Observed.*

One of the most highly-regarded travel writers is Robert Byron, whose *Road to Oxiana* (1937) describes a journey through the Middle East to Afghanistan. Byron had a keen appreciation of architecture. Inspired by Byron, Patrick Leigh Fermor walked from Holland to Constantinople while still in his teens; Fermor later wrote two acclaimed books about this journey, *A Time of Gifts*, and *Between the Woods and the Water.* Peter Fleming's *Brazilian Adventure* (1933) is a popular account of an expedition into Brazil's wild interior, searching for the lost explorer Percy Fawcett. Paul Theroux's *Great Railway Bazaar* (1975) describes a rail journey from London to East Asia. Bruce Chatwin's *In Patagonia* (1977) is also a classic in the travel genre. Chatwin's *Songlines* deals with Australian aborigines. William Dalrymple has written acclaimed travel books and also historical works; his book about Delhi is called *City of Djinns* (1994). Some of the best travel writing is by people who weren't primarily travel writers—novelists like D. H. Lawrence, Graham Greene, Evelyn Waugh, Somerset Maugham, etc.

Robert D. Kaplan is a travel writer and foreign-affairs scholar. Kaplan first became prominent in 1993, after publishing *Balkan Ghosts: A Journey Through History.* In 1994, Kaplan published an essay called "The Coming Anarchy," which painted a grim picture of life in West Africa.

A classic about sea travel is *Two Years Before the Mast* (1840), by Richard Henry Dana; D. H. Lawrence discussed Dana's book in his *Studies in Classic American Literature.* Another notable book about sea travel is *Sailing Alone Around the World* (1900), by Joshua Slocum.

Graham Robb, who wrote several biographies of French writers (Balzac, Hugo, Baudelaire, etc.), also wrote a popular study of Paris, and a book about France as a whole (*The Discovery of France: A Historical Geography*). Like Robb, Alistair Horne is an English writer who specialized in France. He has written books about the French Revolution, Napoleon, the Paris Commune, the French war in Algeria, etc. His *Seven Ages of Paris* is a history of the city.

If you'd like to read a history of London, consider Peter Ackroyd's *London: The Biography* and his *Illustrated London.* Ackroyd is a prolific writer of biography, history, and historical fiction. His biography of Thomas More won the James Tait Black Prize in 1998, and his biography of T. S. Eliot won the Whitbread Award in 1984.

18. Biographies and Autobiographies

Boswell's *Life of Johnson* is widely regarded as the best English biography. Boswell's stately, formal prose reminds one of Gibbon's prose. Boswell describes Johnson's life year by year; Boswell gives a complete, detailed record of Johnson's life. Since much of Boswell's *Life of Johnson* is dry and uninteresting, it should be read in an abridged version.

Boswell recounts Johnson's conversations, in which Johnson expresses his views on a wide range of subjects. Johnson's political and religious views were generally conservative. Johnson didn't agree with his contemporary, Rousseau, that everyone should work: "All would be losers, were all to work for all—they would have no intellectual improvement. All intellectual improvement arises from leisure: all leisure arises from one working for another."[1]

The autobiography of the Italian artist, Benvenuto Cellini, is almost as famous as Boswell's *Life of Johnson*. But Cellini's autobiography is merely an adventure story—sometimes entertaining, but never profound. Benjamin Franklin's autobiography is more interesting than Cellini's; Franklin's autobiography was one of Kafka's favorite books. But Franklin's literary talents were limited, and his autobiography contains some heavy moralizing; it isn't a first rate book.

Van Gogh's letters to his brother, Theo, are a kind of autobiography. They should be read in an abridged version, and they're usually published in an abridged version. Van Gogh's letters are well-written, interesting and moving; they're one of the outstanding works in world literature. Van Gogh vividly describes his struggles with poverty, loneliness, and lack of recognition. "My constitution would be sound enough," writes van Gogh, "if I had not to fast so long, but I have had continually to choose between fasting and working less, and so far as possible I have chosen the former."[2] Van Gogh found solace for his sufferings in painting: "In my opinion I am often as rich as Croesus, not in money, but rich because I have found in my work something to which I can devote myself with heart and soul, and which gives inspiration and zest to life."[3]

One of the most prolific modern biographers is the German writer, Emil Ludwig. Many of Ludwig's full-length biographies (such as his

---

[1] *The Life of Johnson*, by James Boswell, Aetat. 64
[2] *Dear Theo*, New American Library, 1969, p. 226
[3] *Dear Theo*, New American Library, 1969, p. 195

biography of Napoleon) are mediocre. Some of his short biographies, however, are interesting. I recommend his book, *Genius and Character*, which is a collection of short biographies. Ludwig's *Three Titans*—about Rembrandt, Michelangelo and Beethoven—is also interesting.

Lin Yutang is a modern Chinese writer who lived abroad, and spent his career teaching foreigners about China. One of his books is a biography of the eleventh century Chinese poet, Su Tungpo; it's called *The Gay Genius: The Life and Times of Su Tungpo*. This book can teach one much about Chinese civilization. Lin Yutang has some literary talent, but like many modern writers, he doesn't write concisely. His biography of Su Tungpo is considerably longer than it should be.

If you're interested in Chinese civilization, you should also consider the works of Arthur Waley. Waley wrote three books about the life and work of three Chinese poets: Yuan Mei, Li Bai, and Bai Juyi. Waley also published numerous translations of Asian literature, including a book called *170 Chinese Poems*. This book was a favorite of the art historian, Kenneth Clark. "Of all the writers of my youth," Clark wrote, "Arthur Waley was the most valuable. He combined a scholar's feeling for truth (and what a scholar!) with a poet's feeling for language."[1]

Another way to approach Chinese civilization is to experiment with the ancient divination book, the *Book of Changes*, or *I Ching*. Divination means foretelling the future, or getting advice, by a random process, such as rolling dice, or flipping coins. Jung had great respect for the *I Ching*, which draws upon an affinity between the physical world (the falling coins) and the human world, just as Jung's theory of synchronicity draws upon an affinity between the physical world and the human world. The most famous translation/analysis of the *I Ching* is Richard Wilhelm's, but I find it complex and confusing. I recommend a shorter version called *The Illustrated I Ching*, which is pleasurable to read, and easy to experiment with.

If you want to learn about India, consider the works of Nirad Chaudhuri. Chaudhuri wrote two books about his own life and times: *The Autobiography of an Unknown Indian* and *Thy Hand, Great Anarch!* Chaudhuri also wrote a study of Hinduism, studies of modern culture, and biographies of Max Muller and Robert Clive. He won the Duff Cooper Prize for *The Continent of Circe*, a collection of essays about India. Chaudhuri wrote excellent English, and had a deep knowledge of the Western literary tradition.

---

[1] *Another Part of the Wood*, p. 81

The best of all modern biographers is Lytton Strachey. Strachey was a friend of Virginia Woolf, and a member of the so-called Bloomsbury Group, which flourished in London in the early 20th century. Strachey admired French literature, and lamented that England had never produced a biographer capable of

> compressing into a few shining pages the manifold existences of men.... To preserve [a] becoming brevity—a brevity which excludes everything that is redundant and nothing that is significant—that, surely, is the first duty of the biographer.[1]

Strachey is best known as the author of *Eminent Victorians*, which compresses into a few shining and witty pages the lives of four Victorians: Cardinal Manning, Florence Nightingale, Dr. Arnold, and General Gordon. *Eminent Victorians* is a superb literary work. I also recommend Strachey's biography of Queen Victoria, and his *Elizabeth and Essex*, which brings the Elizabethan age alive in just 250 pages. Strachey's *Landmarks in French Literature* might be compared to Gilbert Murray's *History of Ancient Greek Literature* and J. W. Mackail's *Latin Literature*.

---

[1] *Eminent Victorians*, preface

V. Miscellaneous

1. Ruskin

John Ruskin was one of the most influential English writers of the nineteenth century. In the 1840's, while still in his early twenties, Ruskin began his first book, *Modern Painters*. This book was designed as a defense of the English painter Turner, but it gradually grew into a five-volume work on painting in general. Ruskin followed *Modern Painters* with *The Seven Lamps of Architecture* and *The Stones of Venice*. These two works praised Gothic architecture, and contributed to the architectural movement known as the Gothic Revival. Ruskin was the first major writer to devote himself to visual art. The popularity of Ruskin's works on painting and architecture was a factor in the establishment of art history as a branch of study at major universities. The public was ravished by Ruskin's eloquent descriptions of nature and art.

Ruskin teaches his readers to see; after reading *Modern Painters*, Charlotte Brontë said that she felt she had been given a new sense— sight. Ruskin teaches his readers to appreciate nature—to notice clouds, shadows, trees that they hadn't noticed before. Ruskin also teaches his readers to appreciate architecture—to notice cornices, moldings, pediments that they hadn't noticed before. Ruskin educates his readers by giving them a greater appreciation of the world around them—both natural and man-made.

During the nineteenth century, European intellectuals seemed to become more fervent about art as they became less fervent about religion; art was becoming a new religion. Ruskin, the leading art critic of the nineteenth century, was more than a critic, he was a prophet, he stirred people's deepest feelings. Proust had so much admiration for Ruskin that he stumbled through everything Ruskin wrote, despite his scanty knowledge of English. Proust even translated two of Ruskin's books into French. Proust said of Ruskin, "When I see how mightily this dead man lives, I know how slight a thing death is." Tolstoy said, "Ruskin was one of the most remarkable men, not only of England and our time, but all countries and all times. He was one of those rare men who think with their hearts."

Just as Mencius thought that only a good man could write good prose, so Ruskin thought that only a good man could create good art. And if an artist didn't enjoy his work, if his heart wasn't in it, it wouldn't be good art; according to Ruskin, only the happy artist could create good art. Ruskin didn't discuss art by itself, he discussed art in the context of morality, religion, politics, etc. Ruskin connected art to life in general, and thus his art criticism often reaches the level of philosophy. Ruskin believed that modern man couldn't create good art because he didn't lead a good life, because he had no religion except the worship of wealth. "A nation cannot last," said Ruskin, "as a money-making mob: it cannot with impunity... go on despising literature, despising science, despising art, despising nature, despising compassion, and concentrating its soul on Pence."[1]

Ruskin gradually evolved from an art critic into an economist. Just as he had connected art to life, so too he connected economics to life. He insisted that wealth and technology were worthless if they didn't help people to live better. He insisted that, "there is no wealth but life."[2] His best-known work on economics is *Unto This Last*, a short, powerful book that criticized capitalism. *Unto This Last* inspired the founders of the British Labor Party, and also inspired Gandhi, who translated it into one of India's dialects. Many of the ideas expressed in *Unto This Last* have become widely accepted in our time, such as the idea that there should be an *esprit de corps* between labor and management.

Ruskin's complete works fill many volumes because most of his books are lengthy, and many of his lectures have been published. His best short works are the essay "Traffic," *The Seven Lamps of Architecture* and *Sesame and Lilies*.[3] *The Darkening Glass: A Portrait of Ruskin's Genius* is an excellent commentary on Ruskin's works. *The Genius of John Ruskin* is the best anthology of his writings.

---

[1] *Sesame and Lilies*, first lecture

[2] *Unto This Last*, "Ad Valorem"

[3] I recommend David Barrie's abridged version of *Modern Painters* (Knopf, New York, 1987), and Jan Morris' abridged version of *The Stones of Venice* (Little, Brown & Company, 1981).

2. Berenson

Bernard Berenson was born into a Jewish family in Lithuania in 1865, but grew up in Boston. Like many intellectuals, Berenson read voraciously during his teenage years. After studying ancient languages at Harvard, Berenson received a scholarship to continue his language studies in Europe. While he was in Europe, he became interested in visual art, and he discovered that there was much uncertainty about who had painted what. While having breakfast with a friend at an Italian café, he decided to make a thorough study of Italian painting, using the scholarly methods he had learned as a language student. "Here at Bergamo," he said to his friend, "and in all the fragrant and romantic valleys that branch out northward, we must not stop till we are sure that every Lotto is a Lotto, every Cariani a Cariani, every Previtali a Previtali."[1]

Berenson's first books were on Italian painting. The Harvard professor William James, who had taught psychology to Berenson, praised Berenson's early work for its application of psychology to art criticism. One of Berenson's early works, *Italian Painters of the Renaissance*, is a favorite of mine—highly readable and interesting. Like Freud, Berenson turned to more general, philosophical works in his later years. These late works—such as *Sketch for a Self-Portrait* and *Aesthetics and History in the Visual Arts*—might be the best "forgotten books" of the 20th century. Art specialists have little use for these late works, which were written for educated laymen, for generalists. These late works have no audience today because, in our specialized age, generalists are an endangered species.

Though he was a U.S. citizen, Berenson spent most of his life in Italy. He was often consulted by people who wanted to authenticate paintings, and his consulting work made him rich. He bought a spacious home near Florence, *I Tatti*. When World War II broke out, he couldn't bear to leave his beloved home, so he lingered in Italy until it became impossible to leave; eventually the Germans took over his house, and he barely avoided arrest.

Like Hemingway, Berenson was known for his good looks and his numerous affairs. Like Hemingway, Berenson had female descendants who were famous actresses/models. Berenson had the complicated, multi-faceted personality that Hemingway had. Hemingway's first wife, Hadley, said that Hemingway had as many different facets as the

---

[1] *Sketch for a Self-Portrait*, Part 1, Ch. 11, p. 60

sketches in a geometry text. Likewise, Kenneth Clark said, "The personality of Mr. Berenson was so strange and complex."[1]

While Ruskin exemplifies the Victorian age, Berenson represents the intersection of the nineteenth century and the twentieth century. Berenson lived through both world wars, and finally died in 1959 at the age of ninety-four. Berenson tried to carry classical Western culture into the twentieth century. Berenson defended the old values of Western civilization when they were threatened by totalitarian politics and by "modern art." Berenson lacks Ruskin's moral fervor. But Berenson didn't bury himself in the fine points of painting; he believed that visual art should be part of culture in general, and culture should be part of life. Berenson published several volumes of journals, journals that integrate culture and life. His passion for culture didn't flag in his old age; when he was 80, he wrote a book called *One Year's Reading for Fun*.

Like many people before him, Berenson enjoyed life more when he felt it drawing to a close; when he was approaching 90, he said, "I would willingly stand at street corners, hat in hand, asking passers-by to drop their unused minutes into it."[2] He was unwilling to die, and leave his house and library; he wanted to stay around after death, and haunt it. Surrounded by his books, his paintings, his gardens, and his friends, Berenson said, "I have attained Goethe's promise that what one ardently desires when young one will realize in old age.... It is easy now to live in ecstasy."[3]

3. Other Art Historians

It's symptomatic of the decline of modern culture that Berenson's name isn't widely known, and his works aren't readily available. Another modern writer on art, Kenneth Clark, is more widely known than Berenson, partly because he made a television documentary, "Civilization." Clark wrote excellent prose. I recommend all of Clark's books: *Rembrandt and the Italian Renaissance*, *Leonardo*, etc. One might describe Clark as a member of the English school of art history, a school that began with Ruskin; Clark was fascinated by Ruskin, and edited some of his books.

---

[1] *Another Part of the Wood*, p. 133

[2] Kenneth Clark, *The Other Half*, Harper & Row, 1977, ch. 4, p. 107

[3] *Sketch for a Self-Portrait*, Part 3, ch. 11, p. 175

The German school of art history began with Jacob Burckhardt (whom we discussed earlier), and continued with Wölfflin and Panofsky. Burckhardt lived in Switzerland, and during the summer he would walk to Italy to study painting and architecture, then return to Switzerland in the fall, and lecture at the University of Basel about the art works he had seen. Burckhardt wrote *Cicerone*, which attempts to describe all of Italy's major art works. Burckhardt's disciple, Heinrich Wölfflin, was more precise and scientific than Burckhardt, and Panofsky is even more scholarly than Wölfflin. One might compare Burckhardt to a traveler who spends one night in each city, Wölfflin to a traveler who spends the whole summer studying the art works of one city, and Panofsky to a traveler who spends the whole summer studying the works of one artist in one city. Perhaps every branch of knowledge goes through a similar evolution, from broad survey to narrow specialty.

Wölfflin focused on Renaissance and Baroque art, analyzing the differences between these two periods, and attempting to develop a grand theory of artistic forms. Though his work is occasionally dry and dull, it contains a deep knowledge of art, and a patient reader will find it rewarding. Wölfflin writes thus of Michelangelo:

> His interest was in the definition of form, and only the human body seemed worthy of representation to him, for whom the infinite variety of created things simply did not exist. For him, the human race was not the humanity of this world, with its thousands of different individuals, but a race apart, transposed into the colossal.[1]

Erwin Panofsky was born in Germany; only Germany could have produced such an erudite, scholarly writer. Because he was Jewish, Panofsky left Germany in 1933, and came to the U.S.; he ceased writing in German, and began writing in English. He was almost as prolific as Kenneth Clark, treating a wide variety of subjects, including Albrecht Durer, the Renaissance, and Gothic architecture. His specialty was iconology—that is, the meaning of artistic symbols. For example, Durer's *Fall of Man* contains, in addition to Adam and Eve, a variety of animals—a mouse, a rabbit, etc.; Panofsky tries to explain what these animals signify. Panofsky's work is dry and difficult to read; he puts two or three footnotes on each page, as if to test the reader's patience. If the reader has sufficient patience to keep going, he'll find that Panofsky's work is full of profound thoughts and valuable insights.

---

[1] *Classic Art: An Introduction to the Italian Renaissance*, ch. 3

Rudolf Wittkower was also born in Germany, and also spent much of his career in the U.S. Though not as well-known as Panofsky, Wittkower acquired a high reputation among art historians, chiefly for his works on the Italian Baroque. He also wrote a book of short biographies with his wife, Margot; it's called *Born under Saturn: The character and conduct of artists* (it was believed, during the Renaissance, that Saturn's influence caused genius and melancholy).

I can't leave the subject of art without mentioning James Cahill's masterpiece, *Chinese Painting*. Cahill's book is clear, concise, profound, and well suited to both the specialist and the general reader. The evolution of Chinese painting styles and aesthetic theories is a remarkable story, a story that will fascinate anyone interested in culture.

4. Tocqueville

Tocqueville's *Democracy in America* is more than a study of American society, it's a study of democracy in general, and of modern society in general. *Democracy in America* is one of the outstanding works of modern times—profound, philosophical, readable. It's on a par with Ortega's *Revolt of the Masses*, a book which it resembles in many ways. Though Tocqueville, like Ortega, is generally critical of modern society, his goal is to understand, not to criticize, hence he mixes praise with blame. *Democracy in America* would be better if it were written in aphoristic form, or if it were skillfully abridged; some of its chapters are dry, and others are repetitious.

Tocqueville matured rapidly and died young. He wrote *Democracy in America* when he was in his late twenties, and he died before completing the multi-volume work on the French Revolution that he had planned to write. He did, however, complete *The Old Regime and the French Revolution*, which is an excellent book. Many of the features that Tocqueville found in America, such as political and social equality, he also found in France.

Equality, according to Tocqueville, is the fundamental fact of modern times. Formerly, says Tocqueville, people felt themselves to be part of a class, a group, or a guild, they didn't feel themselves to be individuals, and even the word "individuality" was unknown. Modern society, however, is virtually classless, and people don't feel themselves to be part of anything greater than themselves. Even the family has lost its importance, and only the individual remains.

The modern individual, says Tocqueville, cares little about the past or the future, little about religion or culture. The modern individual's chief concern is money. Though his life is filled with activity, he has no high goals, no vast ambitions, no deep thoughts. Tocqueville is pessimistic about the future of Western civilization:

> I fear that the mind may keep folding itself up in a narrower compass forever without producing new ideas, that men will wear themselves out in trivial, lonely, futile activity, and that for all its constant agitation humanity will make no advance.[1]

Tocqueville has been translated into English numerous times; perhaps the best translation is Arthur Goldhammer's.

5. Solzhenitsyn

Solzhenitsyn, in his speech at Harvard in 1978, remarked on several of the same traits in Western society that Tocqueville observed. Like Tocqueville, Solzhenitsyn observed that Western man is obsessed with material things:

> The constant desire to have still more things and a still better life and the struggle to this end imprint many Western faces with worry and even depression.... This active and tense competition comes to dominate all human thought.

Like Tocqueville, Solzhenitsyn observed that there is little intellectual freedom in the West, since the media, academia and public opinion reject and persecute views that are outside the mainstream.

Solzhenitsyn notices several traits in Western society that hadn't yet appeared in Tocqueville's time. For example, Solzhenitsyn notices a decline in the arts, a decline of courage, an invasion of advertising, and an emphasis on individual rights that leaves society at the mercy of criminals. In short, if Tocqueville's picture of Western society is bleak, Solzhenitsyn's is bleaker still.

> Destructive and irresponsible freedom [says Solzhenitsyn] has been granted boundless space. Society has turned out to have scarce defense against the abyss of human decadence, for example against the misuse of liberty for moral violence against young people, such as motion pictures full of pornography, crime, and horror.

---

[1] *Democracy in America*, II, iii, 21

If one considers Solzhenitsyn's Harvard speech to be an essay, it's one of the most powerful essays ever written; one can't praise it too highly. It has brevity, the rarest of literary virtues. I also recommend a speech by Solzhenitsyn called "The Relentless Cult of Novelty," in which he criticizes avant-garde art.[1] Solzhenitsyn's best books are his non-fiction works, *The Gulag Archipelago* and *The Oak and the Calf*; I don't recommend his fiction, which is as harsh and unpleasing as lemon juice.

The purpose of *The Gulag Archipelago* is to tell the story of the prison camps run by the Russian Communists, and to make sure that the sufferings of the prisoners are remembered. The *Gulag* is full of vivid stories and interesting anecdotes. But Solzhenitsyn is so appalled by the crimes of the Communists, and so intent on describing them to the world, that he gives the reader too much detail, and the result is a book about 2,000 pages long. This raises questions: is the *Gulag* a great literary work? Is it a literary work at all? Fortunately, a good abridged version has been made by Edward Ericson. I suggest that the reader start with this abridged version, then continue with *The Oak and the Calf*, which describes how Solzhenitsyn wrote the *Gulag*, how he published it in the face of government opposition, etc. I also recommend Michael Scammell's long biography of Solzhenitsyn.

Solzhenitsyn is a man on a mission; his mission is to tell the world about one of the greatest crimes in the history of mankind, the murder of around 20-25 million Soviets, who were tortured to death, worked to death, frozen to death, and starved to death by the Soviet government.

Another eyewitness account of Stalin's camps is *Journey Into the Whirlwind*, by Eugenia Ginzburg (the sequel is called *Within the Whirlwind*).

6. Bloom and Edmundson

Bloom's *Closing of the American Mind*, published in 1987, discusses some of the same subjects that Solzhenitsyn discussed. But Bloom, being an American, has a more intimate knowledge of Western society than Solzhenitsyn. For example, Bloom understands the importance of rock music in Western society:

> Nothing is more singular about this generation [writes Bloom] than its addiction to music.... Today, a very large proportion of young people between the ages of ten and twenty live for music.... Rock music has one

---

[1] This speech was printed in the NY Times Book Review, 2/7/93.

appeal only, a barbaric appeal, to sexual desire—not love, not *eros*, but sexual desire undeveloped and untutored.[1]

Bloom's chief interest is higher education, hence the subtitle of his book is, *How Higher Education Has Failed Democracy and Impoverished the Souls of Today's Students.* Bloom points out that today's students have little interest in reading serious literature; today's students can see that a knowledge of the humanities won't help them in any career. Today's professors are specialists who have no interest in culture as a whole. Today's colleges divide culture into departments, and fail to provide a general education.

Though Bloom's book is occasionally interesting, it isn't as profound or as concise as Solzhenitsyn's speech. While Bloom has talent, Solzhenitsyn has genius. Though Bloom's book is one of the classics of our time, it isn't one of the classics of all time.

About ten years after Bloom's book appeared, Mark Edmundson wrote an essay that was widely read and widely discussed, an essay that resembles Bloom's book. Like Bloom, Edmundson criticized American higher education, and championed the classics. But while Bloom was fond of Plato and Leo Strauss, Edmundson was fond of Emerson and Whitman. Edmundson's essay ("On the Uses of the Liberal Arts") is a superb literary work, as well as a penetrating critique of the modern soul. Both Bloom and Edmundson argue that modern man doesn't worship heroes, doesn't admire geniuses, because he wants to feel "comfortable in his skin without having to suffer unpleasant comparisons."[2]

7. Matthew Arnold

While Tocqueville, Solzhenitsyn and Bloom have a special interest in American society, Matthew Arnold has a special interest in English society. Arnold was a leading Victorian poet, as well as a literary critic and social critic. Arnold's essays—"Culture and Anarchy," "Democracy," and "Equality"—discuss English society in the late 1800's, just as Bloom discusses American society in the late 1900's. Arnold reminds his contemporaries of the importance of culture; he argues that freedom, the right to speak one's mind, and the right to vote, are of little value if the people lack culture, lack high ideals, and lack great thoughts.

---

[1] I, 3

[2] I, 2

Freedom, according to Arnold, is "one of those things... worshipped in itself, without enough regarding the ends for which freedom is to be desired."[1] Freedom in modern society, says Arnold, isn't leading to any high goal, it's leading only to anarchy. Likewise, Arnold says that physical health is now being worshipped for its own sake, not as part of a higher ideal. Arnold argues that health and fitness shouldn't be ends in themselves, just as wealth shouldn't be an end in itself.

Arnold's essays are more elegant and cultured than Bloom's *Closing of the American Mind*, but they aren't as profound as Tocqueville's *Democracy in America*, or Solzhenitsyn's Harvard speech. Arnold's essays are written for his time, not for all time, hence they're a kind of journalism, not real literature. If you want to read a book about Arnold, consider Lionel Trilling's *Matthew Arnold*.

8. Max Weber

Weber's name has become synonymous with sociology. Weber's most famous book is *The Protestant Ethic and the Spirit of Capitalism*. This book, like many of Weber's writings, opposes the Marxist view that a nation's economy shapes its worldview; Weber argues that, on the contrary, a nation's worldview shapes its economy. In *The Protestant Ethic*, Weber argues that Protestant beliefs shaped capitalism.

Weber discusses the profound impact that ascetic Protestantism had on the Anglo-American peoples. He says that it destroyed their spontaneity, and even affected their facial expression. (Frenchmen have often described Englishmen as gloomy.) Weber blames ascetic Protestantism for creating the most materialistic civilization in history. The Middle Ages had glorified poverty and begging; some monastic orders relied on begging to support themselves. Ascetic Protestantism, on the other hand, glorified work and material wealth.

While *The Protestant Ethic* is an interesting and readable book, most of Weber's other books are dry. One of his books, however, is even more interesting than *The Protestant Ethic*: his book on Confucianism and Taoism. This book not only explores Confucianism and Taoism, it explores Chinese civilization and the Chinese soul. It sheds light on Western civilization by contrasting it with Chinese civilization. And finally, it discusses Weber's central idea, namely, the idea that religion and ethics shape economic life.

---

[1] "Culture and Anarchy," 2

Weber observes that the Chinese have a certain calmness, a placidity, a "striking lack of 'nerves'," an "unlimited patience."[1] Weber ascribes these traits to religion, to the absence of the ascetic religious practices found in the West; he also ascribes these traits to a relatively low usage of alcohol. Weber says that there was no tension in China between "nature and deity," between "consciousness of sin and need for salvation"; such tension was at the heart of Western civilization. While the Chinese quietly adapted himself to the world, the Westerner rejected the world, aspired toward the perfection of God, and tried to transform his own nature.

An interesting sketch of Weber himself can be found in the introduction to a book called *From Max Weber: Essays in Sociology*, edited by Gerth and Mills.

9. Thorstein Veblen

Veblen was an American professor of economics who did most of his writing in the early 1900's. Veblen doesn't deal with economics in the narrow sense, but rather with sociology and cultural anthropology. Veblen is best known as the author of *The Theory of the Leisure Class*, a book which sets forth Veblen's famous theory of "conspicuous consumption." Veblen is one of the three or four most profound thinkers that America has produced. He has a fresh perspective on human affairs, and he sheds light on many aspects of society.

Just as Huizinga interpreted human affairs in terms of play, so Veblen interprets human affairs in terms of status. *The Theory of the Leisure Class* begins by arguing that people desire status, they desire the esteem of other people; only exceptional individuals are satisfied with the contempt of other people. How is status obtained? At an early period of history, says Veblen, status was obtained by trophies, by symbols of success in war or hunting. Status could be lost by manual labor, so some hunters had their wives carry the game they had killed back to their home, lest they lose by working the status that they had won by killing. At a later point in history, status was obtained by titles of nobility, coats

---

[1] *The Religion of China: Confucianism and Taoism*, VIII. It should be mentioned that the latter part of this book is more interesting than the beginning; Part One, "Sociological Foundations", is of little interest or importance.

of arms, etc. Status was also obtained by the possession of numerous women, and numerous slaves or servants.

When Veblen looks at contemporary society, he finds that men who can't afford servants must rely on their wife to symbolize wealth and obtain status. Wives can symbolize wealth by leisure, by not working. If leisure were hidden and inconspicuous, it wouldn't confer status, hence leisure must be flaunted, it must be conspicuous. A woman's leisure can be displayed by having long fingernails, high-heeled shoes, clean clothes, and anything else that's incompatible with manual labor. Men can show they aren't laborers, and acquire status, by wearing clean white shirts, shiny shoes, etc. Veblen says that the Chinese custom of foot-binding was a means of displaying a woman's leisure and obtaining status.

But leisure isn't the only way to obtain status; consumption can also obtain status. But consumption, like leisure, must be flaunted, it must be conspicuous. An expensive car, for example, is a conspicuous form of consumption because it's visible even to people who never see your home or your wife's diamond ring. People strive for wealth, says Veblen, not merely to live, but to obtain status through conspicuous consumption.

Veblen applies his theory of status to religion, and argues that God is the epitome of status. He compares priests to footmen who confer status on their master, and he compares churches to huge palaces that confer status on their owner. He notes that people come to church in their cleanest, most expensive clothes, and they abstain from work on holy days.

The theory of status is Veblen's central theory, but it isn't his only theory. Veblen's writings are full of interesting ideas. I recommend *Imperial Germany and the Industrial Revolution*, "Christian Morals and the Competitive System," "Salesmanship and the Churches," "The Higher Learning," and "Patriotism and the Price System."

10. Morris and Lorenz

Desmond Morris is an Englishman who specializes in the study of animals. During the last few decades, Morris has written many books, some about animal behavior, others about human behavior. Like Veblen, Morris has a fresh and interesting perspective on human affairs. While Veblen viewed human affairs in terms of status, Morris views human affairs from the standpoint of animal behavior. Like Veblen, Morris can deepen one's understanding of man, and of everyday life.

Morris is a student not of human thought, human history, or human nature, but rather of human behavior. He observes how people act—how they walk, how they hold themselves, how they greet each other, etc. He notes that in some primitive societies, people prostrated themselves before their king or their master. Later, kneeling replaced prostration. Later still, curtsying and bowing replaced kneeling. Curtsying is a sort of abortive kneeling, it shows an intention to kneel. Bowing is a way of lowering oneself, and thus showing respect for another. Removing one's hat is also a way of lowering oneself. Saluting is "a stylized modification of the act of removing the hat," just as curtsying is a stylized modification of kneeling. Embracing was once a common form of greeting, and is still found in the Latin countries. Russians, like the ancient Greeks and Romans, greet each other by kissing. Morris says that the British restrict body contacts, and prefer the handshake to the embrace. (As Weber said, ascetic Protestantism had a profound impact on the Anglo-American peoples.) When people stand erect and shake hands, it's a sign of equality, it's the opposite of prostration, which is a sign of inequality. (As Tocqueville said, equality is the distinguishing feature of modern society.)

When we feel uneasy, says Morris, we often "rearrange ornaments, light a cigarette, clean our spectacles, glance at a wrist-watch, pour a drink, or nibble a piece of food."[1] Morris calls these "displacement activities," and he observes something similar in the animal world. Observing a group of chimpanzees, Morris notices that subordinate individuals "can easily be identified by the higher frequency of their displacement self-grooming activities. The truly dominant individual can be recognized by the almost complete absence of such actions."[2]

Morris isn't a literary man, and he has little interest in prose style. Morris won't be as interesting to posterity as he is to us, because human behavior won't be a new and unexplored field to posterity. If Morris' works are classics, they're mortal classics, not immortal classics. *The Naked Ape*, Morris' best-known book, is a good introduction to human behavior. I also recommend *The Human Zoo*, *Intimate Behaviour*, and *Animal Days*.

While Morris writes for laymen, Konrad Lorenz, another student of animal behavior, writes mainly for specialists and scholars. While Morris applies his knowledge of animals to the study of humans, Lorenz generally stays within the field of animal behavior. But some of Lorenz's

---

[1] *The Naked Ape*, 5
[2] *The Naked Ape*, 5

remarks on animals have obvious analogies in the sphere of human behavior. Lorenz says, for example, that

> a young female [goose] that has fallen in love never tries to force her company on the object of her passion. She never follows him directly when he walks away; she merely turns up, as if by chance, in places where she knows he can often be found. [1]

Lorenz notes that animals can communicate through non-verbal means: "It is incredible, what minimal signs, completely imperceptible to man, animals will receive and interpret rightly." [2]

Lorenz's best book is *King Solomon's Ring*. I recommend it highly; it's a fascinating, concise and readable work on animal behavior. I also recommend *On Aggression*, which argues that aggression often plays a constructive role among animals; according to Lorenz, aggression isn't simply the product of the death-instinct, as Freud had argued.

11. Richard Feynman

"Surely You're Joking, Mr. Feynman!" is a book about the life of the American physicist, Richard Feynman. It's an interesting and amusing book that achieved wide popularity. Feynman had an inquiring mind and an abundance of vital energy, and he had many wild adventures during his life. Feynman was more than a Nobel-Prize-winning scientist; he was also a talented artist and musician. One of the people whom he played drums with, Ralph Leighton, was fascinated by his stories, and thought they should be collected in a book; *"Surely You're Joking"* is Leighton's collection of Feynman's stories.

This is a case of a good book being created simply and naturally; this is the oldest form of literature—oral literature, storytelling. Feynman told stories because he loved them; Leighton listened to the stories, and later collected them, because he loved them. Feynman didn't sit down at a desk and say, "I'm going to write a book because I'm a writer," or "I'm going to write a book because I need to make money," or "I'm going to write a book because I can't become a professor if I don't." Some of Feynman's stories are funny, some are thought-provoking, some give the reader an insight into the world of modern science.

---

[1] *On Aggression*, 11
[2] *King Solomon's Ring*

Unfortunately, this book has vices as well as virtues. Like most modern books, it's an un-cultured, un-literary book, and it lacks that rarest of literary virtues, brevity. One suspects that the publisher said, "let's make this a long book, a 350-page book, so that people will be more apt to buy it, and will be willing to pay more for it. Thus, we'll maximize our profits." *"Surely You're Joking"* was written to succeed in the modern marketplace, and to satisfy the casual, modern reader. It's a good modern book, but it falls short of being a classic.

Feynman often wrote for a general audience. If you want to learn about physics, try Feynman's *Six Easy Pieces: Essentials of Physics Explained by Its Most Brilliant Teacher.*

12. Toffler

Alvin Toffler is a contemporary American writer who deals with sociology, economics and "futurology" (that is, forecasting future developments). I recommend Toffler's book, *The Third Wave*, which paints a comprehensive picture of contemporary society. Toffler distinguishes Third Wave civilization from industrial-age civilization, which he calls Second Wave. In Toffler's view, the French Revolution and the Russian Revolution represented the triumph of Second Wave, industrial civilization over First Wave, agricultural civilization. Toffler's book offers the reader a view of modern history through the lens of economics, and it offers the reader a highly readable sketch of the industrial revolution.

Our age is often called the Post-Industrial Age, or the Consumer Age, or the Information Age. According to Toffler, "For Third Wave civilization, the most basic raw material of all—and one that can never be exhausted—is information, including imagination."[1] At the center of the Information Age is the computer; Toffler accurately predicted the personal computer boom. The computer leads to more people working at home; Toffler predicts that, "the home will assume a startling new importance in Third Wave civilization."[2]

While Second Wave civilization was mass-oriented—mass production, mass media, etc.—Third Wave civilization is individualized. Toffler notes that George Orwell predicted a future that was increasingly

---

[1] *The Third Wave*, ch. 24
[2] ibid

mass-oriented. Speaking of Orwell's *1984* and Huxley's *Brave New World*, Toffler says,

> Both these brilliant books... paint a future based on highly centralized, bureaucratized, and standardized societies, in which individual differences are eradicated. We are now heading in exactly the opposite direction.... People today—more affluent and educated than their parents and faced with more life choices—simply refuse to be massified.[1]

13. Riesman

David Riesman was an American sociologist. Riesman's fame rests on a book called *The Lonely Crowd: A Study of the Changing American Character*, which was published in 1950.[2] Riesman's work is more timely than Veblen's and more profound than Toffler's.

While Toffler sees history in terms of three types of economy, Riesman sees history in terms of three types of character: tradition-directed, inner-directed and other-directed. The tradition-directed person follows the traditions of his family and his village. "The tradition-directed person... hardly thinks of himself as an individual. Still less does it occur to him that he might shape his own destiny in terms of personal, lifelong goals."[3] The inner-directed character, which arose around the time of the Renaissance, feels himself to be an individual, with his own goals. The other-directed character, which arose in the 20th century, tries to heed social cues, and get along with his peers. The famous names from history don't move him to envy and emulation.

The Lonely Crowd helps one to understand the modern character, just as *The Third Wave* helps one to understand the modern economy.

14. Philip Howard

The Death of Common Sense: How Law is Suffocating America is a brief, readable analysis of the American legal system. The author, Philip Howard, is a New York lawyer who is active in civic affairs; Howard

---

[1] ibid, ch. 24 and ch. 19

[2] *The Lonely Crowd* was co-written with Nathan Glazer and Reuel Denney.

[3] *The Lonely Crowd*, I, 1

deserves credit for his effort to improve New York. *The Death of Common Sense* emerged from Howard's many years of political experience, and it includes numerous anecdotes culled from the contemporary scene. Many people felt that the American legal system had gone awry, and when Howard's book was published, it jumped to the top of the bestseller list because it described the problem, and explained its causes.

Howard describes how individual rights have multiplied, and how government regulations have multiplied. Government power is reduced by the profusion of individual rights, and government officials are shackled by detailed regulations. Though Howard's style isn't elegant, and his ideas aren't profound, his book is a valuable aid to understanding contemporary society.

In addition to *The Death of Common Sense*, Howard has written three other well-regarded books, *The Collapse of the Common Good*, *Life Without Lawyers*, and *The Rule of Nobody*.

15. Laurens van der Post

Laurens van der Post was born in South Africa in 1906, the thirteenth of fifteen children. When he was 20, he co-edited a student magazine that advocated greater racial integration in South Africa; the magazine was soon shut down by the government. So van der Post and one of his literary friends hitched a ride to Tokyo on a Japanese freighter—an adventure that van der Post discussed many years later in his autobiographical work, *Yet Being Someone Other*.

Returning to South Africa, van der Post began working as a journalist in Cape Town. He was critical of racial separation. Just as Lincoln predicted that, in the U.S., blacks and whites would eventually be amalgamated into one race, so van der Post predicted, "the process of leveling up and inter-mixture must accelerate continually... the future civilization of South Africa is, I believe, neither black or white but brown."

In the early 1930s, van der Post lived in England, and became acquainted with The Bloomsbury Group—John Maynard Keynes, E. M. Forster, Virginia Woolf, etc. Woolf and her husband, Leonard Woolf, published van der Post's first novel, *In a Province*, through their publishing company, Hogarth Press; this novel dealt with race relations in South Africa.

When World War II broke out, van der Post volunteered for the British army (ironically, his father had fought against the British in the Boer War). He served first in East Africa, where his unit led 11,000 camels through difficult terrain, and helped to restore Haile Selassie to the Ethiopian throne, a throne from which Mussolini's troops had expelled him. In early '42, he was sent to Indonesia, where he was taken prisoner by the Japanese; he remained imprisoned until the end of the war.

He played a legendary role in keeping up the morale of troops from many different nationalities. Along with other compatriots, he organized a 'camp university' with courses from basic literacy to degree-standard ancient history, and he also organized a camp farm to supplement nutritional needs.[1]

His prison-camp experience was the basis for his book *The Seed and the Sower*, which became the movie, *Merry Christmas, Mr. Lawrence*.

After the war, colonial authorities twice commissioned van der Post to explore remote areas of South Africa. His first expedition resulted in a bestselling book called *Venture to the Interior*; the second resulted in van der Post's most famous book, *The Lost World of the Kalahari* (and later a book about the Bushmen called *The Heart of the Hunter*). Van der Post's experiences with the Bushmen became the subject of a BBC documentary.

In the late 1940s, van der Post met Jung, who "was to have probably a greater influence upon him than anybody else, and he later said that he had never met anyone of Jung's stature."[2] Van der Post wrote a book called *Jung and the Story of Our Time*. Late in his life, van der Post helped establish a center for Jungian studies in Cape Town.

Van der Post described his travels in the Soviet Union in *A Journey Into Russia* (also known as *A View of All the Russias*). He described his experiences in Indonesia in *The Admiral's Baby* (this book discusses Indonesia after World War II—the independence movement, etc.). His knowledge of Dutch (acquired in South Africa) proved useful in Indonesia, just as his rudimentary knowledge of Japanese (acquired on his early voyage to Japan) proved useful in the Japanese prison camp.

His last years were spent in England, where he advised Margaret Thatcher on African affairs, and became close friends with Prince Charles. Charles viewed van der Post as an older and wiser man—much

---

[1] From the Wikipedia article on van der Post.

[2] ibid

as van der Post had viewed Jung. Charles went on safari with van der Post, and asked him to be the god-parent of his first child, William.

Van der Post's life spanned the twentieth century; he died in 1996, at the age of 90. After he died, debunkers emerged, insisting he was a rascal, a liar, etc., just as debunkers attacked Freud, Jung, Joseph Campbell, Shakespeare, etc. True, every great man has flaws, but why should we spend our time reading debunkers?

16. Frazer, etc.

James Frazer became famous as the author of *The Golden Bough*, which deals with cultural anthropology—that is, the customs, superstitions and religions of primitive societies. Cultural anthropology was a new and exciting field in the late nineteenth century. Nietzsche was fascinated by cultural anthropology; Nietzsche said that what is called "world history" is only current events, and that the real history of mankind is the long history of primitive man that preceded so-called "world history." In *The Golden Bough*, Frazer collected and organized the anthropological research of the late nineteenth century. *The Golden Bough* is a long, dry work, suitable for scholars, but unsuitable for the average reader, for the layman. I recommend the abridged version, which was made by Frazer himself, and which Frazer recommended.

Primitive man, according to Frazer, doesn't distinguish between the internal world and the external world. Primitive man thinks that nature is governed by the same thoughts, feelings and passions that govern his own mind; the primitive worldview is animistic. While the primitive views the world in terms of his own mind, he views his own mind in terms of the world, and explains thoughts and feelings in physical terms. Primitive man thought that sorrows and sins could be transferred to inanimate objects, to other people, to scapegoats. In primitive society, tired walkers would strike themselves with stones, thinking they were transferring their fatigue to the stones, and ridding themselves of fatigue. The stone mounds thus left along trails have become known as cairns.[1]

While *The Golden Bough* is long and dry, *From Ritual to Romance*, by Jessie Weston, is brief and interesting. *From Ritual to Romance* deals with the Holy Grail, first as an ancient ritual, and later as a Christian symbol. Weston argues that many primitive religions were life-affirming: "In the ancient Aryan religion everything is aimed at the

---

[1] *The Golden Bough*, ch. 55

affirmation of life. The phallus can be considered its dominant symbol."[1] Weston's book is best known as one of the sources of T. S. Eliot's poem, *The Waste Land.*

The French archaeologist Salomon Reinach wrote about primitive religion and also wrote *Orpheus: A History of Religions,* a book that's both scholarly and popular. The introduction to *Orpheus* is an excellent summary of the cultural anthropology of the nineteenth century. Later in the book, Reinach discusses the history of religion after primitive times, beginning with the Egyptians and Babylonians, and ending with the early twentieth century. Reinach is a free-thinker, and often treats religion with contempt; he's especially critical of the Catholic Church. Reinach attacks religion with the weapons of anthropology and Biblical criticism. In addition to *Orpheus,* Reinach wrote *Apollo,* a concise and readable history of art, and *Minerva,* an introduction to the Greek and Roman classics.

17. Zen Literature

D. T. Suzuki wrote numerous books on Zen Buddhism, and played an important role in making Zen popular in the West. Suzuki has a deep knowledge of Zen literature, and of Eastern literature in general. He's also familiar with Western literature, and often points out similarities between Zen and Christianity. Born and raised in Japan, Suzuki spent many years in the U.S., and wrote many books in English. Suzuki's work is large in quantity, but uneven in quality; he often repeats in one book what he said in another book. I recommend his *Introduction to Zen Buddhism* and his *Zen and Japanese Culture.*

While Buddhism developed in India, Zen developed in China. After making its way from China to Japan, Zen became more influential in Japan than in China. (It isn't surprising, therefore, that the West learned about Zen from a Japanese writer, not from a Chinese writer.) According to Suzuki, Zen expresses the practical, earthy character of Chinese thought, while other forms of Buddhism express the abstract, metaphysical character of Indian thought.

Zen doesn't emphasize books and learning. Zen steers the individual into himself, into his own mind. If the individual is in harmony with himself and with his own unconscious, he can appreciate the present

---

[1] *From Ritual to Romance,* 4, 2

moment and appreciate nature. When a Zen master was asked about the meaning of Zen, he said,

> Drinking tea, eating rice,
> I pass my time as it comes;
> Looking down at the stream, looking up at the mountains,
> How serene and relaxed I feel indeed![1]

Suzuki's aim is to help the reader to understand Zen, not to practice Zen. If one seeks guidance in practicing Zen, one should turn to a practical book like *Full Catastrophe Living*, by Jon Kabat-Zinn. *Full Catastrophe Living* isn't a literary work, let alone a classic, but it's a useful introduction to meditation, yoga, etc.

Two of Suzuki's Western admirers are Alan Watts and R. H. Blyth. Watts was an American theology professor who specialized in Eastern thought, especially Zen. Watts was a writer of extraordinary talent, and I highly recommend his book, *The Way of Zen*, which is well-organized, profound and poetic. *The Way of Zen* is the best summary of Zen, the best summary of Eastern thought, though somewhat difficult to read. I also recommend two other Watts books, *The Wisdom of Insecurity* and *The Book*; these two books are easier to read than *The Way of Zen*.

R. H. Blyth was an Englishman who traveled to Japan, married a Japanese woman, taught at Japanese universities, and taught English to members of the Japanese imperial family. His knowledge of English poetry and fiction is evident in his book, *Zen in English Literature*, which is saturated with quotations from both Eastern and Western literature. Blyth could read both Chinese and Japanese (as well as numerous European languages), and this helped him to write a 4-volume work on haiku poetry, and a 4-volume work on the history of Zen. Blyth can teach one much about Zen and about world literature.

Another excellent book about Zen is *Zen Flesh, Zen Bones: A Collection of Zen and Pre-Zen Writings*. *Zen Flesh* is made up of four small books, bound together as one 200-page book. The four books that constitute *Zen Flesh* are:

1. 101 Zen Stories
2. The Gateless Gate
3. 10 Bulls

---

[1] Quoted in Suzuki's essay, "On Satori—The Revelation Of A New Truth in Zen Buddhism"; this essay is part of Suzuki's *Essays in Zen Buddhism*, first series.

4. Centering

All four of these mini-books are highly poetic and highly profound, except "The Gateless Gate," which is highly obscure. "101 Zen Stories" is one of the gems of world literature.

Thich Nhat Hanh is probably the chief apostle of Eastern philosophy alive today. Hanh gives many talks/seminars/retreats in the U.S. and elsewhere, and he publishes many books. Hanh has been a peace activist since the 1960s, when he advocated American withdrawal from Vietnam; he terms this activism "engaged Buddhism." His writing is simple, clear, readable, with a certain child-like naivete. "The miracle is not to walk on water," Hanh says, "the miracle is to walk on the green earth in the present moment, to appreciate the peace and beauty that are available now." Hanh has a broad knowledge of the Buddhist tradition and of modern science, but less knowledge of Western philosophy and literature.

Before leaving the subject of Zen literature, I must mention *Zen in the Art of Archery*, by Eugen Herrigel, a German philosophy professor who lived in Japan during the 1930s. This 80-page book describes the author's effort to learn about Zen by studying the art of archery. Like many arts in Japan, archery was permeated by Zen; an archery Master was also a Zen Master. Herrigel describes how he tried to use conscious thought in releasing the arrow, but his teacher insisted that the arrow must be released spontaneously, without conscious thought, like an infant releasing his grip on your finger, like snow falling from a bamboo leaf. *Zen in the Art of Archery* is a powerful, moving work, a work that the reader will never forget.

While Herrigel was studying archery, his wife studied *ikebana*, flower-arranging. She wrote a book called *Zen in the Art of Flower Arrangement*.

18. Tibetan Wisdom

Like Thich Nhat Hanh, Sogyal Rinpoche is a contemporary apostle of Eastern philosophy. Rinpoche was born in Tibet, and spent his early years there; he's steeped in the tradition of Tibetan Buddhism. Rinpoche's most well-known book is *The Tibetan Book of Living and Dying*, which is readable and profound, an excellent blend of parable, anecdote, and argument. It can serve as an introduction not only to Tibetan Buddhism, but to Buddhism in general. It contains doctrines about the after-life that are unique to the Tibetan tradition, but it also has the sort of universal wisdom that anyone would appreciate—Socrates would like it, Confucius would like it, Hoffer would like it.

One might say that *The Tibetan Book of Living and Dying* is a readable, Westernized version of *The Tibetan Book of the Dead*, which appeared in English in the 1920s, and was a bestseller in the 1960s. *The Tibetan Book of the Dead*, also known as *Bardo Thodol*, describes the after-life, or "bardo." The title was modeled after *The Egyptian Book of the Dead*, which also deals with the after-life. What I admire most in Sogyal Rinpoche's book is the universal wisdom about life and death; I'm not as interested in the chapters that deal with the bardo.

Sogyal Rinpoche taught meditation, and he devotes part of his book to meditation techniques. He doesn't treat meditation merely as a way to reduce stress, and sleep more soundly. For him, meditation is a way to reach enlightenment. He tells several stories about the moment of enlightenment. Here's one:

> One great master in the last century had a disciple who was very thick-headed. The master had taught him again and again, trying to introduce him to the nature of his mind. Still he did not get it. Finally, the master became furious and told him, "Look, I want you to carry this bag full of barley up to the top of that mountain over there. But you mustn't stop and rest. Just keep on going until you reach the top." The disciple was a simple man, but he had unshakable devotion and trust in his master, and he did exactly what he had been told. The bag was heavy. He picked it up, and started up the slope of the mountain, not daring to stop. He just walked and walked. And the bag got heavier and heavier. It took him a long time. At last, when he reached the top, he dropped the bag. He slumped to the ground, overcome with exhaustion but deeply relaxed. He felt the fresh mountain air on his face. All his resistance had dissolved, and with it, his ordinary mind. Everything just seemed to stop. At that instant, he suddenly realized the nature of his mind. "Ah! This is what my master has been showing me all along," he thought.[1]

The enlightenment of a Buddhist, or of any mystic, has nothing to do with arguments, reasons, proofs. It's a feeling, a feeling of oneness with the universe, a feeling that comes over you when the barrier between you and the outside world dissolves, when your mind and your individuality rest.

---

[1] Ch. 5, pp. 66, 67

19. Basho

Basho is the Japanese Shakespeare; Basho's contribution to haiku poetry is comparable to Shakespeare's contribution to English drama. But unlike Shakespeare, Basho wrote prose as well as poetry; Basho is the author of several travel diaries, the most famous of which is *The Narrow Road to the Deep North*. *The Narrow Road* is a highly cultured work, filled with references to Chinese and Japanese literature. Prose is interspersed with poetry. The narrative moves swiftly, never stopping on any subject for more than a paragraph or two. Basho uses none of the cheap tricks beloved by modern writers, and some modern readers might be disappointed to find that *The Narrow Road* contains no vulgar anecdotes, no sex and no violence.

20. Joseph Campbell

Joseph Campbell was an American professor who wrote about mythology, psychology and Eastern religion. Campbell's worldview is popular as well as profound; his books are widely read, and his TV appearances generated wide enthusiasm (his interview with Bill Moyers is as good as his books). Campbell influenced American filmmakers, especially George Lucas, creator of the high-tech myth, *Star Wars*.

In his book *The Hero With A Thousand Faces*, Campbell described the typical features of the hero myth. Campbell argued that the rites and customs of primitive societies follow the same pattern as the hero myth: "The standard path of the mythological adventure of the hero is a magnification of the formula represented in the rites of passage: separation—initiation—return."[1] I recommend *The Hero With A Thousand Faces*, *Myths To Live By*, and *The Power of Myth* (the chapter on Zen in *Myths To Live By* may be the best introduction to Zen). Campbell's *magnum opus* is a 4-volume work called *The Masks of God*.

Campbell's books are not great literary works; though Campbell was an excellent public speaker, his prose leaves something to be desired. But though Campbell wasn't a great writer, he was a great reader, and he had a broad culture. One of his favorite writers was James Joyce, and he was an authority on Joyce's *Finnegans Wake*. Jung was another of Campbell's favorites, and Campbell's criticism of Western rationalism often reminds one of Jung.

---

[1] *The Hero With A Thousand Faces*, ch. 3

One of Campbell's teachers at Columbia was Heinrich Zimmer. After Zimmer died, Campbell edited and published several books by Zimmer, including *Philosophies of India, The King and the Corpse*, and *Myths and Symbols in Indian Art and Civilization*. Jung also had a keen interest in Zimmer, and also edited a book by Zimmer.

21. Lovejoy, Kuhn, and the History of Science

Arthur Lovejoy, an American philosophy professor, became famous for his writings on the history of ideas. Lovejoy's best-known works are *The Great Chain of Being* and *Essays in the History of Ideas*. Anyone interested in philosophy should read Lovejoy. Lovejoy believed that philosophical ideas influence other fields, such as literature, and that philosophy is therefore the proper starting-point for an inter-disciplinary approach to intellectual history. Lovejoy's historical approach has thrown light on many branches of the humanities. His style is rough, but his content is extremely interesting. Lovejoy was born in the 1860's, and he has a pre-twentieth-century frame of mind; he concentrates on Rousseau, Darwin, etc. He has a deep understanding of the Enlightenment and of Romanticism, but little understanding of such modern thinkers as Nietzsche and Freud.

Thomas Kuhn was influenced by Lovejoy, and applied Lovejoy's historical approach to scientific ideas. Kuhn's chief work, *The Structure of Scientific Revolutions*, is a popular and respected book in academia. It's a scholarly work, and lacks all poetic qualities, but it's also brief, readable and interesting. Published in 1962, it has become a classic analysis of the history of science, and will surely be read for years to come. Anyone interested in ideas will enjoy Kuhn's book.

Kuhn divides the history of any branch of science into three periods: normal science, crisis, and transition to a new paradigm. A period of normal science is a period in which the specialists in a certain field subscribe to the same general theory, or paradigm. During such a period, scientific work consists of refining the paradigm, and solving the puzzles that exist within it. A period of crisis is a period in which there are so many puzzles, and the puzzles are so difficult to solve, that specialists in the field become dissatisfied with the paradigm. When someone suggests a new paradigm, the specialists compare it to the old one, and if they prefer the new paradigm, it gradually replaces the old paradigm as a foundation for normal science.

Take astronomy, for example. At one time, astronomers accepted Ptolemy's geocentric paradigm. During this period of "normal science," astronomers tried to refine Ptolemy's paradigm, and extend it to all astronomical phenomena. Eventually, however, it became so difficult to match the paradigm to the phenomena, that Copernicus proposed replacing the geocentric paradigm with a heliocentric paradigm. The new paradigm gradually replaced the old one, and then astronomy returned to "normal science."

Those who are trained within a particular paradigm are often reluctant to make the transition to a new paradigm. Kuhn quotes Max Planck: "A new scientific truth does not triumph by convincing its opponents and making them see the light, but rather because its opponents eventually die, and a new generation grows up that is familiar with it."[1]

There were other historians of science before Kuhn. George Sarton was the "founding father" of the History of Science. Sarton planned to write a multi-volume work, bringing the history of science up to his own time, but he died after finishing the volumes on Greek and Arab science. In order to write about Arab science, Sarton learned Arabic, and travelled through the Middle East. Sarton has a broad culture, and discusses Vergil's poems as well as Pliny's observations.

J. D. Bernal wrote a 4-volume history of science (as well as various other science books); Bernal's work has a high reputation, though some say that his communist sympathies influence his views. Bernal was born in 1901, about fifteen years after Sarton. Joseph Needham wrote a famous, multi-volume work on Chinese science and technology. G. E. R. Lloyd compared Greek science and Chinese science in *Adversaries and Authorities*; Lloyd also wrote highly-regarded works on the history of Greek science. Charles Coulston Gillispie was a historian of science at Princeton. His study of Laplace has a high reputation, and he also wrote a general history of science called *The Edge of Objectivity*.

Another notable intellectual historian is Frances Yates, who specialized in the Hermetic Tradition (Giordano Bruno, the Rosicrucian movement, etc.). If you're interested in Hermetism, you should try Yates. Marjorie Nicolson wrote about the Newtonian revolt against Hermetism in books such as *Pepys' Diary and the New Science*.

---

[1] *The Structure of Scientific Revolutions*, ch. 12

VI. Science

1. Biology

Perhaps the best writer in the field of biology is Darwin, whose most famous works are *On the Origin of Species*, *The Descent of Man*, and *The Voyage of the Beagle*. The Norton Critical Edition of Darwin's writings is a useful one-volume abridgement.

For more on Darwin's theory, consider Edward Larson's book, *Evolution: The Remarkable History of a Scientific Theory*. Larson also wrote *An Empire of Ice: Scott, Shackleton and the Heroic Age of Antarctic Science*. Consider also Alan Moorehead's *Darwin and the Beagle*. Moorehead is best known for *The White Nile* and *The Blue Nile*, both of which deal with explorers in Africa.

During Darwin's lifetime, one of his staunchest supporters was the biologist Thomas Huxley, dubbed "Darwin's Bulldog." Thomas Huxley's grandson, Julian Huxley, was a famous biologist in the early to mid twentieth century. Though a leader in the field, Julian often wrote for a lay audience. One of his chief works was *Evolution: The Modern Synthesis*.

Gavin de Beer was a contemporary of Julian Huxley. In the 1930s, de Beer collaborated with Huxley on a study of embryology. De Beer's writings on evolution won high praise from Stephen Jay Gould. For his popular-science writings, de Beer received UNESCO's Kalinga Prize. De Beer was at home in the humanities as well as the sciences. He wrote two books about Hannibal, Rome's nemesis. Perhaps de Beer's chief love was The Alps; he wrote several books about The Alps, and he wrote about people connected to Switzerland and The Alps, such as Gibbon, Rousseau, and Hannibal.

Another famous biologist from this generation was J.B.S. Haldane, whose books are "still thoroughly readable and instructive" (according to Bill Bryson).[1] *Adventures of a Biologist* is one of Haldane's titles; another is *What is Life?*. Haldane's remarks on "test tube babies" influenced Aldous Huxley's futuristic novel, *Brave New World*.

In the 1970s, Lewis Thomas became a popular writer on biology and medicine. His first collection of essays was called *The Lives of a Cell: Notes of a Biology Watcher*. Thomas had a keen interest in words, and wrote a book on etymology called *Et Cetera, Et Cetera: Notes of a Word-Watcher*.

Like Thomas, Stephen Jay Gould was a popular writer on biology, and like Thomas, Gould published several essay-collections that were aimed at a general audience. Gould's first essay-collection, *Ever Since Darwin*, was published in 1977 and became a bestseller. Gould also wrote larger-scale works, such as *Wonderful Life*, *Ontogeny and Phylogeny*, and the massive *Structure of Evolutionary Theory*, which attempts to summarize the current state of evolutionary biology, as Julian Huxley had attempted to do sixty years earlier with his *Evolution: The Modern Synthesis*.

A good general work on biology is *A Guinea Pig's History of Biology*, by Jim Endersby.

If you want to read about man's impact on nature, consider Tim Flannery's *The Future Eaters: An Ecological History of the Australasian Lands and People*. Also consider two books by William Cronon: *Changes in the Land: Indians, Colonists, and the Ecology of New England* and *Nature's Metropolis: Chicago and the Great West*. Cronon also edited a book called *John Muir: Nature Writings*. Muir is a fine stylist and a deep thinker; he deserves comparison with Thoreau and John Burroughs. An interesting book on the watery part of the world is *Cod: A Biography of the Fish that Changed the World*, by Mark Kurlansky.

A popular book by a scientist on the cutting-edge of knowledge is James Watson's *The Double Helix: A Personal Account of the Discovery of the Structure of DNA* (available in a Norton Critical Edition).

One of the leading biology writers today is Colin Tudge. Tudge has found a "happy medium" between scholarly and popular. Tudge has written about trees, birds, genetics, etc. Tudge wrote a tome called *The Variety of Life: A Survey and a Celebration of All the Creatures That Have Ever Lived*, which traces the ascent of life from the first organisms

---

[1] *A Short History of Nearly Everything*, ch. 16, p. 244

to the present time. Richard Dawkins traces the descent of life from the present time to the first organisms in a book called *The Ancestor's Tale: A Pilgrimage to the Dawn of Life*. Dawkins spices science with stories and anecdotes.

Another leading biology writer is Richard Fortey. Fortey became interested in the field as a youngster; he found his first trilobite fossil when he was 14. One of his books is on trilobites, another is on fossils. One of Fortey's books is called *Life: An Unauthorized Biography: A Natural History of the First Four Billion Years of Life on Earth*. Fortey deals with geology in *Earth: An Intimate History*. As Stephen Jay Gould was associated with New York's Museum of Natural History, so Fortey is associated with London's Museum of Natural History (Fortey wrote a book about the museum called *Dry Storeroom no. 1*).

A good book about Mendel is *The Monk in the Garden*, by Robin Henig. Henig also wrote *Pandora's Baby*, which deals with in-vitro fertilization ("test-tube babies").

If you're interested in early man, consider

- Colin Tudge's *The Time Before History*, which has also been published as *The Day Before Yesterday*
- Nicholas Wade's *Before the Dawn*
- Jared Diamond's *The Third Chimpanzee*. This book won the Aventis Prize, as did another book by Jared Diamond, *Guns, Germs, and Steel*, which discusses how Western civilization was able to conquer other civilizations.
- Loren Eiseley's *The Immense Journey*. Eiseley wrote about science with poetic flair and philosophical depth; among his works is *Darwin's Century*.

2. Medicine

If you want to learn about the human body and medical science, consider the works of Sherwin Nuland, such as *The Wisdom of the Body*. Nuland writes about contemporary medicine and also about the history of medicine. He even ventured beyond medicine, writing biographies of Maimonides and Leonardo.

Another medical writer, from a later generation, is Atul Gawande. Gawande is a Boston surgeon who has written several popular books, including *Complications* and *Better*. Siddhartha Mukherjee wrote an award-winning book called *The Emperor of All Maladies: A Biography of Cancer.*

Consider also the alternative-medicine writers, like Gabor Maté, author of *When the Body Says No: Understanding the Stress-Disease Connection.* Robert Sapolsky, who studied baboon groups, wrote a well-known study of stress, *Why Zebras Don't Get Ulcers.*

Tracy Kidder wrote a bestseller about fighting disease in poor nations; it's called *Mountains Beyond Mountains: The Quest of Dr. Paul Farmer, A Man Who Would Cure the World.*

The British writer Roy Porter wrote a history of medicine called *The Greatest Benefit to Mankind: A Medical History of Humanity.* Porter also wrote about the British Enlightenment and British social history.

A classic on the interface of medicine and biology is Paul de Kruif's *Microbe Hunters,* which discusses Pasteur and other explorers of the microscopic world.

Oliver Sacks is a neurologist who has written about people with brain problems. Among his books are *Awakenings, The Man Who Mistook His Wife For A Hat,* and *Musicophilia: Tales of Music and the Brain.*

3. Physics

Gary Zukav makes modern physics accessible to the layman. Zukav's book, *The Dancing Wu Li Masters: An Overview of the New Physics,* was a bestseller in many countries. Zukav is interested in philosophy and the occult, and he brings out the philosophical significance of quantum physics. Another popular book about modern physics is Fritjof Capra's *The Tao of Physics: An Exploration of the Parallels Between Modern Physics and Eastern Mysticism.* David Kaiser, an MIT professor, recently wrote *How the Hippies Saved Physics: Science, Counterculture, and the Quantum Revival.* Another recent book on this subject is *Quantum: Einstein, Bohr, and the Great Debate about the Nature of Reality,* by Manjit Kumar.

George Gamow was a leading physicist who wrote numerous works of popular science, such as *Gravity* and *Biography of Physics.* Stephen Hawking wrote a bestseller called *A Brief History of Time;* later Hawking wrote *The Universe in a Nutshell, A Briefer History of Time,* and other works. Another scientist who wrote for a general audience is Carl Sagan; Sagan wrote *Broca's Brain: Reflections on the Romance of Science, Comet, Cosmos* (a book version of the popular documentary), etc.

Timothy Ferris is a journalist and science writer who often writes about astronomy; his best-known book is *Coming of Age in the Milky Way*. If you want a historical perspective on astronomy, consider *Watchers of the Sky: an Informal History of Astronomy From Babylon to the Space Age*, by Willy Ley.

If you want to learn about Einstein, consider *Einstein: His Life and Universe*, by Walter Isaacson (Isaacson also wrote biographies of Benjamin Franklin, Steve Jobs, etc.). Abraham Pais wrote *Subtle is the Lord: The science and the life of Albert Einstein*. Like Richard Fortey, Pais received the Lewis Thomas Prize, which is given to a science writer whose work is poetic and philosophical. In addition to his study of Einstein, Pais wrote a study of Niels Bohr, a history of modern physics (*Inward Bound: Of matter and forces in the physical world*), a book about twelve physicists (*The Genius of Science: A Portrait Gallery*), and other works.

One of the most popular and readable books about Einstein is $E=mc^2$, by David Bodanis. Bodanis also wrote a history of electricity, *Electric Universe*, which won the Aventis Prize, and a book about the science of everyday things, *The Secret House* (the hardcover version has photos).

One of the few modern novelists who was also an authority on modern science was the British novelist, C. P. Snow. In addition to fiction and literary criticism, Snow wrote *The Physicists*, which contains lively sketches of leading modern physicists. Snow is best known for his lecture "The Two Cultures," in which he laments the rift between the humanities and the sciences in the modern world—laments the fact that literary people are ignorant of science and vice versa.

Another modern novelist who wrote about science is Arthur Koestler. While Snow wrote about modern physics, Koestler wrote about the history of science in general; one of Koestler's books on science is called *The Sleepwalkers: A History of Man's Changing Vision of the Universe*. Koestler is best known for his novel *Darkness at Noon*, which draws on his experiences in a Fascist prison during the Spanish Civil War. Koestler described his adventurous life in a memoir called *Arrow in the Blue*. Koestler had a keen interest in the unconventional and the occult; several of his books, including *The Roots of Coincidence*, deal with the occult. He was particularly interested in what might be called "alternative biology," or "occult biology," and he questioned Darwin's view that evolution can be explained by natural selection alone. In his will, Koestler provided for the establishment of the Koestler Parapsychology Unit at the University of Edinburgh.

Steven Shapin is a Harvard professor and the author of *Leviathan and the Air-Pump: Hobbes, Boyle, and the Experimental Life* (co-written with Simon Schaffer). Shapin also wrote *The Scientific Revolution*. Dava Sobel wrote several popular science books, including *Longitude*, *Galileo's Daughter*, a study of the planets, and a study of Copernicus. Erik Larson wrote about the development of wireless communication in *Thunderstruck*, which tells the stories of the scientist Marconi and the murderer Dr. Crippen.[1] James Gleick discussed the digital revolution in *The Information: A History, a Theory, a Flood*. Gleick is also known for *Chaos: Making a New Science*, and he wrote biographies of Newton and Feynman.

4. Chemistry

Philip Ball has written several well-regarded books about chemistry, including *The Elements: A Very Short Introduction* and *Elegant Solutions: Ten Beautiful Experiments in Chemistry*. Primo Levi (mentioned earlier for his Auschwitz memoir) wrote a fictional work, *The Periodic Table*, which deals with chemistry; in 2006, it won a competition for best science book ever. Cathy Cobb has written some popular books on chemistry, such as *Creations of Fire: Chemistry's Lively History from Alchemy to the Atomic Age* (co-written with Harold Goldwhite). Sam Kean has written several popular science books in recent years: *The Disappearing Spoon* deals with the periodic table; *The Violinist's Thumb* deals with genetics; and *The Tale of the Dueling Neurosurgeons* deals with the brain.

Sharon McGrayne wrote about applications of chemistry in modern industry (*Prometheans in the Lab: Chemistry and the Making of the Modern World*). Another book about applied science is Richard Rhodes' *The Making of the Atomic Bomb*, which is both scholarly and readable, and won numerous awards. A well-regarded book about the space program is Andrew Chaikin's *A Man on the Moon: The Voyages of the Apollo Astronauts*; it's about 700 pages long. A shorter book, focusing on one space flight, is *Lost Moon: The Perilous Voyage of Apollo 13*.

---

[1] Larson has written other popular non-fiction books, including *The Devil in the White City*, which is about a series of murders that occurred in Chicago in 1893, during the World's Fair.

5. General Science

A popular introduction to many different sciences is Bill Bryson's book, *A Short History of Nearly Everything*. Bryson's book is anecdotal rather than profound, fun rather than philosophical. But if you're a stranger to science, Bryson's *Short History* might be the perfect book. The bibliography and footnotes are useful, and can lead you to further study. The illustrated version is also useful; I suggest reading the text-only version first, then flipping through the illustrated version to review what you learned. Like Lewis Thomas, Bryson is interested in words; Bryson wrote a book called *The Mother Tongue: English and How it Got That Way*.

John Gribbin has written numerous books on the history of science. Like Tudge's books, Gribbin's books are both scholarly and popular. While Tudge focuses on biology, Gribbin focuses on physics and astronomy; one of Gribbin's best-known books is *In Search of Schrödinger's Cat: Quantum Physics And Reality*. But Gribbin also deals with biology in books like *The Scientists: A History of Science Told Through the Lives of Its Greatest Inventors*. By the time Gribbin was 60, he had written more than 100 books.

An even more prolific writer on science, from an earlier generation, was Isaac Asimov, who wrote more than 500 books. Asimov is best known for his science fiction, such as The Foundation Trilogy (*Foundation, Foundation and Empire*, and *Second Foundation*); this trilogy has been called the best science fiction ever written. If you want a quick taste of Asimov's science fiction, consider his short story "Nightfall," which is often called the best science-fiction short story.[1] Asimov was considered one of the Big Three of science fiction, along with Robert Heinlein and Arthur C. Clarke.

Asimov also wrote many non-fiction books about science, such as *A Short History of Chemistry* and *Asimov's New Guide To Science*, which attempts to survey all branches of science.[2] Asimov's writing is clear

---

[1] "Nightfall" can be found in various anthologies, including *Nightfall and Other Stories*, and *The Complete Stories Vol. 1* (both by Asimov). In 1990, two years before his death, Asimov expanded "Nightfall" into a novel, with help from Robert Silverberg.

[2] If you want a book that surveys all branches of science, I wouldn't recommend Asimov's *New Guide*, which is dated and overly detailed. I'd recommend Nigel Calder's book, *Magic Universe*, or John Gribbin's book, *Almost Everyone's Guide to Science*.

and readable; he makes science interesting, without sugar-coating it with lots of anecdotes. Asimov wrote many books for young readers. He also wrote many historical works, such as *The Greeks*; some of his historical works are suitable for young readers.

If you want to learn about geology, consider James Powell's *Mysteries of Terra Firma* and Jon Erickson's *Plate Tectonics*. Consider also the books of John McPhee, such as *Rising from the Plains*. Simon Winchester wrote about the history of geology in *The Map That Changed the World: William Smith and the Birth of Modern Geology*.[1]

John Derbyshire has written two well-regarded books on the history of math: *Unknown Quantity: A Real And Imaginary History of Algebra*, and *Prime Obsession: Bernhard Riemann and the Greatest Unsolved Problem in Mathematics*.

6. Science Clubs

In recent years, several books have been written about scientific societies. One of the most acclaimed is *The Lunar Men: Five Friends Whose Curiosity Changed the World*, by Jenny Uglow (also called *The Lunar Men: The Friends Who Made the Future: 1730-1810*). The five friends are

1. James Watt (an engineer and inventor who made improvements to the steam engine)
2. Matthew Boulton (a manufacturer and the business partner of James Watt)
3. Josiah Wedgwood (a manufacturer of pottery and grandfather of Charles Darwin)

---

[1] Simon Winchester began his career as a geologist, then worked as a journalist before becoming an author. He wrote about the making of the Oxford English Dictionary in *The Professor and the Madman* (also called *The Surgeon of Crowthorne*); he also wrote about the Oxford English Dictionary in *The Meaning of Everything*. He wrote about China scholar Joseph Needham in *The Man Who Loved China* (also called *Bomb, Book & Compass*). He wrote about natural disasters in *Krakatoa: The Day the World Exploded*, and *A Crack in the Edge of the World: America and the Great California Earthquake of 1906*. His latest book is *The Men Who United the States*, which deals with explorers, canal-builders, railroad-builders, highway-builders, etc.

4. Erasmus Darwin (a physician, scientist, poet, and grandfather of Charles Darwin)

5. Joseph Priestley (a chemist, clergyman, and political radical)

They called their group The Lunar Society because they met when the moon was full, so the moonlight would facilitate their drive home. They met for about 50 years. In addition to *The Lunar Men*, Uglow has written numerous biographies—George Eliot, Elizabeth Gaskell, Henry Fielding, William Hogarth, etc.

Another book about a scientific club is *The Philosophical Breakfast Club: Four Remarkable Friends Who Transformed Science and Changed the World*, by Laura Snyder. This book deals with four 19th-century English scientists: William Whewell, Charles Babbage, John Herschel, and Richard Jones.

Louis Menand wrote about a group of philosophers in *The Metaphysical Club: A Story of Ideas in America*. The people in this club were William James, Charles Sanders Peirce, Oliver Wendell Holmes Jr., etc. For more on William James, consider the biography by Robert Richardson. Consider also *A Stroll With William James*, by Jacques Barzun. If you want to read James himself, Richardson edited an anthology, *The Heart of William James*.

Lisa Jardine, whom I mentioned earlier in connection with Francis Bacon, wrote a well-regarded book about the Scientific Revolution, *Ingenious Pursuits: Building the Scientific Revolution*. John Gribbin focused on the English role in the Scientific Revolution in *The Fellowship: The Story of a Revolution*.

Richard Holmes wrote *The Age of Wonder: How the Romantic Generation Discovered the Beauty and Terror of Science*. *The Age of Wonder* is a nice blend of history, biography, and science; it pays special attention to the astronomer William Herschel and the chemist Humphry Davy. Holmes also wrote acclaimed biographies of Coleridge and Shelley, and a book called *Dr. Johnson and Mr. Savage*.

Humphry Davy's protégé was Michael Faraday, who in turn was a mentor of the young James Clerk Maxwell. Faraday and Maxwell are the subjects of a book by Nancy Forbes and Basil Mahon: *Faraday, Maxwell, and the Electromagnetic Field: How Two Men Revolutionized Physics*. And Mahon wrote a short, readable book called *The Man Who Changed Everything: The Life of James Clerk Maxwell*.

7. Business and Economics

Todd Buchholz has written some acclaimed books on economics, such as *From Here to Economy: A Shortcut to Economic Literacy*, and *New Ideas from Dead Economists: An Introduction to Modern Economic Thought*. Buchholz is known for predicting economic events, such as the problems in the Eurozone. He has academic experience (he received a teaching award from the Harvard Economics Department), business experience (he was a hedge fund director), and political experience (he served in the White House under Bush *père*).

A similar writer, from an earlier generation, is Robert Heilbroner, who's best known for *The Worldly Philosophers: The Lives, Times and Ideas of the Great Economic Thinkers*. Heilbroner also co-wrote (with Lester Thurow) *Economics Explained*, which went through several editions in the 1980s and 1990s.

Randy Charles Epping deals with the basics of international economics in his popular book *The 21st Century Economy: A Beginner's Guide* (this book is an updated version of Epping's earlier book *A Beginner's Guide to the World Economy*).

Milton Friedman and John Kenneth Galbraith were both born in the early 1900s; Friedman was a leading conservative economist, Galbraith a leading liberal economist. When Galbraith made a 15-hour documentary on economics, Friedman responded with his own documentary. Among Friedman's books are *Money Mischief: Episodes in Monetary History*, and a more general work called *Free to Choose*. Among Galbraith's books are

- *A Short History of Financial Euphoria*
- *The Great Crash, 1929*
- *Money: Whence It Came, Where It Went*

Galbraith was more literary, less mathematical, than today's economists. He wrote several novels, including *A Tenured Professor*.

A classic on the stock market is Edwin Lefèvre's *Reminiscences of a Stock Operator*. Alan Greenspan called Lefèvre's book "a font of investing wisdom." I recommend the edition annotated by Jon Markman and published by Wiley.

Michael Lewis' first book was *Liar's Poker* (1989), which described his experiences on Wall Street. Later he wrote *The Big Short*, which dealt with the economic crisis of 2008, and *Boomerang*, which dealt with how the 2008 crisis affected Iceland, Greece, Ireland, etc. Lewis wrote about baseball in *Moneyball*, and about football in *The Blind Side*. He's a lively writer, and many of his books have been bestsellers.

Nassim Taleb is best known for *The Black Swan: The Impact of the Highly Improbable*. Taleb thinks that people often assume that the future will resemble the past, people make the mistake of predicting the future based on the past. Taleb thinks that unforeseen events, like the 9/11 attacks, have a major impact on the markets, and on history in general; he calls such events "black swans." Although Taleb is an investor, and a very successful one, he often writes in a philosophical vein; he says that only four pages of *Black Swan* deal with investing.

Taleb liked to buy options, which did well if the market collapsed. He criticized sellers of options, saying that they presumed to predict the future, and weren't prepared for black-swan events. One such seller of options was a firm called Long-Term Capital Management, which was ruined as a result of the 1997 Asian financial crisis, and the 1998 Russian crisis. A well-known business writer named Roger Lowenstein wrote *When Genius Failed: The Rise and Fall of Long-Term Capital Management*.

Charles Geisst is a prolific business writer; among his works are *Wall Street: A History* and *The Last Partnerships: Inside the Great Wall Street Money Dynasties*. William Cohan is the author of *The Last Tycoons: The Secret History of Lazard Frères & Co.*, which won an award as the best business book of 2007. Cohan has also written studies of two other Wall Street firms, Bear Stearns and Goldman Sachs. Charles R. Morris is the author of numerous business books including

- *The Tycoons: How Andrew Carnegie, John D. Rockefeller, Jay Gould, and J. P. Morgan Invented the American Supereconomy*
- *The Sages: Warren Buffett, George Soros, Paul Volcker, and the Maelstrom of Markets*
- *The Two Trillion Dollar Meltdown: Easy Money, High Rollers, and the Great Credit Crash*

John Steele Gordon has written about American economic history in such books as

- *Empire of Wealth: The Epic History of American Economic Power*
- *Hamilton's Blessing: The Extraordinary Life and Times of Our National Debt*
- *The Great Game: The Emergence of Wall Street as a World Power: 1653-2000*

James Grant is known for criticizing Fed policy, and advocating a gold standard. He writes well, and has a sharp wit. Among his books are

- *Bernard M. Baruch: The Adventures of a Wall Street Legend*

- *Money of the Mind: Borrowing and Lending in America From the Civil War to Michael Milken*
- *John Adams: Party of One*

One of the most popular business books of recent years is *Barbarians at the Gate: The Fall of RJR Nabisco*, by Bryan Burrough and John Helyar. Another popular book, on a similar theme, is *Predators' Ball: The Inside Story of Drexel Burnham and the Rise of the Junk Bond Raiders*, by Connie Bruck.

That concludes this essay on the Western classics, which has been a cartographer's attempt to meet the needs of miners, and to show them where gold can be found.

Appendix: Criticism and Defense

From the December 12, 2009 issue of my e-zine:

I recently sent a copy of my new book, *Realms of Gold*, to Steven Sage, author of *Ibsen and Hitler*. Steven is a professional scholar. I'm definitely not a professional scholar; I see myself as The Last of the Educated Laymen. Since my new book is very un-scholarly, Steven took a somewhat critical view of it. We exchanged e-mail:

Sage	It's not evident what your purpose is.
Hammond	In his early essay "Richard Wagner in Bayreuth," Nietzsche wrote:
	"The object is not to cut the Gordian knot of Greek culture after the manner adopted by Alexander, and then to leave its frayed ends fluttering in all directions; it is rather to bind it after it has been loosed.... In the person of Wagner I recognise one of these anti-Alexanders: he rivets and locks together all that is isolated....[he] is a Simplifier of the Universe."
	I'm trying to be a simplifier—a simplifier of the world of books, which is perhaps the most important world there is, and the most extensive. Now more than ever, we need to simplify so that the world of culture/knowledge/books doesn't become too specialized, too fragmented. I think Nietzsche would approve of my book. My book is, in a sense, a philosophical project.
Sage	*Realms* would appear to belong to the undergraduate Educational category.
Hammond	I prefer not to put it in any category, I prefer to see it as a book for everyone. It's a personal book, an opinionated book. Isn't every literary work personal? Aren't Montaigne's essays personal? Doesn't Montaigne tell us what books he likes and doesn't like? Doesn't Nietzsche tell us that, too?
Sage	You're competing with Wikipedia and other easily-accessed resources for quick, handy, summary information.
Hammond	I'm a fan of Wikipedia, and I draw on Wikipedia in *Realms of Gold*. But I'm not really doing the same thing: Wikipedia

	isn't personal, or literary. It doesn't try to recommend. And it doesn't try to simplify. On the contrary, it militates against simplification—it fragments, spreads, specializes.
Sage	There are, after all, other digests of great and influential books.
Hammond	I'm not aware of any books that resemble *Realms*. I don't try to write a digest, a summary; for example, I make no attempt to summarize Plato's *Republic*. Hence I can move rapidly, and cover a lot of ground in a small volume. Furthermore, I don't stick to "great and influential books". I mention writers like Steven Sage, who have no influence, but deserve to have influence. I mention Bill Bryson, who doesn't try to be a great writer, but may help the reader to get a broad education. I give short shrift to some Ancient Classics like Aristotle, but have high praise for some modern works like *Zen and the Art of Archery*. I don't aim at completeness; I skip over major writers like George Eliot, Anthony Trollope, Martin Heidegger, etc., etc. I have to skip some writers, I have to be unfair (though I may give these writers their due in a later edition). I can't read everything, or critique everything, just as a travel writer can't tell us about every town in the world. But think of all the writers that I don't skip! Think of all the writers that I try to rescue from oblivion, try to introduce the reader to, try to make enticing for the reader! A book like *Realms* can boost the reputations of many writers. Could it do even more? Could it revive literature in general? Could it make literature more popular—help literature to compete with other media, other pastimes?
Sage	You often use the word "enjoy" in evaluating a book.
Hammond	This is characteristic of a layman; we laymen seek enjoyment, pleasure. On the other hand, a professional scholar like yourself gets enjoyment from a paycheck, so he may not insist that he receive enjoyment from the books that led to the paycheck. Montaigne wouldn't rack his brains over Aristotle because Montaigne was a layman, he wasn't being paid to read, so he read what he enjoyed. On the other hand, Leo Strauss spent many hours poring over Aristotle because he was a professional scholar; his paycheck, and his scholarly reputation, depended on his knowledge.

	My view is that, throughout history, most good books have been written to give the reader pleasure. Homer, Dickens, Tolstoy, Thoreau—they all aim to give the reader pleasure. That doesn't mean, however, that they aim *only* to give pleasure, just as the food you eat may give you pleasure, but not *only* pleasure. From our books, as from our food, we want both nutrition and pleasure.
Sage	If to enjoy is the goal, as you well know there are other, far more intensely gratifying experiences than reading heavy tomes: movies, sex, drugs, drinking, sports, games…
Hammond	My book doesn't focus on "heavy tomes". I seek the light, the witty, the brief, as well as the original and profound. The pleasure that literature offers is different from other pleasures, and can't be replaced by them; even in this video age, many people still read for pleasure. The pleasure that movies afford may not be as intense as that afforded by sex and drugs, but that doesn't mean that no one watches movies.
Sage	The items you've discussed appear to reflect your own training in a particular curriculum.
Hammond	If I was ever "trained", I'm not aware of it. Scholars may be trained, but laymen aren't. Laymen follow their own wayward spirit, their inner voice. Whatever I've learned, I've learned by "free reading." If I hadn't gone to Harvard, I would know as much as I know now.
Sage	In *Realms* the postmodern set of critiques, and the vocabulary of postmodern criticism, are wholly absent and ignored.
Hammond	I was influenced by writers like Nietzsche and Freud, who aren't "postmodern". I was influenced by old books, not current trends.
Sage	Postmodernism is still dominant; the young are inculcated in postmodernism on campuses, and you've stated that your book is ideal for a young philosopher.
Hammond	Every philosopher writes for the next philosopher. I feel that I've discovered some things—for example, when I was about 43, I discovered that E. M. Forster is a great writer, and that quantum physics is relevant to philosophy. I want to share these discoveries. If a 20-year-old philosopher reads my book, I'd like him to learn quickly what I learned slowly.

Sage	If you reject the whole family of postmodern criticism, you need to say why. Or is it that you haven't read any postmodernist thinkers?
Hammond	I've tasted that school of thought, and haven't been captured/enthralled/impressed, so I haven't gone further. But then again, they haven't read my work either. I don't see any need to explain why I ignore the postmodern school. Yes, they're fashionable in academia, but they haven't convinced me that they deserve a close reading and a careful rebuttal.

Feedback

Note: the following e-mail messages react to my books and to my website, LJHammond.com

Hello, I live in Nova Scotia, Canada. I'm 35 years old and just lost my younger brother to complications after Brain Tumor Surgery. He was a self-taught man who knew much about the Humanities.... I cannot begin to describe the loss and the pain I endure on a daily basis. I am completely stuck on the age-old question, What is the meaning of life? The only comfort I get at the present time is to educate myself in more of the great works. I stumbled across your site and it has brought me much comfort. I have made it my home page. I just wanted to say Thank you very much. Tim

If you lack a general liberal education and would like to fill that gap, you may have noticed that it's very easy to get lost. Pick any topic and you are faced with an overwhelming number of classical texts, authors and theories, each requiring a large investment of time and energy to understand and appreciate. What would be really helpful is a high-level overview of entire areas of study, and, incredibly, this very slim book attempts to provide just that.... The book is incredibly easy to read and presents often impenetrably abstract ideas in a comprehensive and entertaining manner. Highly recommended! Mycha, Princeton, NJ (posted on Amazon)

I am a college student at Fudan University, Shanghai, China. I read your book, published by China Film Press. I just want to say thank you. Your book was very easy to understand, but I was amazed by the power in those plain words! I bought your book when I was in high school, and I've been reading it again and again through the years, and it was among the very few books I took to Shanghai with me. Your book made me re-find my interest in philosophy and literature, and also re-find myself. Loretta

Made in the USA
Monee, IL
04 March 2022

92253693R10121